Adjutant General North Carolina.

Muster rolls of the soldiers of the War of 1812: detached from the militia of North Carolina in 1812 and 1814. Published in pursuance of the resolutions of the General Assembly of January 28, 1851 and resolution of the General Assembly of February 25

Adjutant General North Carolina.

Muster rolls of the soldiers of the War of 1812: detached from the militia of North Carolina in 1812 and 1814. Published in pursuance of the resolutions of the General Assembly of January 28, 1851 and resolution of the General Assembly of February 25

ISBN/EAN: 9783337305505

Printed in Europe, USA, Canada, Australia, Japan

Cover: Foto ©ninafisch / pixelio.de

More available books at **www.hansebooks.com**

SOLDIERS OF THE WAR OF 1812:

DETACHED FROM

The Militia of North Carolina,

IN 1812 AND 1814.

PUBLISHED IN PURSUANCE OF THE RESOLUTIONS OF THE
GENERAL ASSEMBLY OF JANUARY 28, 1851 AND
RESOLUTION OF THE GENERAL ASSEMBLY
OF FEBRUARY 20, 1873.

UNDER THE DIRECTION OF THE ADJUTANT GENERAL.

———————

RALEIGH:
STONE & UZZELL, STATE PRINTERS AND BINDERS.

RESOLUTIONS directing the Adjutant General to publish copies of the Muster Rolls of the soldiers of the war of 1812.

Resolved, That the Adjutant General be and is hereby directed to have published a hundred copies, duly certified, of the Muster Rolls of the Soldiers of the war of 1812, which are on file in his Department; and that one copy be sent to the clerk of the county court in each county of this State.

Resolved further, That when it shall be made to appear to the Treasurer that the requirements of the above resolution have been complied with, he shall pay to the Adjutant General, as a compensation for his services, out of any money not otherwise appropriated, the sum of one hundred dollars.

Read three times and ratified in General Assembly, this 28th day of January, A. D. 1851.

J. C. DOBBIN, S. H. C.
W. N. EDWARDS, S. S.

MUSTER ROLL

OF THE INFANTRY DETACHED FROM THE MILITIA OF NORTH CAROLINA, IN PURSUANCE OF A REQUISITION OF THE PRESIDENT OF THE UNITED STATES IN VIRTUE OF AN ACT OF CONGRESS OF THE 10TH OF APRIL, 1812.

DIVISION,

THOMAS BROWN, *Major General, Commanding.*

FIRST BRIGADE, detached from the 1st, 13th, 2d, 3d, 12th, 5th, 4th and 14th Brigades of the Organized Militia of the State—Thomas Davis, Brigader General, Commanding.

FIRST REGIMENT, detached from the 1st and 13th Brigade of ditto.

    JOSIAH FLOWERS, *Lieutenant Colonel Commandant,*
    CALEB ETHERIDGE, *First Major,*
    JOHN M. COTTER, *Second Major.*

First Company of the First Regiment, detached from the Currituck Regiment.

1 John Ship, Captain,
2 Cornelius Jones, 1st Lieut.
3 Amb. Walston, 2d Lieut.
4 Gideon Bonney, Ensign,
5 Joshua White, Private,
6 Samuel Beasley,
7 Dennis Capts,
8 John Smith,
9 Jacob Wichel,
10 John White jr.,
11 Malachi Dudley,
12 Levan Dudley,
13 Jacob Williams,
14 William Beasley,
15 Caleb Wilson,
16 Augustus Linton,
17 James Northam,
18 Merrit Ballance,
19 Thomas Etheridge,
20 Nicholas Elydon,

21 William Garrett,
22 Ivy Halstead,
23 Joseph Sawyer,
24 Charles Sawyer,
25 William Bray jr.,
26 Thomas Mitchell,
27 William Bunnell,
28 Joseph Poyner,
29 Jonathan Wright,
30 Richard Decker,
31 Jesse Parr,
32 Thomas Archland,
33 Merese Jarvis,
34 Henry Spence,
35 Arthur Spence,
36 John Boswell,
37 James Fentns,
38 Bartlett Burton,
39 Charles Fulford,
40 Joseph Fulford,
41 John Gregory,
42 Andrew Heath,
43 James Whitheral jr.,
44 James Nicholson,
45 William Snider,
46 William Perkins,
47 Henry Doxey,
48 Mitchel Gregory,
49 John Baker,
50 John Mayo,
51 William Halstead,
52 James Banks,
53 James Gregory,
54 John Gray.
55 Josiah Taylor,
56 Thomas McMooney,
57 Hollowell Sawyer,
58 Joel Poyner,
59 Frederick White,
60 George Fisher,
61 Benjamin Taylor,
62 Shadrack Kallnm.
63 William Thompson.

Second Company, detached from the Currituck Regiment.

1 Hilliary Bell, Captain.
2 Joshua Baxter, Lieut.
5 Michael Orneal, Private.
6 James Parker,
7 William Spry,
8 Thomas Gregory,
9 Jesse Robeson,
10 William Devont,
11 Jeremiah Gorden,
12 Thomas Whitehall,
13 Thomas Writentt,
14 Elijab Hunnings,
15 John Griffin,
16 Thomas Mercer,
17 Caleb Harress,
18 James Sawyer,
19 Cornelius Mecoy,
20 Jasper Gibson,
21 Thomas B. Jarvis,
22 Ishum Hunt,
23 Thomas Allen,
24 John Demdtund,

25 Josiah Beals,
26 Noah Hobbs,
27 Uriah Simpson,
28 Mark Harris,
29 Jonathan Chapter,
30 Trininger Sandler,
31 William Greves,
32 Nathan Shannon,
33 Peter M. Gray,
34 Thomas Curls,
35 Joseph Sanderson,
36 Matthias Davis,
37 Isaac Dowdy,
38 William Leimpoon,
39 Thomas Parker,
40 Thomas Daniel,
41 David Daniel,
42 Baley Daniel,

43 Avra Daniel,
44 John Daniel,
45 John Shannon,
46 John Credworth,
47 Joseph Baglen.
48 John Barnett,
49 Daniel Stow,
50 Valentine Waite.
51 Joseph Quidley,
52 Thomas Scarborough,
53 Wallis Stirran,
54 Zachariah Burrus,
55 William Gray,
56 Benjamin Stow,
57 John Quidley,
58 Moses Anston,
59 Cornelius Anston,
60 Bartlett Quidley.

Third Company, detached from the Camden Regiment.

1 James S. Garling, Capt.
2 Baley Barco, 1st Lieut.
3 Willis Wilson, 2d Lieut.
4 Wilson Webster, Ensign,
5 James Forbes, 1st Sergt.
6 J. W. Harrison, 2d Sergt.
7 James Godfrey, 3d Sergt.
8 Edward Pugh, 4th Sergt,
9 Wm Godfrey, 1st Cor'l.
10 Simon Jones, 2d Corporal,
11 Jeremiah Jones 3d Cor'l.
12 Isaac Berry, 4th Corporal.
13 Robert Boushel, Private,
14 John Gallup,
15 Edward Curlin.

16 Phillip Morissett,
17 Timothy Berry,
18 Nathan Gregory,
19 Frederick Gregory,
20 Etheridge Standley,
21 William Berry,
22 Joseph McCoy,
23 Jesse Dowdy,
24 Roding Mercer,
25 Dempsey Wilson,
26 John Shorter,
27 James Willis,
28 Caleb Jarvis,
29 Elias McKoy.
30 Henry Gregory,

31 William Dowdy,
32 Peter Seymore,
33 Abner Sanderlin,
34 Jonathan Gregory,
35 Caleb Woodard,
36 Wilson Sikes,
37 Samuel Gregory,
38 John Lewis,
39 Isaac Avery,
40 Jabez Garlington,
41 Edmund Gregory, sr.,
42 Miles Berry,
43 Shipperd Foster,
44 Tully Morrissett,
45 John Mitchell,
46 David Dunken,
47 James Garret,
48 Jacob James,
49 Abner Sikes,
50 Abner Cooper,
51 Lemuel Gregory,
52 James Huit,
53 Cornelius Bryon,
54 Nathaniel Hughes,
55 Owen W. Harrison,
56 Edmund Gregory, jr.,
57 Thomas Portlock,
58 Joshua Gallup,
59 Henry W. Harrison,
60 Wilson W. Nash,
61 Josiah Nash,
62 Archibald Sawyer,
63 Markum Stafford,
64 Joshua Smisson,
65 Joseph Bray,
66 Thomas Gregory,
67 William Proctor,
68 Wilson Duncan,
69 Dempsey J. Burgess,
70 Moses Brock,
71 Bradley Smith,
72 Zebulin Dunkin,
73 Benjamin Carter.

Fourth Company, detached from the Pasquotank Regiment.

1 William Spence, Captain,
2 Richard Muse, Lieut.
3 Joseph Sutton, Ensign,
4 John Graves, Private,
5 Jesse Bray,
6 Edward Greves,
7 Thaddeus Snowden,
8 Peter William,
9 David Griffin,
10 John Low,
11 Holowell Vardell,
12 Thomas Denby,
13 John Keel,
14 Benjamin Lowry,
15 Samuel Overman,
16 Urias Turner,
17 Samuel Spelman.
18 Thomas Woodley,
19 Joshua Benton,
20 Charles Hunt,
21 Jesse Jordan,
22 William Hite,

23 Elijah Munden,
24 Isaac Gallop,
25 Caleb Bundy,
26 Nathan Bundy,
27 Jonathan Garrett,
28 William Turner,
29 Nixon Low,
30 Jesse Bundy,
31 William Munden,
32 Noah Perry,
33 Benjamin Brothers,
34 Josiah Mackey,
35 Henry Cox,
36 Enoch Pritchard,
37 Joseph Harrell,
38 Miles Turner,
39 Arthur Gordon,
40 Henry Raper,
41 Daniel White,
42 Lemuel Cambell,
43 Richard Clark,
44 Christopher Cartwright,
45 Samuel Dozier,
46 Stephen Scott,
47 Adam Deal,
48 Jordan Gray,
49 Thomas Humphis,
50 Samuel Jones,
51 Enoch Sawyer,
52 Britton Temple,
53 Isaac Williams,

54 William Cartwright,
55 Benjamin Gilbert,
56 Lot Fentress,
57 Richard Clayton,
58 John F. Markum,
59 John Lowry,
60 William Nichilson,
61 Cornelius Scott,
62 Lemuel Barrington,
63 Frederick Davis,
64 Michael Phillips,
65 Alexander Whitehouse,
66 Thomas Cartwright,
67 Joshua Cartwright,
68 John Harris,
69 James Davis,
70 William Carter,
71 James Jackson,
72 Joshua Jackson,
73 Robert Spence,
74 David Nichols,
75 Edward Scott,
76 Julian D. Belinger,
77 James Leonard,
78 John Casa,
79 Thomas Allen,
80 Jacob Simpson,
81 John Cartwright,
82 Stephen Chancy,
83 George White,
84 Davis Spelman.

Fifth Company, detached from the Perquimans Regiment.

1 Thomas Myers, Captain,
2 Matthew Jordan, Lieut.
3 Willis Roberts, Ensign,
4 Charles Clay, Private,
5 Exum Nuby,
6 Reuben Overman,
7 Lemuel Tucker,
8 Benjamin Maudlin,
9 Abel Rogerson,
10 Elisha Harreld,
11 Elisha Farles,
12 Henry Garrett,
13 William Standen,
14 Joseph Bagley,
15 Philip Mason,
16 William Tweddy,
17 William Colleson,
18 Harrison Turner,
19 James Turner, jr.,
20 James Turner, sr.,
21 George P. Whidbee,
22 Stephen Twiddy,
23 Jonathan Bogue,
24 Tully Williams,
25 Myles Turner,
26 Thomas Allen,
27 William Hatfield,
28 Joseph Arrenton,
29 Joshua McCoy.
30 Thomas Jones,
31 Thomas Arrenton.
32 Jonathan Smith,
33 Joseph Jackson,
34 Reuben Hobbs,
35 Lemuel Bateman,
36 John Jackson,
37 Francis Wills,
38 Hardy Bateman,
39 Thomas Woodley,
40 Obadiah Reddick,
41 Reddick Hallswell,
42 Lemuel Lain,
43 Tully Moss,
44 Joseph Pike,
45 Samuel Maudlin,
46 Isaac Twiddy,
47 Thomas Allen,
48 Sassel McCoy,
49 Benjamin Bateman,
50 Griffin Brinkly,
51 Joshua Talton,
52 Elisha Eliott,
53 John Moss,
54 Asa Lymous,
55 Nathan Bagley,
56 Moses Webb,
57 Delight Nixon,
58 William Burnham,
59 Abraham Green,
60 Aaron Green,
61 Thomas Hudson,
62 Tully Laden,
63 Jesse Ward,
64 Samuel Barclipt,
65 James Stanton,
66 Saphem Elliott,
67 Benjamin Shinner,
68 Samuel Weeks,

69 Thomas Hendricks,
70 William Barker,
71 Isaac Wilson,
72 Henry Hobbs,
73 John Sylvester,
74 Benjamin Munden,

75 Edward Saunders,
76 Joseph Arrenton,
77 Edward Arrenton,
78 Nathan Nichilson,
79 Exum Newby,
80 John Hardle.

Sixth Company, detached from the Chowan Regiment.

1 John Megnire, Captain,
2 Thomas Tapping, Lieut.
3 Welch Fulierton, Ensign,
4 Thos. Tarlton, 1st Sergt.
5 A. Holloway, 2d Sergt.
6 L. Holloway, 3d Sergt.
7 G. Meredith, 4th Sergt.
8 Job Perkins, 1st Cor'l.
9 Julius Bunch, 2d Cor'l.
10 Neil Sherwood, 3d Cor'l.
11 Joseph Pain, 4th Cor'l.
12 David Welch, Private,
13 James Ward,
14 Duchim Mansfield,
15 Charles Miller,
16 Reddick Wood,
17 Elisha Hurdle,
18 Archibald Leath,
19 William Flnry,
20 Samuel Fitt,
21 Thomas Webb,
22 Abraham Pettigor,
23 Charles Stewart,
24 John Bond,
25 Salter Bunch,
26 John Standing,

27 Nimrod West,
28 Caleb Grant,
29 Peter Markell,
30 John McGlaughlin,
31 Henry Morris,
32 John Bysam,
33 James Braughton,
34 James Crery,
35 William Wingate,
36 Josiah Bogue,
37 Felston Cotten,
38 Nathaniel Bunch,
39 James Robertson,
40 Hana Jorden,
41 Miles Halsey,
42 Noah Smith,
43 Dempsey Trotman,
44 Miles Elliott,
45 John Ward,
46 John Watson,
47 William Walton,
48 Micajah Ward,
49 Daniel Harris,
50 Jacob Perry,
51 Abner Goodwin,
52 George Webb,

53 Levi Persons.
54 James Swan.
55 Elisha Parker,

56 John Middleton,
57 Daniel Liverman.

Seventh Company, detached from the Gates Regiment.

1 Thos. Freeman Captain.
2 Rob't. Reddick, Lieut.
3 Simon Stallings, Ensign,
4 Edwin Ballard, 1st Sergt.
5 Lem. Goodman, 2d Sergt.
6 Lem. Reddick, 3d Sergt.
7 Richard H. Lee, 4th Sergt.
8 Henry Brinkley, 1st Cor'l.
9 Abbey Benton, 2d Cor'l.
10 David Benton, 3d Cor'l.
11 John Hare, 4th Cor'l.
12 William Lunding, Private,
13 Jacob Benton.
14 John Blanchard,
15 Ransom Phillips.
16 Aaron Harrell,
17 Abner Green,
18 Elisha Robertson.
19 Isaac Hiott,
20 Kader Bereman.
21 Dempsey Blanchard.
22 William Green,
23 Henry King,
24 Timothy Robertson,
25 William Spright,
26 Moses Spivey,
27 John Alphin,
28 Luke Parker,
29 Willis Figg,
30 Fader Hurdle,

31 Joseph Phillips.
32 Moses Davis,
33 John Saunders,
34 James Jordan.
35 John Spright,
36 William Matthews,
37 Elisha Matthias,
38 Kader Reddick,
39 Luke Freling,
40 Harman Hays,
41 Abram Parker,
42 William Sumner,
43 Benjamin Morgain,
44 James Spright,
45 Jethro Briggs,
46 Thomas Brown,
47 Jesse Carter,
48 William Haffler,
49 Arthur Boyett,
50 Frederick Alphin,
51 Jacob P. Jones,
52 John Fanney,
53 Elisha Peel,
54 William Benton,
55 Jesse Down,
56 John Outlaw,
57 Richard P. Curl,
58 Miles Parker,
59 Barnard Marsh,
60 John Felton,

61 Stephen Eure,
62 Kinchin Phillips,
63 Benjamin Cross,
64 Cypron Eure,
65 Vinson H. Jones,
66 Robert Parker,

67 Josiah Ellis,
68 Reddick, Peel,
69 Jethro Benton,
70 Henry H. Benton,
71 John Arnold,
72 Frederick Simpson,

Eighth Company, detached from the Hertford Regiment.

1 Irwin Jenkins, Captain,
2 Everard Garrett, Lieut.
3 Benjamin Hill, Ensign,
4 Andrew Oliver, Cadet,
5 James Spires, Cadet,
6 Wm. Walton, 1st Sergt.
7 Hardy Banks, 2d Sergt.
8 Josiah Battle, 3d Sergt.
9 John Scott, 4th Sergt.
10 Arthur Booth, 1st Cor'l.
11 Elisha Horton, 2d Cor'l.
12 Charles Jenkins, 3d Cor'l.
13 J. Witherington, 4th Cor.
14 John Manning, Drummer,
15 Wiley Brown, Fifer,
16 James Early, Private,
17 Lemuel Holloman,
18 James Hayes,
19 Thomas Britton,
20 Luke McGlaulum,
21 Nathan Baker,
22 Cornelius H. Goodwin,
23 Anthony Brown,
24 Anthony Williams,
25 Noah Evans,
26 Jacob Sewell,
27 Jethro Sewell,

28 Jacob Hare,
29 John Baker,
30 John Scull,
31 Thomas Holland,
32 Henry D. Jenkins,
33 John Curl,
34 John Denton,
35 William Ballester.
36 Thomas Clark,
37 Josiah I. Askins,
38 Lewis Carter,
39 Jonas Atkins,
40 Henry Brantly,
41 William Williams,
42 Henry Wiggins,
43 Miles Hobbs,
44 John Everitt,
45 Alexander Booth,
46 Levi Creey,
47 Thomas Thorne,
48 Zachariah Brown,
49 Edward Crump,
50 Anthony B. Lee,
51 John Benthall,
52 Robert Brantley,
53 Thomas Neale,
54 Alexander Smith,

55 William Brown,
56 Isaac Pearce,
57 George Asken,
58 Edward Brantley,
59 Henry Eure,
60 Joseph G. Rea,
61 William Wynns,
62 Thomas Weston,
63 Allen L. Ramsey,
64 Elisha Mints,
65 James Parker,
66 Benjamin Ezell,
67 Britton Sikes,
68 William Andrews,
69 Isaac Foster,
70 John C. Montgomery,

71 Reuben Clark,
72 Lewis Boon,
73 Josiah Robbins,
74 Elijah Archer,
75 Ephraim King,
76 Samuel Boon,
77 Mathuel Archer,
78 James Raleigh,
79 John Weaver,
80 James B. Jones,
81 Hardy Davis,
82 Mills Walters,
83 Abram Boon,
84 West Boon,
85 John Bizzett.

Ninth Company, detached from the Washington Regiment.

1 Henry Garret, Captain,
2 A. Armstrong, Lieut.
3 John Rogers, Ensign,
4 Zachariah Sutton,
5 Joseph Snyder,
6 Benjamin Cullipher,
7 Eliakim Norman,
8 Isaac Cullipher,
9 Davis Biggs,
10 Zebedee Tarkinton,
11 Jehu Ambrose,
12 Enos Tarkinton,
13 Reuben Clifton,
14 Levi Ambrose,
15 Roger Snell,
16 Nathan I. Swain,
17 Edward Nar,

18 Isaac Rawson,
19 Samuel Jones,
20 Isaac Skittlethrop,
21 Edmund Skittlethrop,
22 Joseph Spruill,
23 William Forlan,
24 Enoch Steely,
25 John Simpson,
26 John Airs,
27 Jesse Collins,
28 William Woodley,
29 Miles Hopkins,
30 Andrew Spruill,
31 Arthur Skittlethrop,
32 Isham Pearce,
33 Bethuel Murray,
34 William Allen,

35 Ezekiel Blount,
36 Thomas Smith,
37 Hiram Snell,
38 Frederick B. Jennings,
39 Charles Morse,
40 Edward Parish,

41 Simeon Swain,
42 James F. James,
43 Joseph Sax,
44 Starkey Tarkinton,
45 Thomas Gilbert,
46 Enoch Bundy.

Tenth Company, detached from the Tyrrell Regiment.

1 Wm. Alexander, Captain,
2 Richard Howell, Lieut.
3 James Haysell, Ensign,
4 Benj. Brickhouse,
5 James Davenport,
6 Uriah Spruill,
7 Emri Spruill,
8 Uzzell Brickhouse,
9 Benjamin Clayton,
10 James McAlsten,
11 William Brickhouse,
12 Harman Alexander,
13 Ricardo Rudd,
14 William Steatman,
15 Elisha Strum,
16 Solomon Creed,
17 John West,
18 William Swain,
19 Isaac West,
20 Benjamin Hassell,
21 Spencer Midgitt,
22 Isaac Liverman,
23 James Sivels,
24 Harry Charles,
25 Stephen Powell,
26 Joshua Swain,

27 Ozias Roughton,
28 Zadoch Hassell,
29 James Whitbee,
30 Maxy Davis,
31 Selby Patrick,
32 Asa Barratt,
33 William White,
34 Thomas Sawyer,
35 Peleg Simmons,
36 Selby Armstrong,
37 Bartlett Jones,
38 Ebenezer Cohoon,
39 William Russ,
40 John Banks,
41 Azariah Hutson,
42 Thomas Clayton,
43 William Ward,
44 Mitchel Paine,
45 Joseph Mason,
46 Joseph Man,
47 Hiram Hooker,
48 John Mydgett,
49 Robert Holmes,
50 Michael Hadok,
51 Hezekiah Mariner,
52 John Wynn,

53 Jeremiah Phillip,
54 Noah Dowers,
55 Enoch Davenport.

56 Charles Phillips,
57 Silby Powers.

SECOND REGIMENT.

DETACHED FROM THE 2D, 12TH AND 3D BRIGADES.

SIMON BURTON, *Lieutenant Colonel Commandant.*
NATHAN TISDALE, *First Major.*
JOHN A. LILLINGTON, *Second Major.*

First Company, detached from the Hyde Regiment.

1 Beverly Rew, Captain,
2 Joshua Bell, Lieutenant,
3 James Cheves, Ensign,
4 Moses Windley,
5 Jasper Smith,
6 Enoch Flinn, jr.,
7 Joshua Freeman,
8 John Peartree,
9 Christopher Matison,
10 Maurice Jones,
11 Benjamin Slade,
12 James Daniels,
13 Winfield Davis,
14 Oden Wilkinson,
15 Joshua Muse,
16 John Winfield,
17 Benjamin Smith,
18 Selden Henderson,
19 Willam Banks,
20 John Fortiscue,
21 John Russell Fortiscue,
22 Jeremiah Warner,
23 Burrige Selby,
24 Thomas Winfield,
25 Jacob Caffee,
26 Hugh Foddree,
27 Richard Migett,
28 James Owens,
29 Jordan Carrow,
30 Thomas Simons,
31 Edward Fuller,
32 Levi O'Neals,
33 William Berry,
34 Thomas Daniels,
35 Clement Daniels,
36 William Bunn,
37 Shadrick Daniels,
38 Benjamin Bunn,
39 Zephaniah Sawyer,
40 William Cohoon,

41 Jeremiah Hall,
42 Joy Sanderson,
43 Robert Hopkins,
44 Robert Jennett,

45 Selby Spencer,
46 Solomon Thornton,
47 William Casons.

Second Company, detached from the Beaufort Regiment

1 Frederick Brooks, Capt.
2 Richard Barner, Lieut.
3 John Vines, Ensign,
4 Will Grist,
5 John Booner,
6 Richard Bonner,
7 John Langley,
8 Thomas Heures,
9 George C. Burbage,
10 William Loveland,
11 David C. Clark,
12 Samuel Campbell,
13 George Congleton,
14 James Howard,
15 Jonathan Wallace,
16 Jonathan Waters,
17 Frederick Waters,
18 Charles Waters,
19 Eleazer Jackson,
20 William Archibald,
21 Absalom Price,
22 James M. Mahow,
23 James Boyd,
24 James Eborn,
25 Alfred Lanir,
26 James Cowper,
27 Abram Cox,
28 Moses Evett,
29 Jonathan Giddins,
30 Thomas Morris,

31 Jesse Evett,
32 John Jones, sr.,
33 Samuel Vines,
34 Gibbin Dickson,
35 Thomas Vines,
36 William M. Moreland,
37 Meshart McReel,
38 John Barrow,
39 Arnett Latham,
40 Henry Woodard,
41 William Albird,
42 Talbing Equals,
43 John Barnett,
44 Humphrey Cherry,
45 Benjamin Cherry,
46 James Brown,
47 Zachariah Ferrell,
48 Alfred Latham,
49 Gideon Fannet,
50 James Wood,
51 William Rawts,
52 Ephraim Dickson,
53 Jesse Robeson,
54 Samuel Philpot,
55 Rowland Mayo,
56 John Grist,
57 Henry Harding,
58 Cannon Smith,
59 Bryan Archlin.

Third Company, detached from the Pitt Regiment.

1 Reading Shipp, Captain,
2 Henry Smith, Lieutenant,
3 John Smith, Ensign,
4 William Browning,
5 Eliphlet King,
6 Sampson Wauley,
7 David Smith,
8 Elisha Holloman,
9 Robert Thomas,
10 Kinyan Downs,
11 William H. Griffin,
12 Henry Wright,
13 Jeptha May,
14 John Pumphrey,
15 Newman Dunn,
16 Allen Chance,
17 Edward Arnold,
18 Major Boid,
19 William Mumford,
20 Joshua Robertson,
21 Lewis Burney,
22 Jesse Boyd,
23 Joseph Sanders,
24 Edward Browning,
25 James Spivey,
26 Absalom Cox,
27 Abram Smith,
28 Frederick Litchworth,
29 Samuel Smith,
30 John Cannon,
31 William Mooring,
32 John Hardee,
33 Dennis Cannon,
34 Freeman McDowell,
35 William Chance,
36 Henry Cannon,
37 Grove Corbett,
38 Frederick Mills,
39 Allen Smith,
40 Asa Starks,
41 Samuel Corbett,
42 Samuel Knight,
43 Cannon Chaner,
44 Samuel Venters,
45 Zachariah Cox,
46 Kennedy Smith,
47 Willie Smith,
48 Palmer Cannon,
49 Redding, Peters,
50 Obed Roundtree,
51 Benjamin Bently,
52 Isaac Robertson,
53 Levi Stocks,
54 John Roy,
55 Nehemiah Dixon,
56 Samuel Merrell,
57 Stephen Right,
58 Cannon Stocks,
59 John Mattocks,
60 Fred Mills, jr.,
61 John Vanpelt,
62 Cullen Tripp,
63 Warren Andrews,
64 Witham Casson,
65 Simon Barney,
66 William Parkes,

67 George Bland,
68 Edward T. Salter,

69 Richard F. Macklewain.

Fourth Company, detached from the Craven Regiment.

1 Horatio Dade, Captain,
2 David Murdock, Lieut.
3 Abner Neale, 2d Lieut.
4 Daniel McRean, Ensign,
5 William H. Ives.
6 Thomas Leath, Corporal,
7 James Delamar,
8 William Caraway,
9 Jeremiah Bateman,
10 James Carney, sr.,
11 Vine Allen,
12 George Washington,
13 John Gettig,
14 Thomas Skidmore,
15 James Lewis, 1st Sergt.
16 Jonathan Perkins,
17 Darius Amyett,
18 Ephraim Simpkins.
19 Hardy L. Jones,
20 Silas Miller,
21 Jesse Vendrich,
22 James Tingle,
23 Major Tingle,
24 Iredell Burnett,
25 John Rice,
26 Thomas Green,
27 William Butler,
28 Reuben Clark,
29 Jeremiah Washington,
30 Nathan Slade,
31 John Dowdy,
32 Smith Jones,
33 William Shines, Corporal,
34 Cornelius Bateman,
35 Seldon Delamar,
36 Jesse Broadway,
37 Barney Wadsworth,
38 William J. Loftin,
39 Henry Carrow,
40 Equilla Pollard,
41 Hardy Willis,
42 Radford Ernell,
43 Allen Ernell,
44 Alexander Prichard,
45 Alderson Thomas,
46 Lewis McKoy,
47 Zadock Woods,
48 James White,
49 Daniel Humphrey,
50 Lewis Humphery,
51 Fred Jones,
52 Samuel Smith,
53 Asa Purity,
54 John Everington,
55 John Forns,
56 Charles Nelson,
57 Joseph Polyard,
58 William Taylor, 2d Sergt.
59 William Ward,
60 John Parks,
61 John Parker,
62 Joseph Fulshire,

63 Paul Berbank,
64 Jesse Barrington,
65 Jebediah Dixon,
66 James Sewell,
67 Thomas Purify,
68 William Stableford,
69 Frederick Powers,
70 Joseph Wiggins,
71 Reuben Hobbs,
72 Abner Cooper,
73 Southey Weatherington,
74 William Williams,
75 James Atherly,
76 Matthew Williams, Drum.
77 David Lewis,
78 Moses Nichols, 3d Sergt.
79 David Russell,
80 Toloson Ryal,
81 Robert Carney, 4th Sergt.
82 Abner Whitehead,
83 John T. Baily,
84 James Lovick.
85 Sylvester Brown,
86 William Edgar, Corporal.

Fifth Company, detached from the Lenoir Regiment.

1 Francis Kilpatrick, Capt.
2 Nathan Bird, 1st Lieut.
3 Benj. Britton, 2d Lieut.
4 Gabriel Parker, 1st Sergt.
5 James Uzzell, 2d Sergt.
6 John Wooten, 3d Sergt.
7 Francis Bright, 4th Sergt.
8 James Walford, 1st Cor'l.
9 William *Mullin, 2d Cor'l.
   *Miller in one return.
10 Spencer Phillips, 3d Cor'l.
11 Robert Murray, 4th Cor'l.
12 Joshua Bird, Drummer,
13 Isaac Walters, Fifer,
14 Henry Parker,
15 Peter Phillips,
16 William Kittral,
17 John Wiggins,
18 Curtis Phillips,
19 John Byrd,
20 James Davis,
21 James B. Miller,
22 William Mosely,
23 William Wayne,
24 Samuel Abbot,
25 Richard Jones,
26 Zachariah Pate,
27 Thomas Brown,
28 Lewis Falkner,
29 Francis Benton,
30 John Goodman,
31 John Whitfield,
32 Henry Pickle,
33 James Davis,
34 Richard Pickle,
35 Cornelius Harper,
36 Alexander Thompson,
37 William Carter,
38 Ashael Herring,
39 William Gray,
40 Jacob Jackson,
41 John Andrews,

42 John Gray,
43 William Miller,
44 William Herring,
45 Edwin Taylor,
46 Francis Brown,
47 William Gray,
48 John Ritter,
49 Francis Benton,
50 Martin Hill,
51 Richard Hill,
52 Robert Mitchell,
53 Nathaniel Walters,
54 Joshua Mosely,
55 George P. Lorrik,

56 Kinnon Taylor,
57 Selathiel Potts,
58 John B. Hartsfield,
59 Blount Coleman,
60 Benjamin Hearing,
61 Robert Wiggins,
62 Nathaniel Hearing,
63 Vinsten Andrews,
64 Walter Allen,
65 Rayman Surls,
66 Joseph Henson,
67 William Campbell,
68 Shadrick Campbell.

Sixth Company, detached from the Wayne Regiment.

1 David *Watson, Captain,
 *Wasdon, in one return.
2 N. Whitfield, 1st Lieut.
3 Wm. Killegrew, 2d Lieut.
4 Hatch Whitfield, Ensign,
5 John Ammonds, Cadet,
6 Alexander Hines,
7 Burwell Rowse,
8 John Howell,
9 David Jennigan,
10 Bryan Barfield,
11 Raphael Bird,
12 Frinitold Manly,
13 Amer McCullen,
14 Henry Phillips,
15 William Adam,
16 David McDaniel,
17 Need Pipkin,
18 Joseph Pipkin,

19 Morris Wyse,
20 Thomas Fowler,
21 Thomas Coor, jr.,
22 William Rose, jr.,
23 George Collins,
24 Elias Harrell,
25 Enos Toler,
26 Charles Bendon,
27 John Motton,
28 Law Jackson,
29 Joel Harrell,
30 Needham Grantum,
31 Daniel Bennett,
32 John Musgrove,
33 William Pipkin,
34 William Bass,
35 Aaron Lean,
36 James Strilling,
37 John Brogdon,

38 Jesse Floid,
39 Josiah Brown,
40 John Casey,
41 Samuel Flowers,
42 Stephen Reeves,
43 William Jones,
44 Jesse Bass,
45 Richard Falkim,
46 Wiben Lewis,
47 Ully Lewis,
48 John Giddins,
49 William Measles,
50 Jehabud Herring,
51 Abner Wiggs,
52 Barna Cotten,
53 James Johnston,
54 William Wilson,
55 Robert Jones,
56 Levi Skipper,
57 William Johnston,
58 Edward Holmes,
59 John Thompson,
60 Philip Hooks,
61 Job Rooks,

62 Mathew Daniel,
63 George Mitchel,
64 Thomas Pindar,
65 Enos Holland,
66 Joseph Fulghum,
67 Joseph Taylor,
68 Peter Rice,
69 David Thompson,
70 Jesse Harper,
71 John Harrel,
72 John Dean,
73 William Hooks,
74 Jacob Newsom,
75 Joseph Newsom,
76 John Britt,
77 Wright Smith,
78 Woodard Howell,
79 Jason Macbau,
80 Dawson Smith,
81 Curtis Daniel,
82 John Sasser,
83 Giles Ham,
84 Oliver Donell.

Seventh Company, detached from the Green Regiment.

1 Hymerisk Hooker, Capt.
2 Thomas Hooker, Lieut.
3 Wm. Hooper, 1st Sergt.
4 John Harper, 2d Sergt.
5 Wm. Doughty, 3d Sergt.
6 J. H. Albritton, 4th Sergt.
7 Jos. J. House, 1st Cor'l.
8 Lemuel Speigpt, 2d Cor'l.
9 Patrick Dickson, 3d Cor'l.
10 Absalom Tyler, 4th Cor'l.
11 Readin Jones,
12 Joseph Harrell,
13 Wiley Dale,
14 Caleb Spivy,
15 John Jackson,
16 Calvin Mage,
17 Right Canady,
18 Rinchen Hollowday,

19 Simeon Albritton,
20 James Armond,
21 Person Tutton,
22 Benjamin Scaborough,
23 John Minshew,
24 Peter Eppes,
25 Jesse Pope,
26 Thomas Edwards,
27 Stephen Cooke,
28 James Hooker,
29 Bryant Kilpatrick,
30 Michael Coward,
31 John Brand,
32 Alfred Hart,
33 James Butts,
34 John Craft,
35 George Belcher,
36 Henry Barfield,
37 Samuel Hay,
38 Kinchen P. Epes,
39 Jesse Coward,
40 Stephen Johnston,
41 John Burord,
42 Alexander Williams,
43 Stephen Chester,
44 Abner Cox,
45 Elijah Newsom,
46 John Mayton,
47 Robert Hinson,
48 Robert Hall,

49 Winston Garland,
50 Crewry Rogers,
51 Hardy Dain,
52 Kinchen Faircloth,
53 Gideon Britt,
54 Samuel Whitby,
55 James Elmore,
56 Gabriel Sherod,
57 Giles Smith,
58 Elijah Smith,
59 William Hamm,
60 Haywood Hamm,
61 Noah Peacock,
62 John Peacock,
63 James Aycock,
64 Silas Lamb,
65 Jesse Peacock,
66 Elisha Davis,
67 Cullen Haywell,
68 John Peacock,
69 Nathan Turrell,
70 Edwin Holswell,
71 Hezekiah Smith,
72 Joseph Hollowell,
73 William Lovering,
74 Harrison Love,
75 Daniel Ellis,
76 William King,
77 James Woodard,
78 Peter Wooten.

Eighth Company, detached from the Johnston Regiment.

1 Thomas Folsome, Capt.
2 Jarrat M. Jelks, 1st Lieut.
3 Henry Guy, 2d Lieut.
4 John C. Guy, Ensign,
5 A. S. Ballenger, 1st Serg
6 Willis Hinton, 2d Sergt.

7 Nicholas Lynch, 3d Sergt.
8 Newit Bridges, 4th Sergt.
9 Mabry Richison, 1st Cor'l.
10 Jesse Wellons, 2d Cor'l.
11 Stephen Hicks, 3d Cor'l.
12 Reddick Hews, 4th Cor'l.
13 Thaddeus Duck, Drum.
14 James Jordan, Fifer,
15 Braswell Bridges,
16 Jacob Avera,
17 Needham Lambert,
18 Samuel Frost,
19 Stephen Brown,
20 Stephen Makins,
21 Josiah Hinnant,
22 Lewis Godwin,
23 Amos Batten,
24 Hardy Batten,
25 William Batten,
26 Micajah Wilkinson,
27 Elam Smith,
28 Jacob Walker,
29 Etheldred Bagly,
30 Reuben Pope,
31 John Allen,
32 Kedar Farmer,
33 Joshua Daniel,
34 Joseph Farmer,
35 Benjamin, Sellers,
36 Jones Davis,
37 Benjamin Johnston,
38 Bryan Adams, jr.,
39 Hardy Adams,
40 Ridly Porter,
41 Absalom Woodall,
42 Reeves Joy,

43 Myrick Joy,
44 John Barber,
45 Brittain Barber,
46 Bright Bird,
47 Jeremiah Blackman,
48 Mathew Hinton,
49 John Filgo,
50 David Filgo,
51 Nathaniel Johnston,
52 John Killingworth, jr.,
53 Richard Rollins,
54 Thomas Simpkins,
55 Edward Lee, sr.,
56 John Brunt,
57 Bold Robin Hood,
58 Samuel Engram,
59 Nathan Bryan,
60 Noah Barefoot, jr.,
61 Benjamin Simpkins,
62 Burnel Cole,
63 Francis Harrell,
64 John Kean,
65 John Sellers,
66 Henry Lee,
67 Frederick Biggener,
68 Oliver Raines, jr.,
69 William Holt,
70 Hervey Raines, sr.,
71 Amos Peden,
72 John Peden,
73 Willis Woodard,
74 Benjamin Bridges,
75 Thomas Hollowell,
76 Malichi Humphrey,
77 Reuben Perry,
78 John Lee,

79 Nathan Stancel,
80 David Bailey,
81 Jonathan Fuller,
82 Frederick Oneal,
83 John Pender,
84 Martin Hall,
85 Drury Baley,
86 Bud Price,
87 William Green,
88 Jacob Adams,
89 Micajah Woodard,
90 William Richardson,
91 Thomas Gerald,
92 Thomas Taylor,
93 Jonathan Hinnant,
94 Hardy Hinnant,
95 Loved Pearce,
96 Bannister Grissel,
97 Tobias Goodwin,
98 Levi Richardson,
99 William Pender,
100 John Richardson,
101 Lewis Hayly,
102 Reddin Green,
103 Nathan Stansill,
104 Benjamin Martin,
105 James Stevenson,
106 Richard Whittington,
107 George Mainard,
108 Silas Goodwin,
109 Brittain Honecut,
110 Brittain Johnston,
111 Bartley Stevens,
112 Reuben Gower,
113 James Johnston,
114 Kiah Copeland.

Ninth Company, detached from the Duplin Regiment.

1 Bryan Glissen, Captain,
2 Stephen Williams, Lieut.
3 Samuel Cherry, Ensign,
4 James Grimes,
5 James Sullivan,
6 Joseph Osburn,
7 Jonathan Jones,
8 Richard Bradley,
9 William Frederick,
10 Thomas Bennett,
11 Charles Gibbs,
12 John Denmark,
13 Buk Jernigan,
14 John Blanchard,
15 David Rouse,
16 Abram Connegay,
17 David Carr,
18 John Greer,
19 Moses Manchy,
20 James M. Cam,
21 Elijah Mallard,
22 George Bray,
23 Felix Candy.
24 Robert Sand,
25 Owen Lanier,
26 David Brooks,
27 John Hankin,
28 Elijah Tucker,
29 William Best,
30 Lewis Bowen,

31 John Bowen,
32 Nathan South,
33 Andrew Wallace,
34 James Evans,
35 Richard Sellers,
36 Thomas Lee,
37 John Lanier,
38 Henry Matthews,
39 Richard Rusley,
40 James Matthews,
41 Samuel Sumner,
42 Isaac Weston,
43 Stephen Grimes,
44 John Peale,
45 Isaac Phips,
46 Robert Williams,
47 John Grimes,
48 Joseph Dickson,
49 James Gaylor,
50 Stephen Duncan,
51 Warren Blount,
52 Reuben Blanchard,
53 Jacob Harrell,
54 David Allen,
55 Amos Walder,

56 Daniel Jernigan,
57 Jacob Gilmore,
58 Jesse Outlaw,
59 James Carter,
60 Zachariah Carter,
61 Lott Batts,
62 Owen Hale,
63 Stephen Herring,
64 John Glisson,
65 Harget Kornegay,
66 James Flannigan,
67 Stephen Carmon,
68 James Brown,
69 William West,
70 Isaac Powell,
71 Jacob Powell,
72 John Manor,
73 Fountain Brown,
74 Daniel Kethly,
75 David Collins,
76 William Sellers,
77 Joshua Murett,
78 William Smith,
79 David Noles.

Tenth Company, detached from the Jones Regiment.

1 Anthony Hatch, Captain,
2 James Huston, Lieut.
3 Donald C. Burkly, Ensign,
4 Zadock, Cox,
5 Hall Bags,
6 James Rhodes, jr.,
7 John Jones,
8 John Saunders, jr,

9 Urban Williamson,
10 James Williamson,
11 Thomas Hay,
12 George Hay,
13 Joseph Hay,
14 William Wise,
15 Simeon Simons,
16 Barge Gooding,

17 Asa Fasene,
18 John Stanly,
19 Benjamin Miller,
20 Peter Elliot,
21 David Jones,
22 Joshua Davis,
23 James McDaniel,
24 David Ketchum,
25 James Frazier,
26 James Masburn,
27 William Hop,
28 Hardy Saunders,
29 John McKenny,
30 William Giles,
31 John Pitman,
32 Stephen Conaway,
33 David Berry,
34 James Perry,
35 Jesse Lee,
36 Westly Davis,
37 Edmund Howard,
38 William Simmons,
39 George Koonce,
40 John Morris,
41 Edward Bryan,
42 Samuel Hatch,
43 James Wood,
44 Rigden Hewit,
45 Edmund Jones,
46 George Smith,
47 Wm. Hubbard Houston,
48 Theophilus Best,
49 Masburn Raimer,
50 David King,
51 Theophilus Williams,
52 William Richerson,
53 Abraham Spencer,
54 David Jones,
55 Asa Sumner,
56 Bryan Smith,
57 Lewis Smith,
58 Benjamin Brittain,
59 Felix Jones,
60 Andrew Adams,
61 James Sandline,
62 Lewis Mariner,
63 James Daffin,
64 Jordan Moore,
65 William Lewis,
66 Joshua Shepperd,
67 Isaac Coverton,
68 Benjamin Wooten,
69 William Mason,
70 William Anderson,
71 Isaac James Jones,
72 John Rue,·
73 Sherwood Faulk,
74 Benjamin Gause,

Eleventh Company, detached from the Onslow Regiment.

1 Jacob Galden, Captain,
2 William Mitchell, Lieut.
3 Hardy Pitts, Ensign,
4 Benjamin Scott,
5 Isaac Scott,
6 David Scott,
7 James Wade,
8 Aaron Fox,

9 Washington Hamnor,
10 Jacob Hufman,
11 Nathan Thompson,
12 Robert Wallace,
13 James White,
14 Hardy Wood,
15 Jess Gregory,
16 Bryant Williams,
17 Ebrey Sanding,
18 Henry Shepherd,
19 James Saunders,
20 Elijah Hardeson,
21 Neal Grisson,
22 Burney Humphrey,
23 Samuel Jones,
24 Bray Harrell,
25 Lewis Stenkman,
26 Ephraim King,
27 Thomas Alphin,
28 Micajah King,
29 Thomas Garnto,
30 James McCullok,
31 Benjamin Barrow,
32 William Phillips,
33 Abner Anders,
34 Isaac Henderson,
35 Beverly Simmons,
36 Isaac Huggins,
37 Henry Henderson,
38 Hillory Henderson,
39 Joseph Simmons,
40 Hardy Newton,
41 Elijah Russel,
42 Alexander Nelson,
43 Thomas Ennett,
44 Joshua McDonald,

45 William Williams,
46 Francis Venters,
47 Whitchurst Ennett,
48 Edward Pearson,
49 Stephen Hawkins,
50 Benjamin Ward,
51 Aldridge Hicks,
52 Humphrey Marshall,.
53 Seth Hadnok,
54 William Howard,
55 John Milson,
56 Ezekiel Askins,
57 Edward Fonville,
58 Dempsy Wilson,
59 Calvin Howard,
60 John Willis,
61 John Grant,
62 William Grant,
63 John Stephenson,
64 Isaac Gilbert,
65 Bazzel Grant,
66 Isaac Riggs,
67 John Crane,
68 Aquilla R. Hill,
69 Walter Hellen,
70 Hill Williams,
71 William Humphrey,.
72 Lewis Oliver,
73 Moses Cox,
74 Samuel Davis,
75 William Ennett,
76 John Hawkins,
77 Malachi Wilder,
78 Nicodemus Gargamy,
79 Daniel Mitchell,
80 Abram Burnett.

Twelfth Company, detached from the New Hanover Regiment.

1 John Mitchel, Captain,
2 John Watson, Lieutenant,
3 D. W. Griffith, Ensign,
4 Collin Blue,
5 Levi Chace,
6 Henry Farrand,
7 John Holmes,
8 Jacob Levy,
9 Ezekiel Trussel,
10 James Marshall,
11 Ezra Peck,
12 Niel Robeson,
13 Peleg Pierce,
14 Jesse Wingate,
15 John M. Wright,
16 John McFarland,
17 William Branch,
18 Jesse Saunders,
19 Frederick George,
20 William Larkins,
21 James Stanly
22 Josiah Piner,
23 Joseph Clifford,
24 John Howell,
25 John Hulett,
26 Hardy Micks,
27 Jacob Caston,
28 Frederick Quinby,
29 Henry Quinby,
30 Oliver Caston,
31 William Smith,
32 Joseph Quinby,
33 William Parmer,
34 Alexander McAlister,
35 Walter Simpson,
36 Samuel Moore, jr.,
37 Joseph Simpson,
38 William Berring,
39 William Moore,
40 Thomas Sharpless,
41 James Goff,
42 James Pinner,
43 William Hand.
44 Ambrose Smith,
45 Luke Townly,
46 Jeremiah Sutherland,
47 Henry Williams,
48 John Filyaw,
49 Abram Hall,
50 Lewis Hall,
51 William Pegford,
52 Nathaniel Wheeler,
53 Angus Kurr,
54 George Corbett,
55 William Jones,
56 James Fennell,
57 Bennet Fellows,
58 Arthur Evans,
59 William Hawsley,
60 William New,
61 Zachariah F. Burfield,
62 Joseph Picket,
63 Israel C. Burdeaux,
64 Hiram Brocket,
65 James Price,
66 John St. George,

67 Kinchen Nicholas,
68 John Messick,
69 Lean Messick,
70 Owen Hansley,
71 Woodham Shepherd,
72 William Jones Larkins,

73 James Walker,
74 Swinson Gurgarmus,
75 Moses Moore,
76 Cornelius Murphy,
77 James L. White,
78 Abijah Hanson.

THIRD REGIMENT.

DETACHED FROM THE FIFTH BRIGADE.

JEREMIAH SLADE, *Lieutenant Colonel Commandant.*
JAMES J. HILL, *First Major.*
ANDREW JOYNER, *Second Major.*

First Company, detached from the First Halifax Regiment.

1 James Overstreet, Capt.
2 Wil. C. Whitaker, Lieut.
2 William Brickle, 2d Lieut.
4 John Vaughan,
5 William Crowell,
6 John Riks,
7 James Whitaker,
8 Thomas Applewhite,
9 Moses Grimmer, Fifer,
10 Wallis Nicholson,
11 Timothy Connell,
12 Samuel Simmons,
13 John Parker,
14 John Scott,
15 James Gaskins,
16 Henry Bradford,
17 Thomas Bradford,

18 William Willey,
19 John Bradford,
20 George Goodwin,
21 Willie Watson,
22 Thomas B. Parker,
23 David Douglass,
24 Wilson Brantly,
25 John Glover,
26 Hall Hudson,
27 John W. Branch,
28 John Knight,
29 James Merrit,
30 Washington Turner,
31 Samuel Brickle,
32 John Shields,
33 James Youngs,
34 John Bryant,

35 James Brantly,
36 James Lawrence,
37 Benjamin Pearce,
38 John Matthews,
39 Hansel Horne,
   Cullen Grimmer,
41 Jethro Parker,
42 Miles Cross,
43 Willis Shelton,
44 Robert Saunders,
45 Patrick McDaniel,
46 Wilson W. Carter,

47 John Scott,
48 John Clark,
49 Edward King,
50 Hiram King,
51 Jesse A. Brooks,
52 Blake Baker,
53 Lewis Lewis,
54 Joseph Pully,
55 Rinchen Harriss,
56 Jacob Bartholomew,
57 James Abington.

Second Company, detached from the Second Halifax Regiment

1 Isham Matthews, Captain.
2 Thomas Nichilson, Lieut.
3 John Alston, Ensign,
4 Zachariah Sullivan,
5 Francis Anderson,
6 Halvin Ash,
7 William Brown,
8 James Ash,
9 William H. Ballance,
10 Robert Brinkley,
11 Jesse Blackburn,
12 Asa Blackburn,
13 William J. Bradie,
14 John Cooley,
15 John Curling,
16 Jesse Christie,
17 Samuel Carter,
18 Gideon Dameron,
19 William R. Daniel,
20 Rhoderick Easley,
21 Allen Easley,

22 Eaton F. Allen,
23 Allen Flood,
24 Wilson Green,
25 Thomas Green,
26 William Gurly,
27 Thomas Y. Grimsted,
28 Benjamin Green,
29 Jesse Hamblet,
30 Miley Harbin,
31 David Harriss,
32 Jesse Harlow,
33 Gabriel Hawkins,
34 John Hawes,
35 Hansel Hathcock,
36 Edmund Jackson,
37 Beverly Jackson,
38 Robert Jones,
39 John Jordan,
40 John King,
41 Solomon Locklear,
42 Exum Low,

43 Samuel Locklear,
44 John Lee, jr.,
45 John A. Losset,
46 Jesse Moore,
47 Alfred Moore,
48 John Moore, jr.,
49 William Montford,
50 William Moore,
51 John Mann,
52 James Mason,
53 Arthur Manly,
54 Guilford Nicholson,
55 Thomas H. Green,
56 William Onions,
57 Eaton Powell,
58 Rica Pullin,
59 John Pugh,

60 Ransom Powell,
61 Frederick Pully,
62 John Porter,
63 Allen Powell,
64 Michael Rand,
65 Joseph Studivant,
66 Abner Spear,
67 Thomas Sammons,
68 Benjamin Saunders,
69 Peter Ship,
70 Whiles Studivant,
71 Arthur Spear,
72 John Thrower,
73 Lemuel Wilkins,
74 John Wright, sr.,
75 Caleb Woodard,
76 Thomas Ward.

Third Company, detached from the Northampton Regiment.

1 Jas. C. Harrison, Captain,*
2
3 Sterling Milton, Lieut.
4 Whitmel Rulland, Ensign*
*2 Capt. and 2 ensigns ret'nd
5
6 William Erwin,
7 Willis Jasey,
8 Samuel Bryan,
9 John M. Williams,
10 James Slightfoot,
11 John Bryan,
12 Obediah Bowing,
13 Elisha Boon,
14 David Boon,
15 James Vaughan,

16 Willis Edge,
17 Kinchen Murrel!,
18 John Sandefur, jr.,
19 Cullen Mitchell,
20 Bynum Harriss,
21 John Woodruff,
22 John Jones,
23 Charles Love,
24 Zachariah Allen,
25 Solomon Holmes,
26 John Norworthy,
27 John Warwick,
28 Randolph Newsum,
29 John Simons,
30 John Umphreys,
31 Williby Hastey,

32 George Garris,
33 Henry Smith,
34 Barnaba Bunn,
35 John Benton,
36 Jiles Jewter,
37 Abel Gay,
38 Nathan Pope,
39 Newit Morgan,
40 Richard Pilano,
41 Lewis Short,
42 Alexander McGridor,
43 William Friear,
44 Thomas Norworthy,
45 Reuben Scott,
46 Elisha Ryno,
47 Cullen Artis,
48 Robert Burnett,
49 Thomas Williams,
50 Calson Futtrell,
51 Robert Warren,
52 Morris Parker,
53 James W. Davis,
54 Nehemiah Vinson,
55 Rhodes Gary,
56 Drury Britt,
57 Francis Parker,
58 Drew Walden,
59 Hardy Hart,
60 Henry Gilham,
61 Riggan Newsom,
62 James Valentine,
63 Willie Wilkinson,
64 Edmund Thompson,
65 Benjamin Newsom
66 Barnes Bridges,
67 James Warwik,
68 Benjamin Griffin,
69 John James,
70 Dennis O'Conner,
71 Thomas Norman,
72 Hermon Rowell,
73 William Boon,
74 James Griffin,
75 Gilbert Griffin,
76 Shadrack Grant,
77 Lewis Boon,
78 Stephen Wimborne,
79 Henry Evans,
80 Joiner Boon,
81 Austin Kindrik,
82 Henry E. Simons,
83 Joel Price,
84 Stott Watson,
85 Jep Boon,
86 Cordal Newson,
87 John Newson,
88 Seamore Newsom,
89 Kinchen Artis,
90 Herbert Scott,
91 Whitfield Cross,
92 Aaron Fly,
93 Warren Bridges,
94 Brittain Lassiter,
95 Daniel Futrell,
96 Samuel Parker,
97 Micajah Futrell,
98 Moab Underwood,
99 Benjamin Vaughan,
100 Isham Curl,
101 Sterling Dupree,
102 Arthur Tyner,
103 Robert Thompson,

104 James Love,
105 James Smith,
106 Richard Harrison,
107 Lemuel Vaughan,
108 James Morriss,

109 Jones Glover,
110 John Richards,
111 Benjamin Edwards,
112 William Collier,
113 Littleton Tooke.

Fourth Company, detached from the Edgecombe Regiment.

1 David Barnes, Captain,
2 John B. Walten, Lieut.
3 Josiah Wood, 2d Lieut.
4 James Knight, Ensign,
5 Paul Randolph, 1st Sergt.
6 Alex. Cotten, 2d Sergt.
7 J. L. Southerlin, 3d Sergt.
8 L. Barfield, 4th Sergt.
9 Pelasky Dudley, 1st. Cor'l.
10 Jonathan Bailey, 2d Cor'l.
11 Etheldred Gray, 3d Cor'l.
11 Joshua Warren, 4th Cor'l.
13 Jonathan Thigpen, Drum.
14 Pitman Worsley, Fifer,
15 Bythel Staton,
16 John Garrett,
17 Thomas Edmondson,
18 James Knight, Ensign,
19 William Savage,
20 Thomas Baton,
21 Noah Cushing,
22 Lawrence Mayo,
23 John Rhodes,
24 Whitmell Hardy,
25 James Alsobrook,
26 Spear Bradley,
27 Kader Hales,
28 Bartholomew Bryan,

29 Theophilus Parker,
30 John Parker,
31 Samuel Parker,
32 Stephen Harper,
33 Benjamin Portis,
34 Samuel Portis,
35 Joseph Portis,
36 Charles Cobb,
37 Abner Eason,
38 David Rayner,
39 Rading Sugg,
40 Bartholomew Bowers,
41 Andrew Clark,
42 Wilie Cotton,
43 David Dancy,
44 Gideon Jolley,
45 James Bilberry,
46 Samuel Wood,
47 Gray Thigpen,
48 James Thigpen, jr.,
49 Howell Thigpen,
50 John Nowell,
51 James Cobb,
52 John Blackburn,
53 David Tennison,
54 Benjamin Barfield,
55 Michael Parker,
56 David Morris,

57 Brittain Pitman,
58 Reuben Pitman,
59 James Teat,
60 Kalib Warren,
61 Isaac Horne,
62 Jacob Brake,
63 Henry Horne,
64 Theophilus Thomas,
65 David Brake,

66 Elisha Thomas,
67 Thomas Price,
68 Thomas Haughton,
69 Lott Stalling,
70 Josiah Crocker,
71 Noah Davis,
72 William Morgan,
73 Eli Vann,
74 John Hines.

Fifth Company, detached from the Martin Regiment.

1 Durham Davis, Captain,
2 James Reddick, Lieut,
3 James Howell, Ensign,
4 J. C. Williams, 1st Sergt.
5 George Harrison, 2d Sergt.
6 Luke Bennett, 3d Sergt.
7 Jesse Lolly, 4th Sergt.
8 Hosea Lanier, 1st Cor'l.
9 James Hardeson, 2d Cor'l.
10 Selathiel Sherod, 3d Cor'l.
11 Jehu Pearce, 4th Cor'l.
12 Jesse Hardeson, Drummer,
13 Samuel Robeson, Fifer,
14 James Garrott,
15 William Bultry,
16 Thomas Lassiter,
17 John Amis,
18 William Applin,
19 Harmon Girkin,
20 John Smithwrick,
21 Joshua Hardeson,
22 Silas Wollard,
23 Nathaniel Wollard,
24 James Cottram,

25 Timothy Brogden,
26 Westley Floid,
27 Edmond Rogers,
28 Seth Meazel,
29 Aaron Meazel,
30 Jesse Meazel,
31 John Rogerson,
32 James Ward,
33 Benjamin Futrell,
34 John Rowbuck,
35 William Everitt,
36 David Roberson,
37 Nathan Morris,
38 Darling Cherry,
39 William Beach,
40 James Caraway,
41 Whitmel Pierce,
42 Richard Airs,
43 Henry Best,
44 William Rogers,
45 Raleigh Rowbuck,
46 Newton Coburn,
47 Arden Taylor,
48 Perry Brewer,

49 Solomon Kelly,
50 John Hawkins,
51 James Stalls,
52 Balentine Page,
53 William Smith,
54 Henry Smith,
55 Willie Hoard,
56 Thomas Ross,
57 Chancey Davenport,
58 William Correl,
59 William James,
60 William Whorton,
61 Jonathan Calloway,
62 John Wheatley,
63 William Hines,
64 Moses Weaver,
65 Lawrence Hyman,
66 Thomas Bryan,

67 Elias Bryan,
68 Nicholas Lord,
69 Augustus Wood,
70 Benjamin Amis,
71 David Baston,
72 Jesse Peal,
73 David Cooper,
74 David Rogerson,
75 Micajah Perry,
76 Thomas Cary,
77 John Manning,
78 Robert Daniel,
79 Noah Robeson,
80 James Hynes,
81 Daniel Medford,
82 Reuben Griffin,
83 John Beach,
84 Henry Robeson.

Sixth Company, detached from the Nash Regiment.

1 Francis Drake, Captain,
2 Isaac Watkins, 1st Lieut.
3 David Daniel, 2d Lieut,
4 W. Manning, Ensign,
5 Samuel Sorsby, 1st Sergt.
6 William Lepford, 2d Sergt.
7 Samuel Williams, 3d Sergt.
8 Alfred Bunn, 4th Sergt.
9 Henry Bridgers, 1st Cor'l.
10 Archb'd. Wheless, 2d Cor'l.
11 Jos. Whitehead, 3d Cor'l.
12 Thos. Beckwith, 4th Cor'l.
13 Guilford Whitfield, Drum.
14 Green Henry, Fifer,
15 Thomas Davis,

16 Levi C. Arrington,
17 Richard Carlisle,
18 Jinnes Hackney,
19 Joseph Green,
20 William Griffin,
21 Nathan Evans,
22 Edward White,
23 John Evans,
24 Henry Hunt,
25 Bennett Jones,
26 George Evans,
27 Wilson Hammons,
28 Nathan Sikes,
29 Thomas Bryant,
30 Woody Tucker,

31 David Wall,
32 Kader Bass,
33 Loody Ferrell,
34 Thomas Lloyd,
35 Hutchins Ferrell,
36 Burton Ferrell,
37 Henry Morgan,
38 James Ferrell,
39 Gillum Cone,
40 Archibald Lemon,
41 Claton Mann,
42 Samuel Davis.
43 Edward Crowell,
44 Benjamin Gloveyer,
45 James B. Crowell,
46 Thomas Brown,
47 Eli Tisdale,
48 Jacob Atkins,
49 Richard Triggler,
50 John Poulan,
51 Daniel Bachelor,
52 Joseph Tucker,
53 John Williams,
54 Jacob Row,
55 Elijah Wiggins,
56 Elen Mecome,
57 Edwin Brantly,
58 Harrell Horn,
59 Richard Stallings,
60 Alston Gandy,
61 Sampson Sikes,
62 John Grandy,
63 Thomas Valentine,
64 Griffin Ganday,
65 Solomon Thomas,
66 Peter Gray,
67 Amor Beckwith,
68 Newit Edwards,
69 John Hawks,
70 William Richards,
71 Jorden Barrow.

Seventh Company, detached from the Warren Regiment.

1 Charles Allen, Captain,
2 Thos. Stackhouse, Lieut.
3 John Motholand,
4 Micajah T. Hawkins,
5 Nathan Turner,
6 Amos P. Sledge,
7 Doct M. Robertson,
8 Samuel Dowtin,
9 Wilmot F. Egerton,
10 Owen F. Myrick,
11 Richard Ward,
12 Thomas Davis,
13 Ivy Allen,
14 William Breadlove,
15 Philemon Perdue,
16 William Oliver,
17 William Turner,
18 Arthur Tussell,
19 Ransom Stroud,
20 Lemuel Mitchel,
21 Thomas Harton,
22 Joseph Wren,
23 William Powell,
24 Allen Wren,

25 Wiles Person,
26 James C. Bennet,
27 Joshua Harper,
28 Ransom Acock,
29 Cudburth Neal,
30 Henry Pearson,
31 Richard Davis,
32 James Powell,
33 Peter Randolph,
34 John Robertson,
35 William Sherrin,
36 Charles Stoddard,
37 Lewis Sherrin,
38 Kinchen Williamson,
39 George Hazlewood,
40 Jasper Capps,
41 Thomas Walker,
42 Elisha Sherod,
43 Buck Robertson,
44 Jiles Carter,
45 Joshua Davis,
46 Benjamin Davis,
47 Thomas Newman,
48 Pleasant Ellington,
49 John Allen,

50 Daniel A. Perdue,
51 Charles Bennet,
52 Joel Ellington,
53 James Thompson,
54 D. G. Williams,
55 Anderson Peebles,
56 James Alston,
57 Solomon Jenkins,
58 Hardeway Davis,
59 William Pertilla,
60 Edward Pertilla,
61 Richard Beach,
62 Joel Tally,
63 Miles Ellis
64 James Tally,
65 Thomas Tally,
66 Simes Ellis,
67 Claton Lambert,
68 John Hawks,
69 Henry James,
70 Daniel White,
71 Obadiah Ellis,
72 James Smith,
73 Leonard King,

Eighth Company, detached from the Franklin Regiment.

1 Marma. M. Jeffreys, Capt.
2 Benj. Stewart, Lieutenant.
3 Nathaniel Hunt, 2d Lieut.
4 James Harrison, Ensign,
5 Richard Wright,
6 Winson Cook,
7
8 Newsome Bridges,
9 Stephen Davis,
10 Nathaniel Hayes,
11 Thomas Tharington,
12 William D. Jones,
13 Dabney M. Duke,
14 William T. Dent,
15 Izekiah Stephens,
16 Benjamin G. Richards,

17 William Baker,
18 Martin Murphy,
19 James Bridges,
20 John C. Perry,
21 Benjamin Lanier,
22 Duncan McLean,
23 William Bird,
24 R. Nellsmall 1st Sergt.
25 Kinchen Boon,
26 Thomas B. Arendel,
27 Elijah Izzard,
28 Julius Hill,
29 Robert Thomas,
30 John Baker,
31 James Murphy,
32 Willie Hight,
33 Green D. House,
34 John Prince,
35 Breedlove Pippen,
36 John Mullins,
37 Reddick Haswell,
38 Thomas Haswell,
39 Ignatius Goldsberry,
40 Albert Perry,
41 John M. Sherod,
42 Willie O. Davis,
43 Thomas Davis,
44 Jesse Collins,
45 David Collins,
46 John Hill,
47 Guilford Lewis,

48 James Nelms,
49 Willis Cook,
50 Joseph Stevens,
51 James Barrow,
52 Henry Thomas,
53 Joseph C. Harris,
54 Alexander Carson,
55 James Vincent,
56 Guilford Bass,
57 Bennett Perry,
58 Miles Carv,
59 Joseph B. Flemming,
60 John Wichidht,
61 Green Wood,
62 Simeon Jenkins,
63 Eaton Freeman,
64 Mathew Walker,
65 Alsey Young,
66 John Young,
67 William Simmons,
68 Macomb Alfred,
69 William C. Perry,
70 Julius Alford,
71 James Hunt,
72 Hugh Hayes,
73 John J. Lancaster,
74 Drury Denton,
75 John Jones,
76 William Alford,
77 William Debnam,
78 Dilworth Sledge,

FOURTH REGIMENT,

DETACHED FROM FOURTH AND FOURTEENTH BRIGADES.

ALFRED ROWLAND, *Lieutenant Colonel Commandant.*
JOHN A. CAMERON, *First Major.*
DAVID GILLESPIE, *Second Major.*

First Company, detached from the Bladen Regiment.

1 John Nicholson, Captain,
2 J. C. Cumming 1st Lieut.
3 Robert McKee, 2d Lieut.
4 James Campbell, Ensign,
5 Alex. McIver, 1st Sergt.
6 Thos. Smith, 2d Sergt.
7 Neil McMillan,
8 Thomas Clardy,
9 Turpin Cheshire,
10 Colin Shaw,
11 Anguish McMillan,
12 Evan Rice,
13 David Davis,
14 Julius High,
15 Mercer Grimes,
16 William C. Singletary,
17 David Singletary,
18 Jasper Hester,
19 Daniel Gooden,
20 Thomas Averit,
21 Abel Burney.
22 Wilie Adkison,
23 Edward Pemberton,
24 James Kelley,
25 John Campbell,
26 David White,
27 James McLelland,
28 Sampson Davis,
29 Arthur Butler.
30 Patrick Murphy,
31 William Davis, jr.,
32 William Davis, sr.,
33 William McKay,
34 Thomas Brown,
35 John B. Cowen,
36 George B. Thomas,
37 Archibald Pattison.
38 Samuel Plumber,
39 Dennis Kelleham,
40 John Kelleham,
41 Pierce Kelleham,
52 John Taylor,
43 James Stredy,
44 John McFalten,
45 Dugald McKitchen,
46 John Savage,
47 James Salter,
48 Alexander Lamer,
49 Barnabas Brown,
50 Joseph Hester,

Second Company, detached from First Cumberland Regiment.

1 Arch'd. McCraine, Capt.
2 Daniel Shaw, 1st Lieut.
3 John Shaw, 2d Lieut.
4 John Hodges, Ensign,
5 Robert Shaw,
6 John Steele,
7 Jesse Betha,
8 Owen Boon,
9 James Sorrel,
10 William Hodges,
11 Neil McNeil,
12 William McKinsie,
13 John Gordon,
14 John McLelland,
15 Ebenezer Folsome,
16 Murdoc McRae,
17 Hector McAuthur,
18 Benjamin Morrison,
19 Samuel Searsey,
20 Rowland Fauckner,
21 Aaron Searcy,
22 Peter Munro,
23 August Ray,
24 John McKellar,
25 Neel Munro,
26 Theophilus Denny,
27 Cornelius Colefield,
28 John McDougal,
29 John Wilkinson,
30 Hector McNeil,
31 Richard Cade,
32 Richard Wilkinson,
33 Absalom Hammonds,
34 James Norris,
35 David Bone,
36 Richard Bone,
37 John Jackson,
38 Thomas Gill,
39 Joshua Jesop,
40 Samuel Reeves,
41 John Taylor,
42 Robert Harwell,
43 Francis Hobby,
44 Thomas Paine,
45 Drury Massey,
46 Frederick Yarborough,
47 Wilson Ray,
48 Darius Cox,
49 Murdock Campbell,
50 Elisha Brown,
51 Jesse Northington,
52 Alexander Mckellan,
53 Sion Tedder,
54 Allen Campbell,
55 Neil Bowie,
56 Malcolm Pattison,
57 William Lathom,
58 Needham Moore,
59 Horatio Griffin,
60 Lewis Moore,
61 Benjamin Moore,
62 James Stephens,
63 Allen Northington,
64 Neil McNeil,
65 Bogle Ferrand.
66 Thomas H. Massey,
67 Joshua Carman,
68 Arthur Core,

69 Shadrack Johnson,
70 William Daniel,
71 John Lewis,

72 John Johnston,
73 John Moore.

Third Company, detached from the Cumberland Regiment.

1 David Evans, Captain,
2 George Jones, 1st Lieut.
3 John Leonard,
4 John Evans,
5 James Rush,
6 Phillip Horton,
7 Samuel Salmon,
8 Etheldred Syke,
9 Thomas McMurray,
10 Phillip McRae,
11 Council McCullin,
12 Pitkin McCullin,
13 John Carver,
14 Sion Horne,
15 Waddell Cade,
16 Mathew Hayes,
17 Gilbert McColl,
18 William Taylor,
19 Willam Nunnery,
20 John Bryan,
21 Robert Olery,
22 William Anderson,
23 John Thagard,
24 Samuel Reeves,
25 James McDaniel,
26 Zachariah Butler,
27 Norman McNeil,
28 John McKinzie,
29 Samuel Butler,
30 John Langdon,

31 John Shaw,
32 Douglass McLaughlan,
33 James Denton,
34 Hugh McGuire,
35 Thomas Bowen,
36 Jonathan Evans,
37 John Ray,
38 James Kirkpatrick,
39 Murdock Orchillred,
40 William Tillingast,
41 Jesse Anson,
42 Thomas Evans,
43 Murwin Carrington,
44 James Stevens,
45 John B. Smith,
46 Murdock McLeod,
47 German Seawell,
48 George Holmes,
49 William Horn,
50 Thomas Cole,
51 Jacob Seawell,
52 John Burgess,
53 Jonathan Hare,
54 Dugald McIntyre,
55 John Johnston,
56 Duncan Pharis,
57 Jacob Faircloth,
58 Daniel Everitt,
59 Joshua Edwards,
60 Mathew Freeman,

61 Richard Everitt,
62 Thomas Richardson,
63 John Everitt,
64 Malcomb Patterson,
65 Allen Dudley,
66 John Law,

67 Isaac T. Cushing,
68 Samuel Smith,
69 John B. Troy,
70 William Adkinson,
71 Thomas Wilkinson.

Fourth Company, detached from the Sampson Regiment.

1 George Lassiter, Captain,
2 Robert Lassiter, 1st Lieut.
3 Josias Lee, 2d Lieut.
4 Abram Nailor, Ensign,
5 Pharo Lee, first Sergeant,
6 Sion Danfoot, 2d Sergt.
7 Starling Otary,
8 Jacob Mannels,
9 George Warwick,
10 Joseph Two,
11 Granbury Goodwin,
12 John Warwick,
13 James Jones,
14 Gardner Keen,
15 Isaac Manner,
16 Bryant Flowers,
17 Jesse Mannor,
18 Hugh Burke,
19 Whiting Ryolds,
20 Lewis Johnston,
21 Jesse Ezzel,
22 John Bird,
23 Herrin Gregory,
24 Landen Two,
25 Daniel Hall,
26 Samuel Gavin,
27 Owen Shorton,

28 Samuel Standly,
29 John White,
30 Nathan Young,
31 William Lee,
32 Joab Whiley,
33 John House,
34 Robin Pope,
35 James Harden,
36 Jonathan Edge,
37 David Ryold,
38 Elias Two,
39 Jacob Stanly,
40 Thomas Jacobs,
41 Edmond Goodwin,
42 Reddick Jones,
43 Owen Ryold,
44 Daniel Two,
45 Laban Williams,
46 Stephen Maner,
47 Hardy Stephens,
48 William Turner,
49 Joshua Bell,
50 Samuel Robeson,
51 Arthur Hare,
52 Joseph Herrin,
53 Stephen Herrin,
54 Phelix Chesnut,

55 Samuel Gavin,
56 Edmund Mannel,
57 Nathaniel Boyet.
58 Elias Whilly,
59 Jonas Quinby,

60 Warren Jackson,
61 James Hobbs,
62 Raiford Faircloth,
63 Henry Lee,
64 Joel M. Lamb.

Fifth Company, detached from the Sampson Regiment..

1 Thomas Boykin, Captain,
2 Jas. Williamson, Lieut.
3 T. Williamson, 2d Lieut.
4 Lavis Spell, Ensign,
5 Reyney McIlwines,
6 Laban Morgan, 2d Sergt.
7 Hartwell Porter, 3d Sergt.
8 Peter Ryon, Drummer.
9 John Boykin,
10 Daniel Cooper,
11 Simon Reynolds,
12 John Porter,
13 Michael Porter,
14 Core Cooper,
15 Thomas Stephens,
16 William Ryon,
17 Henry Pope,
18 Solomon Boykin,
19 Edward Broy,
20 Allen Parker,
21 John Ammonds,
22 David Underwood,
23 Zachariah Williams,
24 Rayford Cooper,
25 Willis Royal,
26 Angus Johnston,
27 Lewis Pope,
28 Israel Tarlington,

29 Henry Hart,
30 Joshua Herring,
31 John Pope,
32 Hardy Royall,
33 James Porter,
34 Owen Crumpler,
35 Jesse Strickland,
36
37 John Blackwell,
38 William Turner,
39 William Pope,
40 Neil Campbell,
41 James Frazier,
42 John Simonds,
43 Rayford Grist,
44 Noah Faircloth,
45 Aaron Cummings,.
46 William Miller,
47 Thomas Frazier,
48 Sander Fisher,
49 Sutton Grist,
50 John Manor,
51 John Orion,
52 Blackman Tews,.
53 Samuel Revells,
54 John Carter,
55 Aaron Peterson,
56 Abram Sellers,

57 Thomas Green,
58 Luke Parker,
59 David Whitney,
60 Mathew Hall,

61 Isaac Carter,
62 Charles Butler,
63 Henry Hall,
64 John Blount.

Sixth Company, detached from the Moore Regiment.

1 Nathaniel Tucker, Capt.
2 Neil Morrison, 1st Lieut.
3 Hugh McDaniel, 2d Lieut.
4 John Garner, Ensign,
5 Dougald Mathews,
6 Robert Kennedy,
7 Erwin Stephens,
8 John Tyson,
9 Alexander Black,
10 William Goings,
11 William Jackson,
12 Stephen Berryman,
13 Edward Goings,
14 Neil Thompson,
15 David Jones,
16 George Anderson,
17 John Myrick,
18 Andrew Anderson,
19 Malcolm McGilvery,
20 William Wilson,
21 Charles Smith,
22 John Phillips,
23 Drury Richardson,
24 Raiford Phillips,
25 Joab Cheek,
26 John McLeod,
27 Benjamin Pope,
28 William Page,
29 George Carlton,

30 John Laughon,
31 Elisha Rogers,
32 Sampson Muse,
33 Malcolm McDuffy,
34 John Medlin,
35 John White,
36 William Gillmore,
37 Alexander Medlin,
38 John McDonald,
39 John Spicer,
40 Isom Sowell,
41 Everitt Sheffield,
42 Daniel Hollin,
43 Simon Lewis,
44 James Morgan,
45 Jacob Gargle,
46 Frederick Antry,
47 James Owen,
48 Aben Brown,
49 James Garner,
50 Edward Moore,
51 Bralley Garner,
52 Angus McAuley,
53 John Bird,
54 John Martin,
55 John Graham,
56 John Patterson,
57 Donald McLean,
58 Argus Morrison,

59 John Richardson,
60 John McLeod,
61 William Williamson,
62 Lauchlan McKinnon,
63 Daniel Love,
64 Duncan Blue,
65 John Blue,
66 Malcolm McNeil,
67 Duncan McLean,
68 Hugh Cameron,
69 Edward Patterson,
70 Archibald Blue,
71 Neil McLeon,
72 Nathan Maples,
73 Thomas Maples,
74 John Maples,
75 James Maples,
76 John Cole,
77 John Johnston,
78 William Sterling,
79 William Koy,

80 Thomas Rhodes,
81 Joseph Stephens,
82 Duncan Smith,
83 Benjamin Morris,
84 Robert Tapley,
85 Benjamin Bushup,
86 Malcolm Fulsum,
87 Mathew Wicker,
88 Charles Crawford,
89 Benjamin Huckaby,
90 John Bushup,
91 Josiah Hogwood,
92 William Oliver,
93 John Underwood,
94 John Baker,
95 John Bledsoe,
96 William Dalrymple,
97 Benjamin C. Bennett,
98 William Murchinson,
99 Archibald Bue,
100 Benjamin Wicker.

Seventh Company, detached from the Columbus Regiment.

1 Caleb Stephens, Captain,
2 John White, 1st Lieut.
3 Alexander Taylor Ensign,
4 James Smith, 1st Sergt.
5 Thos. B. Wooten, 2d Sergt.
6 Michael High,
7 David Baldwin,
8 Prosper Forma Duval,
9 Thomas Hobbs,
10 Amos Allen,
11 James Baldwin, jr.,
12 Elijah Reynols,

13 John Reynols,
14 William Hooks,
15 Daniel Fowler,
16 Richard Reynols,
17 Anthony Cribb,
18 Elijah Warley,
19 Richard Folk,
20 John Carteret,
21 Frederick Door,
22 Archibald Bogleman,
23 Aaron Floid,
24 Robert Carlisle,

25 John Gore,
26 Richard Fowler,
27 Isaiah Smith,
28 Thomas Cribb,
29 Hardy Duncan,
30 Moses Duncan,
31 Isaiah Sessions,
32 Willis Lamberton.

33 John Folks.
34 Frederick Sasser.
35 Josiah Powell,
36 Archibald Taylor,
37 Allen Barfield,
38 Eli Nichols,
39 Isaac Nichols,
40 Amos Tyson,

Eighth Company, detached from the Anson Regiment.

1 Frederick Staton, Capt.
2 Solomon Trull, 1st Lieut.
3 Henry James, 2d Lieut.
4 James White, Ensign,
5 James King,
6 Thomas Ward,
7 William Anderson,
8 John Walden,
9 Benjamin Williams,
10 Francis Mullis,
11 Isaac Watson,
12 William James,
13 Newbern Williams,
14 Richard Manes,
15 Mathew Rumage,
16 David James,
17 Elisha Griffin,
18 Hosea James.
19 Balis Carr,
20 John Hagler,
21 Asa Baggott,
22 Robert Preston,
23 John Fornberton,
24 Moses Thomas,
25 Reuben Vinson,

26 William Gurley,
27 Jesse Lacy,
28 Needham Curley,
29 Jesse Barnett,
30 Alsey Hyatt,
31
32 John Winetuster,
33 Abram Wimberly,
34 James Perkins,
35 James Morris,
36 Lewis Collins,
37 John Brown,
38 Asa Rushing,
39 David Hendrick.
40
41 Arris Rosser,
42 Micajah Taylor,
43 Absalom Stegall,
44 Moses Pearce,
45 Anson Pearce.
46 William Sikes,
47 William Pearce,
48 William Mulder,
49 George Mulder.
50 William Oniel.

Ninth Company, detached from the Anson Regiment.

1 James Tindall, Captain,
2 Boggan Cash, 1st Lieut.
3 Malach Goulde, 2d Lieut.
4 Hezekiah Billingsby, En.
5 William Jasper,
6 John Goodwin,
7 Thomas C. Threadgill,
8 Austin Fort,
9 William German,
10 John German,
11 Lemuel Ingram,
12 John Ingram,
13 John Rushing,
14 John Jones,
15 Charles Strother,
16 James Copeland,
17 John Webb,
18 Benjamin Sinclair,
19 Orrin Sinclair,
20 Jacob Phillips,
21 Jesse Turner,
22 William West,
23 Stephen Nash,
24 Westly Wortrind,
25 Booky Dickson,
26 Isham Ingram,
27 William Worhine,
28 Howell Threadgill,
29 Nathaniel Davis,
30 William Dabbs,
31 Mathew Bushnell,
32 Jeremiah Gullidge,
33 Mills Ballie,
34 John Moore,
35 Mathew Hubbard,
36 William Fielding,
37 Jesse Cox,
38 Christopher McRae,
39 John Julding,
40 James Brooks,
41 Benjamin Teal,
42 Harman Adams,
43 Jurguhard McRae,
44 Isaac Little,
45 John Chewning,
46 John Ross,
47 Thomas Tyson,
48 Bennet Williams,
49 William Lewis,
50 William Julke,
51 Thomas Slay,
52 Jesse Ratiff,
53 Francis Downer,
54 James Capel,
55 William Wood,
56 Handy May,
57 James Miller,
58 James Martin,
59 Thomas Handcock,
60 John Barber,
61 John Williams,
62 James Briley,
63 Henry Adcock,
64 William Scott,
65 Thomas Jones,
66 Neel McBride,
67 Samuel Ratliff,
68 Daniel McLearn,

69 John Russon,
70 John Short,
71 James Mersham,

72 Neil McLeran,
73 Benjamin Hanley,
74 Hezekiah Ingram.

Tenth Company, detached from the Richmond Regiment.

1 John Blue, Captain,
2 John McAlston,
3 Daniel McAuley,
4 Alexander Brown,
5 James Torry,
6 James Watkins,
7 Fenly McSween,
8 William Wakins,
9 John James,
10 Alexander McLeod, sr.,
11 Amos Corbett,
12 Luke Barnett,
13 Elisha Crowson,
14 Lorick Stephens,
15 Alexander McRae,
16 Dempsey Pitman,
17 James Williams,
18 John Bostwick,
19 William Harris,
20 Stephen Jones,
21 Angus McLoud,
22 John McSween,
23 Charles Hawley,
24 Donald McSween,
25 Kenneth McInnis,
26 David Britt,
27 James Dawson,
28 Cannor Weaver,
29 Edward Gantlin,
30 Martin James,

31 Luke Woodle,
32 James Smith,
33 Berry Norton,
34 Elias Pate,
35 Hanly Snead,
36 Henry Covington,
37 William Robeson,
38 Isaac Vaughan,
39 James Brown,
40 Alexander McDonald,
41 Daniel McNair,
42 Daniel Carmichel,
43 John McRae,
44 John McMillan,
45 John McEwen,
46 Peter Patterson,
47 William Bringham,
48 Alexander Shaw,
49 Duncan Buie,
50 James McDonald,
51 Daniel Watson,
52 Archibald McLeod,
53 Josiah Bozeman,
54 Gilbert McEachin,
55 Roderick Campbell,
56 Alexander McPherson,
57 Malcolm Shaw,
58 Mathew Rainwater,
59 John Chase,
60 James Molton,

61 John Migginson,
62 Daniel Williams,
63 James Mask,
64 Samuel Mallock,
65 John Black,
66 Wader Shepherd,
67 Josiah Shepherd,
68 John McDonald,
69 Archibald McDonald,
70 Donald McDonald,
71 Lochlin McLennan,
72 Jess Williams,
73 Benjamin Thomas,
74 Kennith McKinsie,
75 Moody Ingram,
76 John McLeod,
77 Isaac Mason,
78 Calloway Stephens,
79 Eli Northam,
80 John Stogner.

Eleventh Company, detached from the Robeson Regiment.

1 Isaac Sullivan, Captain,
2 Wm. Brown, 1st Lieut.
3 Benj. Blount, 2d Lieut.
4 Elias Thomas, Ensign,
5 John Stewart,
6 John McMillan,
7 Archibald Stewart,
8 Charles Campbell,
9 Jesse Musslewhite,
10 Spencer Porter,
11 William Council,
12 John Wilkerson,
13 Allen Buie,
14 Stephen Banley,
15 Charles Oxendine,
16 Thomas Locklier,
17 Silas Strickland,
18 John McNeil,
19 Daniel Chrisholm,
20 Alexander Chrisholm,
21 William Edward,
22 Ralph Revelis,
23 Isaac Streeter,
24 Hugh Locklier,
25 Joseph Walters,
26 James Ivey,
27 William Davis,
28 William Bodiford,
29 Harman Cox,
30 William Britt,
31 Charles Storm,
32 John Cox,
33 Hardy Cox,
34 Nathaniel Hawthorn,
35 Daniel Pate,
36 Duncan Baker,
37 Isham Ivey,
38 John Wilkins,
39 John McKellar,
40 Martin Lewis,
41 Lemuel Thompson,
42 John Drake,
43 Peter McCormick,
44 Daniel Stewart,
45 Smith Dease,
46 Amos Taylor,

47 James McKay,
48 Hardy Pope,
49 Josiah Ratley,
50 John Walters,
51 John Drinkwater,
52 Thomas Pope,
53 Thomas Lowe,
54 Jacob Pitman,
55 William Walters,
56 Dawson Walters,
57 Moses Bass,
58 Daniel McPhallair,
59 Raiford S. Witherell,
60 Francis F. Varnum,
61 William Purvis,
62 John Thompson,
63 William Bullard,
64 Reading Blount,
65 Solomon Thomas,
66 James Reeves,
67 Charles Ivey, sr.,
68 Elijah Hammons,
69 Joseph Blount,
70 Duncan McMillan,
71 Roderick Sutherland,
72 Angus McCulland, sr.,
73 Angus McQueen,
74 Alexander McKay,
75 Hector McLeon,
76 John McKay,
77 Angus McCullum,
78 Archibald Morrison,
79 Daniel Nicholson,
80 Daniel McRae.

SECOND BRIGADE,

DETACHED FROM THE SIXTH, SIXTEENTH, SEVENTH, ELEVENTH, EIGHTH, NINTH, TENTH AND FIFTEENTH BRIGADES OF THE ORGANIZED MILITIA OF THE STATE.

EPHRAIM DAVIDSON, *Brigader General*

FIFTH REGIMENT,

DETACHED FROM THE SIXTH AND SIXTEENTH BRIGADES.

RICHARD ATKINSON, *Lieutenant Colonel Commandant.*
SIMPSON SHAW, *First Major.*
BENJAMIN ELLIOTT, *Second Major.*

First Company of the Fifth Regiment, detached from the First Orange Regiment.

1 Hugh Munhollon, Capt.
2 James Latta, Lieutenant.
3 James Smith, Ensign,
4 J. Munhollon, 1st Sergt.
5 George Mebane, 2d Sergt.
6 Thos. Bradford, 3d Sergt.
7 George Tate, 4th Sergt.
8 Joseph Bradford,
9 James Bird,
10 Joseph Bird,
11 William Reddin,
12 John Wilson,
13 Robert Barnhill,
14 Nathaniel Beane,
15 Joseph Hodge,
16 James Wilson,
17 John Warren,
18 Lewis Simpson,
19 William Smith,
20 William Glinn,
21 William Cherenhall,
22 James Browning,
23 Royal Willis,
24 Elisha Glenn,
25 James Wood,
26 Samuel Willis,
27 Lewis Durning,
28 John Sikes,
29 Joel Parish,
30 Bird Lean,
31 Miles Jones,
32 Richard Howard,

33 Francis Crocker,
34 John O'Neal,,
35 Moses Atwater,
36 Gardner Ballard,
37 Benjamin Bridges,
38 James Chambers,
39 George Smith,
40 Charles Canley,
41 William Bishop,
42 John Curthington,
43 Benjamin Price,
44 Abner Jackson,
45 Bradley Collins,
46 William Jacobs,
47 William Clemons,
48 Scearly Docherty,
49 James Lindsey,

50 Theophilus Thompson,
51 John Crabtree,
52 Uriah Crabtree,
53 William Mebane,
54 John Jones,
55 Thomas Thomas,
56 Richard Wilson,
57 Joseph Wilkinson,
58 Martin Liggett,
59 James White,
60 Richard Jones, sr.,
61 William R. Tate,
62 John Wood,
63 Alexander Patten,
64 Elijah Hart,
65 William Price,
66 Gabriel Finn,

Second Company, detached from the First Orange Regiment.

1 Robert Thompson, Capt.
2 Samuel Strahorn, Lieut.
3 Wm. Bradshaw, Ensign,
4 William Kirkland,
5 Davis Davis,
6 Asa Couch,
7 William Herndon,
8 Isaac D. Dollar,
9 John Horn,
10 Robert Allen,
11 John Turner,
12 William Allen,
13 James Dollar,
14 John Ivy,
15 William Harris,
16 John Hunt,

17 William Lingo,
18 Thomas Patterson,
19 Thornton McFarlin,
20 Francis Roberts,
21 Levin Ellis,
22 Harrison Parker,
23 Henry Newton,
24 Andrew Gray,
25 Amos Nichols,
26 John Horner,
27 John Nichols,
28 George Riggs,
29 Wilson Ball,
30 Isaac Morris,
31 Mathew Durham,
32 Edward Howington,

33 Thomas F. Cardwell,
34 Henry Shepherd,
35 Pleasant Herndon,
36 Nathan Marcomb,
37 James Ashley,
38 Henry Trill,
39 William Lyhn,
40 John Hart,
41 William Kirland,
42 William McDaid,
43 Alfred Hill,
44 William Woods,
45 Fisher Clendenning,
46 Archibald Pugh.

47 John Thompson.
48 Jacob Green,
49 James Ray, jr,
50 Samuel Stuart,
51 Thomas Lynch,
52 Robert Jeffries,
53 Hugh Wood,
54 John D. Covington,
55 Thomas Cate,
56 Adam Douglass,
57 James Lindsey,
58
59 William Ragans,

Third Company, detached from the Second Orange or Haw River Regiment.

1 John Stockard, Captain,
2 John Albright, Lieut.
3 Jacob Efland, Ensign,
4 John Proxter,
5 Jacob Jackson,
6 Henry Loy,
7 Thomas Steel,
8 Mathew Baswell,
9 Edward Baswell,
10 Hugh Baglas,
11 Thomas Moore, 2d Sergt.
12 Joseph Cable,
13 Drewry Ballard,
14 John Ireland,
15 William Moore,
16 David Barber,
17 Peaton Wilson,
18 Ziah Horniday,

19 John Foust,
20 James Upson,
21 Thomas Bevers,
22 Joseph Murray,
23 Alexander Filmar,
24 Ned Heathcock,
25 Palmer Freeman,
26 William Hughs,
27 Abraham Hawey,
28 Henry Hurdle,
29 John Wallis,
30 Joel Tate,
31 John Lewis,
32 James Burrage,
33 Lemuel Thompson,
34 James Grimes,
35 Osborn James,
36 Daniel Criscow,

37 Elisha Willis,
38 Philip Hodge,
39 Charles Shanks,
40 John Wilson,
41 John Cable,
42 Nehemiah Thomas,
43 John Cook,
44 Adam Long,
45 Boston Graves,
46 Daniel Thomas,

47 David Spoon,
48 John Hornady,
49 Nathaniel Robeson,
50 William Holt,
51 James Turner,
52 Joel Albright,
53 Alexander Taddis,
54 John Long,
55 Isaac McAdams,
56 Michael Ryke.

Fourth Company, detached from the Randolph Regiment.

1 Joshua Craven, Captain,
2 Adam Winningham, Lieut.
3 Jacob Worthington, En.
4 Raley Spinks, 1st Sergt.
5 Peter Kivet, 2d Sergt.
6 Marma. Swean, 3d Sergt.
7 Fred. Brown, 4th Sergt.
8 Absalom Harper, 1st Cor'l.
9 Wm. Patterson, 2d Cor'l.
10 Daniel Jackson, 3d Cor'l.
11 Henry Johnston, 4th Cor'l.
12 James McMasters, Drum.
13 James Unde, Fifer,
14 Lewis Martin, Private,
15 Robert Haskin,
16 Abel Winningham,
17 Silas Davison,
18 Isaac Vinson,
19 Solomon Luther,
20 Asa Peacock,
21 Jacob Lassiter,
22 Isham Harris,
23 William Jackson,

24 Thomas Shaw,
25 Hezekiah Andrew,
26 Lewis Scarlet,
27 Henry Boss,
28 James Wade,
29 Martin Chandler,
30 Archibald Dunbar,
31 Thomas Nelson,
32 Seth Wade,
33 Duncan Harvey,
34 William Brown,
35 Campbell Powell,
36 John Ferguson,
37 William Cole,
38 Isaac Miller,
39 Frederick Fentress,
40 Alexander Robins,
41 Alexander Cunnigan,
42 Frederick Steed,
43 John Steed,
44 Elijah Williams,
45 John Malone,
46 Stephen Hervey,

47 John Smitherman,
48 Alexander Dockery,
49 Isham Steed,
50 John Reid,
51 John Pierce,
52 Garrat Spinks,
53 Joseph Argoe,
54 James Harris,
55 Lewis Garner,
56 Thomas Bray,
57 Ezekiel Mills,
58   illiam Conner,
59 West Hicks,
60 Jacob Briles,
61 Rudolph Weymire,
62 Ezra Bukerdite,
63 Will Acborn,
64 Abram Elliott,
65 James Sweany,
66 Henry Lamm,
67 Samuel Beson,
68 Dun Lamm,
69 Henry Burton,
70 James Barker,
71 Michael Jackson,

72 Jeremiah Barker,
73 George Wilson,
74 John Chaplain,
75 Enoch Williams,
76 John Wood,
77 William Maples,
78 Henry Underwood,
79 Henry Kivett,
80 Miles Stephens,
81 James Savage,
82 John Burgess,
83 William Nelson,
84 Anderson Roach,
85 Nathan York,
86 William Howe,
87 Thomas Alexander,
88 Larkin Curtis,
89 Henry Curtis,
90 William Gay,
91 George Black,
92 John Brown,
93 Abijah Moore,
94 John Johnston,
95 George Lean,
96 John Bryan.

Fifth Company, detached from the Chatham Regiment.

1 Carney Cotton, Captain,
2 Daniel Smith, 1st Lieut.
3 John M. Gee, 2d Lieut.
4 Riddick Burns, Ensign,
5 Jonathan Rickets,
6 William Sloan,
7 George McDaniel,
8 John Coley,

9 James Burns, jr.,
10 Aaron Bryan, jr.,
11 Benjamin Dowdy, sr.,
12 Frederick Phillips,
13 Elisha Jackson,
14 Michael Welch,
15 Robert Barker,
16 Lemuel Underwood.

17 John Bray,
18 John Lawler,
19 Thomas Mullins,
20 Edom Edwards,
21 John Purvis,
22 Joab Brooks,
23 Benjamin Emmerson,
24 George Smith,
25 James Eastis,
26 Ezekiel Mazey,
27 William Matthews.
28 William Jordan,
29 Guilford Gardner.
30 Elisha Kurby,
31 Isaiah Cole,
32 George Merrett,
33 Samuel Harris,
34 Larkin Straughn,
35 James Edwards,
36 Josiah Kurby,
37 Cornelius Myrick,
38 Wm. F. Richardson,
39 Joseph Elliot,
40 Joseph Hart,
41 James Myrick,
42 Azel Myrick,
43 James Dixon,
44 James Wamble,
45 Johnston Barber,
46 Daniel Nevin,
47 Stephen Upchurch,
48 Matt Jinks,
49 Jesse Patridge,
50 Alexander Moore,
51 William Spivey,

52 Moses Archer.
53 James Perry,
54 John Noblet,
55 John Eastbridge.
56 John Whitehead,
57 Leonard Johnston,
58 Duty Dorset,
59 John Craton,
60 Henry Harris.
61 John Evans,
62 Joseph Alston,
63 Josiah Tomison,
64 Milliner Burk,
65 Reuben May,
66 David Blacklock,
67 Isaac Field,
68 William Stedman,
69 James McMath, jr.
70 Edward Buckner,
71 John Taylor,
72 John Gear,
73 Isaac Richison,
74 Benjamin Curl,
75 Jesse Davis,
76 John Carton,
77 Mathew Hogan.
78 John Boon,
79 Banston Chaves,
80 Benjamin Pytent,
81 Armstead Haynes.
82 James Tidder,
83 Richard Evans,
84 Charles Evans,
85 John Cullerson,
86 David Fox, jr ,

87 Aaron Stout,
88 David Vestal,

89 Barnell Fox,
90 John Davis.

Sixth Company, detached from the Wake Regiment.

1 William McCullers, Capt.
2 John Walton, Lieut.
3 Critton Sanders, Ensign,
4 Littleton Hutson,
5 Burtess Upchurch,
6 Nathaniel Ward,
7 John Scott,
8 John Pride,
9 William Harwood,
10 Little John Utley,
11 Whitmill Hunter,
12 Alvin Utley,
13 Jyre Parish,

14 Wiley Womak,
15 John Watson,
16 John Rand,
17 Darling Jones,
18 Giles B. Bledsoe,
19 Miller Sexton,
20 Anthony Pilkinton,
21 Isma Kellum,
22 Noel Norris,
23 William Holland,
24 Peter Angel,
25 Arthur Reves,

Seventh Company, detached from the Wake Regiment.

1 John T. C. Wiatt, Capt.
2 Lewis S. Muse, 1st Lieut.
3 Nicholas Sheffield, Ensign.
4 Samuel Combs, 1st Sergt.
5 Thomas Rice, 2d Sergt.
6 Samuel Pearson, 3d Sergt.
7 Daw. Atkinson, 4th Sergt.
8 David A. Knott, 1st Cor'l.
9 John R. Kart, 2d Cor'l.
10 John Carney, 3d Cor'l.
11 A. H. Roylan, 4th Cor'l.
12 Preston Pearson,
13 Ilie Nunn,
14 William W. Seaton,
15 Mark Cook,

16 Robert Harrison,
17 Alfred Jones,
18 Jonathan Busbee,
19 Willis Parker,
20 Martin Adams,
21 James B. Ruth,
22 John Rice,
23 Thomas Powers,
24 Edmond R. Pitt,
25 William Brown,
26 Robert Calum,
27 James G. Mitchel,
28 William Harrison,
29 Littleberry Williams,
30 Nelson Andrews,

31 William Davis,
32 Allen Parks,
33 John Olive,
34 James Olive,
35 Elias Gay,
36 Allen Griffin,
37 Thomas Bowden,
38 Jesse Gibbs,
39 John Dodd,
40 Oran Vincent.
41 Samuel Blake,
42 William W. Bell,
43 William Brantley,
44 Christopher Woodard,
45 Joseph Woodard,
46 William Bell,
47 Shadrack Haywood,
48 Jeremiah Bell,
49 Willis Nelms,
50 Josiah Davis,

51 Cader Nutt,
52 Robert Rutherford,
53 James Morris,
54 Wiley Roberts,
55 John George,
56 Wylie Carpenter,
57 John Burges,
58 Daniel George,
59 John Lynn,
60 James Thorn,
61 Brittain Stephenson,
62 Willis Holderfield,
63 James Head,
64 Little John Utley,
65 William Harwood,
66 John Pride,
67 John Scott,
68 Nathaniel Ward,
69 Bentess Upchurch,
70 Littleton Hutson.

Eighth Company, detached from the Granville Regiment.

1 Willis Johnston, Captain.
2 William G. Brown, Lieut.
3 William Dolby, Ensign,
4 Wilie M. Spears,
5 Green B. Walker,
6 Tandy Walker,
7 James G. Tate,
8 John Bass,
9 Richard Wood,
10 Francis Clark,
11 Wiat Johnston,
12 John Barnett, jr.,
13 John Barnett,

14 Solomon Hayes,
15 Kinchen Higgs,
16 Kinchen Bynum,
17 Thomas Cole,
18 James Mayson,
19 William W. Ananias,
20 Valentine Mayfield,
21 John Davis,
22 Kade Kittrell,
23 William Parks,
24 John Roberts,
25 Abram Lawrence,
26 George Lienter,

27 John Lyod,
28 John Paskill,
29 James Allen,
30 James Gill,
31 Moses Winston,
32 Wiat Kennedy,
33 Newmon Robertson,
34 Jehu Spear,
35 Benjamin Huffman,
36 Arthur Fuller,
37 Lain Moore,
38 Thomas Lile,
39 Henry Morris,
40 Flecher Taylor,
41 John Sherril,
42 Asa Green,
43 James Sewit,
44 David Byers,
45 William Bock,
46 Henry Avery,
47 Lazarus Minor,
48 George Byers,

49 William White,
50 Wiat Cazart,
51 Samuel Clemons,
52 James Medders,
53 Michael Christon,
54 John Stephenson,
55 Jesse Acock,
56 Benjamin H. Wortham,.
57 Henry Chambles,
58 Samuel Persyth,
59 Henry Jones,
60 Mertin Freeman,
61 Payten Madison,
62 Merkle Tom Kithrell,.
63 Egreppy Nance,
64 Edward Weathers,
65 Henry Hendley,
66 William Adcock,
67 Arthur Fuller,
68 Asa Green,
69 Nicholas Green,
70 John Mitchell,

Ninth Company, detached from the Granville Regiment.

1 Lestly Gilliam, Captain,
2 William Gilliam, Lieut.
3 Thomas Hunt, Ensign,
4 Thos. Howard, 1st Sergt.
5 John Downey, 2d Sergt.
6 Thos. Downey, 3d Sergt.
7 Moses Petitord, 4th Sergt.
8 Horatio Bass, 1st Cor'l.
9 Charles Pratt, 2d Cor'l.
10 Benjamin Ward, 3d Cor'l.
11 William Oakley, 4th Cor'l.

12 Peyton Hayes, Private,
13 William Terry,
14 Charles Duncan,
15 Scarlet Anderson,
16 Ransom Hester,
17 Solomon Satterwhite,.
18 William Daniel,
19 Overton Haines,
20 Thomas Daniel,
21 Phillip P. Pool,.
22 Charles Smith,.

23 Meredith Lampkin,
24 William Blanks,
25 Elkshel Ellis,
26 Robert Wilson,
27 Robert Jenkins,
28 William Hargrove,
29 William Collins,
30 John Norwood,
31 Reuben Hawkins,
32 William Barnes,
33 Pleasant Mangum,
34 Rowland Perdue,
35 John Daniels,
36 John Montague,
37 Robert Stamper,
38 John Chavis,
39 Thomas Evans,
40 William Evans,
41 Jeremiah Anderson,
42 Lemuel Tyler,
43 Meredith Lampkins,
44 William Griffin,
45 Thomas Lewis,
46 William Seares,
47 Benjamin Grissom,
48 Reuben Parish,
49 Zachariah Mitchel,
50 William Johnston,

51 Robert Elliston,
52 Robert Gordon,
53 Robert Longmire,
54 David Jones,
55 Thompson Hedgepith,
56 Bewdie Howard,
57 William Gordon,
58 James G. Tate,
59 Lervey Pettiford,
60 John T. Peace,
61 Thomas House,
62 Ransom Harris,
63 Wilie Grissom,
64 Barnett Higgs,
65 Edward Setton,
66 Payton Madison,
67 Samuel Persithe,
68 Miston Freeman,
69 Henry Jones,
70 Henry Chambles,
71 Benjamin H. Wortham,
72 Jesse Adcock,
73 John Stephenson,
74 Michael Christian,
75 James Meddows,
76 Samuel Clement,
77 Wyat Cazart,
78 William White.

Tenth Company, detached from the Person Regiment. No. 2 Returns.

1 Sampson Glenn, Captain.
2 John Glenn, 1st Lieut.
3 Robert Williams, 2d Lieut.
4 Solomon Pain, Ensign,

5 Gabriel Davey, 1st Sergt.
6 Edmond Dixson, 2d Sergt.
7 Hosea Fuller, 3d Sergt.
8 Lewis Ramsay,

9 Philip Singleton,
10 Alexander Elixor,
11 Asa Hudgins,
12 William Nelums,
13 Samuel Nipper,
14 Philip Day,
15 John Cooper,
16 Joseph Rogers,
17 Isaac Vanhook,
18 William W. Chambers,
19 John Mann,
20 Robert Cochran,
21 Hutchens Burton,
22 John Rainey,
23 Charles Ward,
24 John R. Eskridge,
25 William Gill,
26 Giles Rogers,
27 Jeremiah Stanfield,
28 John W. Graves,
29 Solomon Walker,
30 William Jones,
31 Jesse Bull,
32 Thomas Lawson,
33 Robert Mann,
34 John Ingram,
35 John Pullam,
36 John Atkinson,
37 James Branch, 4th Sergt.

38 John Stanfield,
39 Duncan Rose,
40 Bird Walker,
41 Thomas Gordan,
42 Thomas Dancey,
43 Edmond Mitchel,
44 David Nellum,
45 Aaron Chrisenburg,
46 William Pope,
47 William Singleton,
48 Jeremiah Blanchard,
49 Thomas Halley Burton,
50 John Carton,
51 James Mann,
52 Jeremiah Rimer,
53 John Filmond,
54 James Jacobs,
55 William Buchannon,
56 Leonard Morris,
57 Vinson Tapp,
58 John Elmore,
59 John Moore,
60 David Lareson,
61 John Fuller,
62 Walter Fuller,
63 Reuben Corner,
64 James Waddy,
65 John Toler,
66 Walter Buchannon,

Eleventh Company, detached from the Caswell Regiment.

1 Joseph Benton, Captain,
2 John Mitchell, Lieut.
3 John Lea, 2d Lieut.
4 Wm. B. Graves, Ensign,

5 Allen Gunn,
6 Joshua Hightower,
7 Samuel Wood,
8 Richard Jones,

9 Armstead Watington,
10 Carter Malone,
11 Goodwin Evans,
12 Moses Simpson,
13 Alexander Watson.
14 Oliver Brintle,
15 Hiram Parks,
16 John Nighton,
17 Tilmore Stone,
18 William Night,
19 William Martin,
20 Lemuel Chilton,
21 Isham Normand,
22 Turner Nighton,
23 Isaac Patterson,
24 Robert Ware,
25 Josiah Stanfield,
26 Isaac West,
27 Westly Normand,
28 Richard Swift,
29 Lewis Ballard,
30 Bartholomew Ellis,
31 Thomas Fielder,
32 Benjamin Cantrall,
33 Henry Collier,
34 John Brown,
35 John Shackletord,
36 Robert Bruce,
37 Spencer Jackson,
38 William Johnston,
39 James Bruce,
40 James Somers,
41 John Badget,
42 Eli Snarp,
43 Hiram Wetherford,
44 Daniel Morgan,

45 Baldy Ramson,
46 Edward Jones,
47 Walter Brayfield,
48 Hugh Howard,
49 Francis Wattington,
50 Henry Booker Hailey,
51 Jeptha Parks,
52 George Brooks,
53 Jonathan B. Wattington,
54 William H. Wattington,
55 John Williams,
56 James Scott,
57 Parabo Bozwell,
58 William Terrell,
59 John H. Humphries,
60 John Stadler,
61 Haroway Swift,
62 Joseph Burrough,
63 Stewart Farley,
64 George Randolph,
65 Mathew Hubbard,
66 William Kersey,
67 Robert Stadler,
68 Lewis Hall,
69 Yunger Hardwick,
70 William Nipper,
71 Edward Glore,
72 Sandy Smith,
73 Robert Wilson,
74 William Fullington,
75 James Johnston,
76 William Harwell,
77 Virgil M. Rainey,
78 John B. Farley,
79 Stephen Burton,
80 William Gordon,

81 Noel Burton,
82 Benjamin Crider,
83 James Atkins,
84 Zenas Martin,
85
86 Daniel Smith,

87 Joshua Butler,
88 Laban Hunt,
89 William Singleton,
90 Pleasant Rudd,
91 Benjamin Loafmand,

SIXTH REGIMENT,

DETACHED FROM THE EIGHTH BRIGADE.

John Martin, *Lieutenant Colonel Commandant.*
George Lemmond, *First Major.*
James Johnston, *Second Major.*

First Company, detached from the Second Guilford Regiment.

1 William Mears, Captain,
2 William Dinkey, Lieut.
3 Grovesnor Marsh, Ensign.
4 Elias Prickhard,
5 John Chance,
6 Arthur Forbez, sr.,
7 Elijah Lingold,
8 John Clark,
9 Frederick Sheaver,
10 David Story,
11 Andrew Law,
12 Stephen Griffin,
13 Reuben Anderson,
14 Maxwell Wilson,
15 Aaron Sprouts,
16 Jacob Wilker,
17 John Barnhart,

18 John J. Matthews,
19 William Forster,
20 Alanson Forster,
21 Daniel Cobb,
22 Ludwith Seabold,
23 William Smith,
24 Henry Swing,
25 Henry Greason,
26 David Glass,
27 Henry Bowman,
28 Henry Shaw,
29 John Charles,
30 John Shepperd,
31 Lewis May,
32 Christian Cline,
33 Daniel Mitchel,
34 William Tate,

35 Shadrack White,
36 Christian Isley,
37 Peter Wamick,
38 Bartin Garringer,
39 Richard Fentress,
40 John Wilson,
41 Robert Elkins,
42 Thomas Jackson,
43 Joash Reynolds,
44 Levin Sullivan,
45 Obediah Leonard,
46 Samon Wilson,
47 Robert Parsons,
48 Thomas Elkins,
49 Solomon Ward,
50 George Montgomery,
51 William Jackson,
52 Dempsey Whitney,
53 James Leonard,
54 John Howell,
55 John Strickland,
56 James Williams,
57 John Thomas,
58 Andrew Thomas,
59 John Spoon, jr.,
60 Ebenezer Whitney,
61 Thomas Lane,
62 William Spoon,
63 Samuel Horney,

64 Isaac Leonard,
65 Samuel Montgomery,
66 Stewart Hardin,
67 Benjamin Field,
68 Daniel Kirkman,
69 James Witherly,
70 Thomas Lincheum,
71 Johnston Alexander,
72 Daniel Gladson,
73 Robert Fields,
74 Fisher B. Taylor,
75 William Hacket,
76 William Meed,
77 Elias Bowen,
78 Francis Wrightet,
79 Gradathan Harper,
80 Isaac Rolan,
81 William Dunning,
82 William Watson,
83 Thomas Ross,
84 Elijah Ward,
85 John Buchannon,
86 Charles Clemer.
87 James Walker,
88 Peter Wetherby,
89 Wilkins Lucans,
90 John Starks, jr.,
91 Israel Brown,

Second Company, detached from the First Guilford Regiment.

1 Samuel Hunter, Captain,
2 Abraham Riples, 1st Lieut.
3 John Moore, 2d Lieut.
4 Thomas Bevill, Ensign,
5 Nicholas Ogborn, Cadet,
6 Levy Ross, 1st Sergt.
7 Thos. L. Moody, 2d Sergt.
8 Miat Carter, 3d Sergt.

9 Alex. Bevill, 4th Sergt.
10 Philip Bevill, 1st Cor'l.
11 James Cole, 2d Cor'l.
12 Noel Parish, 3d Cor'l.
13 Alfred Branner, 4th Cor'l.
14 Charles H. Harris, Private.
15 Henry Maga.
16 Wilson Patterson,
17 Kinchen Vaughan,
18 John Osburn,
19 Nathan Barham,
20 Aaron Walker,
21 Parrum Ray,
22 Peyton Ray,
23 Felix M. Binco,
24 Elijah Beasel,
25 Sihon Turner,
26 William Billingsby,
27 Jonas Case,
28 William Walker,
29 David Fairbanks,
30 John Walker,
31 Walker Dowet,
32 Levin Caulk,
33 James Gaugh,
34 Reuben Parish,
35 Harbert Tatum,
36 John Willy,
37 George W. Bell,
38 John Flemming,
39 Enoch Tumlinson,
40 James Nelson,
41 Valentine Garoll,
42 Caleb Lawrence,
43 Edward Wilson,
44 John Doak,

45 David Lanin,
46 Isaac Howlet,
47 William Winchester,
48 William Parmer,
49 Thomas Maga,
50 Charles Case,
51 Reuben Garlick,
52 Archibald Whitworth,
53 Bryant Pearcy,
54 Lodwick B. Wilson,
55 Thomas Jackson,
56 Robert H. Brinkle,
57 William A. Stephens,
58 David Archer,
59 James Archer,
60 Zenas Bunker,
61 Peter Brown,
62 Henry Reed,
63 Thomas Dunning,
64 John Pegg,
65 David Beason,
66 Jacob Lovell,
67 William Shelly,
68 George Middleton,
69 Jesse Pegg,
70 Joab Pegg,
71 Martin Pegg,
72 Danut North,
73 Absalom Williams,
74 Jacob Riggins,
75 Joseph Edoll,
76 Hezekiah Lock,
77 Robert Bevill,
78 Morton Riggins,
79 William Riggins,
80 Thomas Hunt,

81 Daniel Barnell,
82 Jacob Waggoner,
83 Argis Suthard,
84 John Kindle,
85 Nathan Underwood,
86 William Dunning,

87 Valentine Waggoner,
88 Isaac Lee,
89 Malcomb Morrison,
90 Andrew Cain,
91 Wist Lane,
92 Sihon Turner.

Third Company, detached from the Rockingham Regiment.

1 William Lenmon, Captain.
2 Reuben Lindsay, Lieut.
3 Thomas Galoway, Ensign,
4 J. Vermillion, 1st Sergt.
5 Elijah Thomas, 2d Sergt.
6 Enock Hinston, Private.
7 William Berwick,
8 Robert Walker,
9 Edward Massey,
10 Thomas Botts,
11 William Hosford,
12
13 William W. Brown,
14 James Hudson,
15 Valentine Morgan,
16 Robert Barnes,
17 Pleasant Barnes,
18 John Bundrant,
19 Reece Watkins,
20 William Griffith,
21 Samuel Jelton,
22 Zera Summers,
23 Joseph Maye,
24 Archills Wynn,
25 William Henderson,
26 James King,
27 Matthew Covey,

28 Peter Wall,
29 Abram Jerald,
30 James Young,
31 Chesley Wooders,
32 David Heron,
33 Stewart Dramond,
34 Joshua Jarrall,
35 Reason Waters,
36 James Sparks,
37 Baldy Rice,
38 Durham Pearce,
39 William Sharp,
40 Ambrose Joice,
41 Pleasant Joice,
42 Thomas Barfield,
43 Thomas Eloner,
44 Peter Horn,
45 William Haynes,
46 James Lemon,
47 William Alexander,
48 Bartlet Gregan,
49 Thomas Godsey,
50 William Smothers,
51 David Chadwell,
52 Robert Hall,
53 David Buchannon,
54 William W. Burk.

Fourth Company, (Grenadiers,) detached from the Rockingham Regiment.

1 James Campbell, Captain.
2 William J. Mongus, Lieut.
3 David Barry, 2d Lieut.
4 George Adkins, Ensign.
5 Wm. Wardlow, 1st Sergt.
6 John Shivers, 2d Sergt.
7 George Cantrill, 3d Sergt.
8 Eli Coram, 4th Sergt.
9 John H. Taylor, 1st Cor'l.
10 Morgan Lillard, 2d Cor'l.
11 James H. Scales, 3d Cor'l.
12
13 Martin Jones, Drummer,
14 Richard Coram, Fifer,
15 John Serkin,
16 Jeremiah Nichols,
17 James W. Olington,
18 William Grogan,
19 William Mobly, jr.,
20 William Brown, jr.,
21 John Molesby,
22 John Hancock,
23 William Miller,
24 John Wall, jr.,
25 Joseph Berry,
26 Elijah Cantrill,
27 Daniel Ellington, jr.,
28 Fedding Wright,
29 Grieff Ellington,
30 John Barry,
31 Skipwith Wray,
32 William Williams,
33 Joseph Woldrige,
34 Daniel Carter,
35 Henry Miller,
36 John Mount, jr.,
37 William Coram, jr.,
38 George Coffer,
39 Davis Heron,
40 James Wardlow,
41 James Barry,
42 John Sinclair, jr.,
43 Robert Cantrill,
44 Lewis Dodson,
45 John Cantrall,
46 Daniel Forster,
47 James Walker,
48 Lelin Molenby,
49 Frederick Miller,
50 Edward Godsey,
51 James Mackey,
52 John Wollington,
53 James Taylor,
54 Jesse Thomas,
55 Isaac Pitle,
56 Pleasant Mount,
57 Allen Caldwell,
58 Thomas Wammot,
59 John Jones,
60 Lemiah King,
61 John King, .
62 Edward Nunon,
63 Joseph Asbrige, jr.,
64 John Powell,
65 Matthias Mount, jr.,
66 William King,

67 William S. Haney,
68 James B. Rice,'
69 Robert S. Stewart,
70 John Sims, jr.,
71 Zacha Lewis,
72 Eli Young,
73 Daniel Tucker,

74 John Griffin,
75 Reuben Grady, jr.,
76 Thomas Jarold,
77 George Stewart,
78 William Lewis,
79 Robert Grady.

Fifth Company, detached from the Second Stokes Regiment.

1 Alexander Moody, Capt.
2 Thomas Yarrell, Lieut.
3 William G. Haynes, En.
4 Henry Fry,
5 Thomas Westmoreland,
6 James Cooper,
7 William Cox,
8 William Hubbart,
9 James Hargrove,
10 John Cox,
11 William Dalton,
12 Jesse Stewart,
13 Henry Doube,
14 Henry Briggs,
15 John Stofel,
16 Jacob Teats,
17 Peter Moses,
18 Robert Hill,
19 Samuel Aldrige,
20 John Binkley,
21 Henry Stide,
22 Leonard Conrad,
23 Simon Croon,
24 Jacob Miller, sr.,
25 Jacob Hixt,
26 Elijah Purdon,

27 Charles Anderson,
28 Austin Smith,
29 Charles Chitty,
30 Christopher Zimmerman,
31 Archibald Davis,
32 William Boly Jack,
33 Henry Hitner,
34 John Hyor,
35 Elisha Stator,
36 Andrew Krowse,
37 Abram Beck,
38 Edward Tatom,
39 Stephen Riddle,
40 John Barr,
41 John Rick,
42 Joseph Holbrook,
43 David Linvill,
44 William Holbrook, jr.,
45 William Holbrook, sr.,
46 Willis Cooper,
47 Daniel N. Repton,
48 James Ham,
49 James Reid,
50 George Hubbard,
51 John Wright,
52 John Smith,

53 George Kennemon,
54 Jesse Swim,
55 Kelan Pittcord,
56 Campbell Sutton,
57 Francis Jackson,
58 John S. Leight,
59 Asbury Arnett,

60 James Crews,
61 John Harald,
62 William Beason,
63 Daniel Huff,
64 John McPherson,
65 Solomon Fulp,
66 Elijah Gerrell.

Sixth Company, detached from the First Stokes Regiment.

1 William Goode, Captain.
2 David Dalton, 1st Lieut.
3 Samuel Martin, Ensign.
4 Robert Young,
5 Berryman Knight,
6 James Fountain,
7 Joshua Southam,
8 William Ward,
9 Elijah Night,
10 Richard Flynt,
11 Bradford Vanter,
12 James Marshal,
13 William Smith,
14 Michael Smith,
15 William Riggs,
16 Joel Smith,
17 William Welch,
18 Thomas Reddick,
19 Benjamin Morgan,
20 William Daggins,
21 Richard Vernon,
22 Samuel Heath,
23 William Eads,
24 William Sisk,
25 Aurelua Wooldrige,
26 Thomas Westbrook,

27 William Harris,
28 Benjamin Haynes,
29 Hezekiah Torc,
30 William Oliver,
31 Lambert Dodson,
32 Henry Baker,
33 William Cannon,
34 Samuel Neil,
35 Pillis Priddy,
36 Lewis Tilly,
37 James Young,
38 Benjamin Hutchison,
39 Thomas Wilkins,
40 John Priddy,
41 Elisha Vernon,
42 Thomas Jinkins,
43 James Griffin,
44 Clifford Yates,
45 George Wilkins,
46 James Beasley,
47 Joel Kitchum,
48 Elisha Nelson,
49 Lewis Bower,
50 William Nelson,
51 Benjamin Fry,
52 Henry Bulling,

53 Larkin Burge,
54 Pleasant Bridgmore,
55 Moses Hiett,
56 William Gregory,
57 Daniel Scotte,
58 James Bavick,
59 Isaac Jackson,
60 Samuel Jackson,
61 Christopher Spoonse,
62 James Eaton,
63 Raleigh Darnold,
64 Thomas Franklin,
65 Solomon Spanchour,

66 Joseph Zimmerman,
67 John Prather,
68 William Stone,
69 Henry Alberty,
70 Jesse Brown,
71 Clisby Robertson,
72 John Crammer,
73 Jesse Childress,
74 John Cook,
75 John Segimore,
76 James Walker,
77 Mereday Bennet,
78 Nicholas Frost.

SEVENTH REGIMENT,

DETACHED FROM THE SEVENTH AND ELEVENTH BRIGADE.

JESSE A. PEARSON, *Lieutenant Colonel Commandant.*
DAVID KERR, *First Major.*
JOHN STILL, *Second Major.*

First Company, detached from the First Rowan Regiment.

1 Jacob Krider, Captain.
2 Hugh McKnight, Lieut.
3 James Gelispee, Ensign.
4 Frederick Cauble,
5 Henry Lippart,
6 George Fisher,
7 John Tinkle,
8 Conrad Smitteds,
9 Henry Casey,
10 Jacob Lane,

11 Daniel Brown,
12 Pleasant Tapley,
13 Sion Keeth,
14 James Ross,
15 Philip Hootman,
16 John Kastor,
17 William Snow,
18 Solomon Miller,
19 Charles Ryer,
20 George Hodge,

21 John Ross, sr.,
22 Mertin Miller,
23 Mertin Happner,
24 Andrew Holshouse, jr.,
25 Henry Caulans,
26 Adam Cauble,
27 John Lingle,
28 John Lane,
29 John Clutz,
30 Jacob Lingle,
31 Meihall Delow,
32 Phillips Carter,
33 Jacob Skussing,
34 Peter Deal,
35 Peter Albright,
36 Henry Sudler,
37 Leonard Craigh,
38 John Hauston,
39 Hiram Davidson,
40 Edward Heulin,
41 John Rudisil,
42 John Smith,
43 Morris Pinkston,
44 Peter M. Smith,
45 William H. Horoh,
46 John Utzman,
47 George Utzman,
48 Jacob Utzman,
49 Jesse James,

50 William Dickson,
51 Robert Wood,
52 John Wood,
53 Ralph Kasler,
54 David Ewell,
55 Eps Robertson,
56 Skiles Foster,
57 Daniel Cress,
58 John B. Lonona,
59 Daniel Shuford,
60 John Holshouser,
61 George Withellene,
62 Moses Lamb,
63 John Lance,
64 Philip Lytiker,
65 Samuel Felker,
66 Peter Upright,
67 Jacob Rary,
68 Malikiah Bowers,
69 Henry Singenwinder,
70 Andrew Kincade,
71 James Gleen,
72 Samuel Rice,
73 Samuel Kincade,
74 Thomas Hutson,
75 William Bar,
76 William Cowin,
77 John Patterson,
78 Isaac Cowin.

Second Company, detached from the Second Rowan Regiment.

1 Henry Katts, Captain.
2 John Beard, Lieutenant.
3 James Lowe, Ensign.
4 Julius Strange, 1st Sergt.

5 Barna. Bowers, 2d Sergt.
6 John Brinkhart, 3d Sergt.
7 Wil. Wiseman, 4th Sergt.
8 Jacob Stoner, 1st Cor'l.

9 Thomas Ceicel, 2d Cor'l.
10 Elijah Northern, 3d Cor'l,
11 Even Thomas, 4th Cor'l.
12 James Wiseman, Drum.
13 Jacob Bringle, Fifer,
14 James Silvers, Private,
15 Benjamin Sincunger,
16 Josiah Cuningam,
17 Adam Hendrick,
18 George Birkhart,
19 Christian Sink,
20 Alfred Owens,
21 Shadrick Hill,
22 Christian Lucanbill,
23 George Bowers,
24 George Myers,
25 Henry Hepler,
26 John Myers, sr.,
27 James Jones,
28 James Moss.
29 Bryant Fiy,
30 Abram Shular,
31 Abraham Hunt,
32 Oliver Hunt,
33 Jonathan Davis,
34 Michael Myers,
35 Samuel Williams,
36 John Sims,
37 Edmond McCarn,
38 Jesse Lane,
39 Joseph Warford,
40 Barnard Living,
41 Thomas Workman,
42 William Workman,
43 Peter Livenger,
44 Philip Headrick,
45 Micajah Hill,
46 Smith Hill,
47 Abram Johnston,
48 Isaiah Hicks,
49 James Lacey,
50 Zachariah Coggins,
51 Thomas Davis,
52 Lewis Beard,
53 James Ziveley,
54 John Stoutenberg,
55 Barzilla McBride,
56 John Delow,
57 John B. Crump,
58 James Owen,
59 Walter Northern,
60 Isaac Grist,
61 Moses Holmes,
62 John Williams,
63 James Gallimore,
64 James Green,
65 Charles Savage,
66 Henry Cline,
67 Philip Cline,
68 Cornelius Smith,
69 Jonathan Walk,
70 David Bierly,
71 Philip Willis,
72 Reuben Nunby.

Third Company, detached from the Third Rowan Regiment.

1 John Frost, Captain.
2 William Duffy, Lieut.
3 Charles Anderson, Ensign.
4 James Wilson, 1st Sergt.
5 John Ford, 2d Sergt.
6 James Gamble, 3d Sergt.
7 Samuel Dial, 4th Sergt.
8 William Wiatt, 1st Cor'l.
9 Samuel Frost, 2d Cor'l.
10 John Hodgers, 3d Cor'l.
11 William Hutson, 4th Cor'l.
12 James Warren, Drummer,
13 Samuel McGuire, Fifer,
14 William Bissent, Private,
15 Daniel Lark,
16 George Claybrook,
17 Thomas Horn,
18 Howell Horn,
19 William Chapman,
20 Conel James,
21 Isaac James,
22 Inley Smith,
23 Caleb Brock,
24 Edward Williams,
25 Richard Haxwood,
26 Robert Clark,
27 Thomas Smith,
28 Oliver Griffin,
29 Richard Jarvis,
30 John Speak,
31 Dennis Jarvis,
32 Clare Maxlin,
33 Thomas Gears,
34 Baker Johnston,
35 Elwin Howard,
36 James Orton,
37 Richard Luckey,
38 Henry Luckey,
39 Gustavus Boswell,
40 Francis Kinshaw,
41 Teneson Cheshen,
42 George Taylor,
43 Thomas Taylor,
44 Thomas Leach,
45 Richard Jones,
46 Joseph Lewis,
47 Brice W. Isam,
48 William Brogdon,
49 Alfred Brogdon,
50 Jonathan West,
51 John Becketh,
52 Daniel Cane,
53 Virtue Sweat,
54 Richbell Mott,
55 Samuel Beaman,
56 Jacob Newton,
57 William K. Aire,
58 Jacob Gawood,
59 Isaac Gawood,
60 Edward Buckner, jr.,
61 Zachariah Booth,
62 James Owens,
63 Aaron Tucker,
64 Enoch Chamberlain,
65 David Hampton,
66
67 James Park,
68 John Douthet,

69 Thomas Gentle,
70 Freeman Bate,
71 George Smith,
72 John James,
73 Zachariah Tenneyhill,
74 Christopher Erwin,
75 John Graham,
76 John Buck,
77 Andrew Morrison,
78 Arthur Smith.

Fourth Company, detached from the Fourth Rowan Regiment.

1 Thos. M. Times, Captain.
2 Jones Enoch, Lieutenant.
3 George Lowry, Ensign.
4 John Wilborn, 1st Sergt.
5 Micajah Eagle, 2d Sergt.
6 William Cerill, 3d Sergt.
7 Benjamin Pain, 4th Sergt.
8 Geo. Snider, jr., 1st Cor'l.
9 Brummel Sap, 2d Cor'l.
10 George Kelly, 3d Cor'l.
11 Edmond Cawil, 4th Cor'l.
12 John Farrington, Drum.
13 Micajah Haworth, Fifer,
14 George Saner, Private,
15 Jacob Douthit,
16 Abraham Brindle,
17 Ransom Ellis,
18 David Marklan,
19 Abner Brown,
20 William Swim,
21 James Kelly,
22 Philip Smith,
23 Daniel Chriswell,
24 Jaret Wood,
25 Jeremiah Haworth,
26 William Welborn,
27 John Cerill,
28 Obadiah Twidwell,
29 William Twonay,
30 Samuel Cerill,
31 Daniel Waworth,
32 Meredith Pearce,
33 Barnabas Idol,
34 Hugh Robertson,
35 Matthias Idol,
36 John Donaway,
37 Jacob Miller,
38 Francis Barncastle,
39 Henry Hill,
40 Christian Fash,
41 Henry James,
42 Larkin Scott,
43 John Oaks,
44 Joseph Farabee,
45 Andrew Clinard,
46 Abraham Everitt,
47 William Pain,
48 Samuel Weer,
49 Samuel Spurgin,
50 William Weer,
51 Jacob Williams,
52 John Merick,
53 Adam Frits,
54 David Darr,
55 Henry Long,
56 John Grub,

57 Jacob Averhart,
58 Jacob Sowens,
59 Jacob Grub,
60 James Skider,
61 George Myers,
62 Jacob Kesler,
63 Richard Graham,
64 Macoy Gallispie,
65 Daniel Lynch,
66 Moses Thompson,

67 Jonathan Burns,
68 James McLaughlen,
69 Richard Foster,
70 Andrew Morrison,
71 Caleb Webb,
72 William Dickey,
73 John Hugey,
74 Andrew Renshaw,
75 William Summers.

Fifth Company, detached from the Iredell Regiment

1 John Moody, Captain.
2 William Carson, Lieut.
3 William Moody, Ensign.
4 Thos. Prather, 1st Sergt.
5 Caleb Combey, 2d Sergt.
6 Jos. Duporster, 3d Sergt.
7 Samuel Hayes, 4th Sergt.
8 Henry Marshall, 1st Cor'l.
9 Milus Privitt, 2d Cor'l.
10 David Fox, 3d Cor'l.
11 Richard Privitt, 4th Cor'l.
12 Richard Cook, Drummer,
13 Harris Swivit, Fifer,
14 William Millsaps, Private.
15 William Martin,
16 William Gordon,
17 James Martin,
18 Samuel McKoy,
19 George W. Robertson,
20 Erwin Privitt,
21 George Lackey,
22 Richard Sparks,
23 William Blackenship,

24 Sake Harris,
25 John Teague,
26 James Lack,
27 Walter Beill,
28 John Cash,
29 Henzy Giddens,
30 Thomas Green,
31 James Templeton,
32 Samuel Templeton,
33 Hugh B. King,
34 Joseph Edson,
35 John McConnel,
36 Solomon Claywell,
37 Samuel Mitchel,
38 Hugh Currant,
39 Greenbury Haire,
40 John Hath,
41 Reuben Barnard,
42 Turner Welch,
43 Ashley Johnston,
44 John Rector,
45 Pleasant Owen,
46 Benjamin Moody..

47 Bresom Heziah,
48 Benjamin Bently,
49 Henry Carson,
50 John M. Clerland,
51 Nathan Baker,
52 Michael Tague,
53 Lovet Phelps,
54 Abram Cook,
55 Samuel Henderson,
56 William Looper,
57 Allison Gapp,
58 Richard Mears,
59 Hiram Flecher,
60 Thomas Lovelus,
61 Reason Beill,

62 Elias Luzenbury,
63 Thomas Galloway,
64 Alexander Read,
65 Andrew Well,
66 Joseph Moon,
67 John Young,
68 Philip Phillips,
69 Randolph Roads,
70 Benjamin Brown,
71 Richard Booker,
72 Henry Buck,
73 Joseph Donalson,
74 George Masters,
75 Samuel Hart.

Sixth Company, detached from the Iredell Regiment.

1 Neil McCoy, Captain.
2 Abram Nelson, Lieut.
3 Alexander McCoy, Ensign.
4 Thos. Davidson, 1st Sergt.
5 James Jones, 2d Sergt.
6 Wm. Freeland, 3d Sergt.
7
8 A. Kilpatrick, 4th Sergt.
9 Benj. Sterns, 1st Cor'l.
10 John Fenster, 2d Cor'l.
— Elijah Tucker, 3d Cor'l,
11 Thos. Campbell, 4th Cor'l.
12 Daniel Rector, Drummer,
13 William Arthur, Fifer,
14 George L. Davidson,
15 Thomas Crawford,
16 Robert Allison,
17 Theophilus Simonton,

18 Theophilus Falls,
19 John Cleton,
20 John Parker,
21 John Beil,
22 John Murdock,
23 Ephraim Ewin,
24 James Parker,
25 William Preil,
26 James Templeton,
27 Henry Conner,
28 Robert Westmoreland,
29 David McCrery,
30 Andrew Caldwell,
31 Joseph Rogers,
32 Joseph Templeton,
33 Robert Rankin,
34 Edmond Taylor,
35 Robert M. Hughs,

36 William Horsliam,
37 John Scott,
38 Neil Brawlie, jr.,
39 Robert West,
40 David Mulholland,
41 David Currell,
42 John Bector,
43 Michael White,
44 Hezekiah Grey,
45 Neil McCastle,
46 William Wintosh,
47 Thomas Morrison,
48 David Moore,
49 Archibald Essleman,
50 Samuel McMillan,
51 John Wintosh,
52 Alexander Wintosh,
53 Joseph Alexander,
54 Mosey Stephenson,
55 John Houp,
56 James Hill,
57 Samuel Freeland,
58 James reeland,
59 Thomas Morrison,
60 Andrew Watts,
61 Andrew Morrison,
62 Samuel Wah,
63 John Morrison,
64 Alexander Kilpatrick,
65 George Braddy,
66 Andrew McAdams,
67 Joel Bruce,
68 Hugh Copland,
69 David Potts,
70 Levi Moore,
71 Laban Bracker,
72 Ninian Steel, sr.,
73 Thomas Archibald,
74 John Gay,
75 Reason Bell,
76 John Hait,
77 Samuel Chambers.

Seventh Company, detached from the First Mecklenburg Regiment.

1 Jos. Douglass, Captain.
2 William M. Kary, Lieut.
3 William Walker, Ensign.
4 Ham. Brevard, 1st Sergt.
5 David Gibony, 2d Sergt.
6 Samuel Brown, 3d Sergt.
7 Wm. M. Barrett, 4th Sergt.
8 Thos. Allen, 1st Cor'l.
9 John Solon, 2d Cor'l.
10 Isaac V. Pitt, 3d Cor'l.
11 R. Duchworth, 4th Cor'l.
12 Adam Harrison,
13 Hugh Wiley,
14 James Moore,
15 John Caldwell,
16 Junius Hood,
17 David Alexander,
18 James Parker,
19 Mathew Wallace,
20 Thomas McRae,
21 John Phillips,
22 Henry Farr,

23 Hugh Todd,
24 Hugh Elliott,
25 Arthur Jimison,
26 Nicholas Parish,
27 Andrew Walker,
28 Upton Roden,
29 David B. Wilson.
30 Joseph Love,
31 Isaac Beaty,
32 Joseph Bingham.
33 William Sharply,
34 Hugh Greggs,
35 Francis Erwin,
36 Richard Mason,
37 John B. Elliott,
38 John L. Darnell,
39 William Camerson,
40 Samuel J. Hutchison,
41 Joshua Clark,
42 James Hutchison.
43 John McLure,
44 John Darnell,
45 Benjamin Thompson,
46 Alexander Moore,
47 Alexander Smith,
48 Wilham Darnel,
49 David Darnel,

50 Jacob I. Cunnigham,
51 Hugh Harris,
52 Eli Alexander,
53 Mitchel Johnston,
54 Allen Lucas,
55 William Downy,
56 Samuel Graham,
57 Will Bushbey,
58 Thomas Shepherd,
59 Allen Sloan,
60 John Fat,
61 Andrew M. Lane,
62 Alexander Washam,
63 Howard Weir,
64 William Sullivan,
65 John Ferret, sr.,
66 David Henderson,
67 Arthur Garretson,
68 Will Robertson,
69 James Simmimer,
70 Drury Solomon,
71 Hugh Holmes,
72 Thomas McIlie,
73 Hugh Stevenson,
74 William Munteeth,
75 Will Scott,
76 Palan Alexander.

Eighth Company, detached from the Second Mecklenburg Regiment.

1 Robert Wood, Captain.
2 Jacob Shaver, Lieut.
3 Peter Mape, 2d Lieut.
4 John Wilson, Ensign.
5 Wm. Flenigan, 1st Sergt.

6 John Hooker, 2d Sergt.
7 John Barnes 3d Sergt.
8 James Watson, 4th Sergt.
9 John Hummuns, 1st Cor'l.
10 Obed Dafter, 2d Cor'l.

11 Will John, 3d Cor'l.
12 Charles Hart, 4th Cor'l.
13 Allen Stewart, Drummer.
14 John Rice, Fifer.
15 James Walker, Private.
16 John Brown,
17 Robert Flenigan,
18 William Sharp,
19 Elias Flenigan,
20 Randolph Cheek,
21 Samuel E. Flanigan,
22 Elias McCallok,
23 Andrew Stewart,
24 Samuel Wiley,
25 Ash John,
26 Cunningham Sharp,
27 John Wiat,
28 John Black,
29 Paten Bambow,
30 Joseph Bryan,
31 Antheris Purvins,
32 Henry Cloutz,
33 Charles Crowell,
34 John Cathberton,
35 Wm. L. Lemmond,
36 John Flow,
37 Jacob Starns,
38 Robert Boid,
39 Daniel McLoyd,
40 Roderick McReley,
41 Moses Stunford,
42 Allen Broom,
43 Charles Lancey,
44 John None,
45 Brelon Belk,
46 Samuel Holden,
47 Valentine Prifly,
48 Michael Flenigan,
49 Henry Moser,
50 Eli Coughran,
51 James Robertson,
52 William Redford,
53 Jesse Yandles,
54 Will Rea,
55 Thomas Henley,
56 Samuel Ormand,
57 John Fobes,
58 Adam Ormand,
59 Lewis Howard,
60 John McCorkle,
61 Will U. Irvey,
62 James Thompson,
63 John Long,
64 Thomas Miller,
65 Samuel Givens,
66 William Martin,
67 Robert Shannon,
68 William Barns,
69 Solomon Morris,
70 William Pirant,
71 William Pool.

Ninth Company, detached from the Second Mecklenbury Regiment.

1 John Garretson, Captain.
2 Isaac Wiley, Lieutenant.
3 Natheil Sims, Ensign.
4 Arch. Sawyer, 1st Sergt.
5 Ire B. Dixon, 2d Sergt.
6 William Smith, 3d Sergt.
7 Joro Kimmons, 4th Sergt.
8 William Mays, 1st Cor'l.
9 John Holbrooks, 2d Cor'l.
10 Frederick Kiser, 3d Cor'l.
11 A. M. Grady, 4th Cor'l.
12 George Kenty, Drummer.
13 John Jaccour, Fifer.
14 John Irwin, Private,
15 Saml. H. Harris,
16 James Ross,
17 Houston Harris,
18 John Alexander,
19 Isaac Harris,
20 Laid Alexander,
21 Cyrus Campbell,
22 Robert M. Cochran,
23 John Morrison,
24 Robert C. Morrison,
25 Hugh McCain,
26 Daniel Bost,
27 Jacob House,
28 Henry Miller,
29 Jacob Rinehart,
30 Henry Rowe,
31 Matthias Bost,
32 Michael Owrey,
33 John Light,
34 Robert Carrigan, sr.,
35 Robert Carrigan, jr.,
36 Theophilus Gayler,
37 John Carrell,
38 Joseph Hamilton,
39 David Houston,
40 Andrew Neele,
41 James Neele,
42 George Flemming,
43 Martin Icehour,
44 George Dove,
45 William Smith,
46 George Linker,
47 Daniel Smith,
48 John Barnhard,
49 Son Fink,
50 Andrew Carriher,
51 Philip Fink,
52 John S. Taylous,
53 John Johnston,
54 Rufus Johnston,
55 David H. Black,
56 John Black,
57 Johnston N. Biggers,
58 William Newit,
59 George Right,
60 Josiah Gilmore,
61 Edward Martin,
62 William Kelly,
63 William Wines,
64 Ebanezer Keelough,
65 James Hall,
66 Jacob Gaugus,

67 John Goodnight,
68 Adam Freeze,
69 John Freeland,
70 John Clisk,
71 Jesse Chaple,
72 Reuben Sneed,

73 John Goodman,
74 James McGraw,
75 Charles Walter,
76 Martin Shank,
77 Daniel Luther,
78 Jacob Simmon.

Tenth Company, detached from the Montgomery Regiment.

1 Elijah Hattam, Captain.
2 William Moor, Lieutenant.
3 Hardy Morgan 2d Lieut.
4 Wyett Scott,
5 Hamlin Freeman,
6 Stephen Morton,
7 William Folks,
8 Sion Pearce,
9 William Gillan,
10 Jacob Cockram,
11 Allen McKackle,
12 James Hellen,
13 Hector McKinsie,
14 Mathew Ingram,
15 Joseph Killis,
16 Nimrod Bradley,
17 Robert B. Wood,
18 Richard Urry,
19 William Thompson,
20 William Trusty,
21 William Eights,
22 Daniel Hurley,
23 Robert Berton,
24 James Wiot,
25 James Stephens,
26 Zachariah Collins,
27 William Johnst^{m},

28
29 Etheldred Blake,
30 Micajah Rogers,
31 Abraham Cochran,
32 Daugle McDuffy,
33 Colin Pall,
34 Joseph Blake,
35 Benjamin Johnston,
36 Hennith McKinsey,
37 Myerdoh Loyd,
38 Abel Rolan,
39 John McRae,
40 Aulas McCalar,
41 Patrick Thompson,
42 Joseph Hattom,
43 Marrel Suggs,
44 James Bennett,
45 David Blallock,
46 William Morgan,
47 Nathaniel Mckins,
48 John Still,
49 William Morton,
50 William Holton,
51 George Heair,
52 Rolen Crump,
53 Wiley Harris,
54 John Crump, jr.,

55 West Harris, jr.,
56 Allen Harris,
57 Ezekiel Hearn,
58 Daniel Redwine,
59 William Hurley,
60 Banister Porter,
61 Frederick Randle,
62 John Smith,
63 John Durgan,
64 Jeptha Milton,
65 John Merrett.
66 Abram Trusty,
67 Robert G. Steele.
68 James Balton,
69 Joseph Morgan,
70 Ephraim Coker,
71 Majro Russell,
72 Francis Jordan,
73 Brantly H. Gallihan,
74 Terrel Blalock,

75 Drury Bennett,
76
77 Reuben Hicks,
78 George Martin,
79 John Beaves,
80 Green Harris,
81 Thomas Morris, jr.,
82 Eli Harris, son, of J.,
83 William Hanisen,
84 Darby Jones,
85 John Hancock,
86 Jesse Bell,
87 Elijah Grisham.
88 Elias Morris,
89 John Cotton,
90 William Harris, son of K.
91 David Tillman,
92 Nelson Smith,
93 John Poplin.

EIGHTH REGIMENT,

DETACHED FROM THE NINTH, TENTH AND FIFTEENTH BRIGADES.

NATHAN HORTON, *Lieutenant Colonel Commandant.*
MERRITT BURGIN, *First Major.*
SAMUEL DAVIDSON, *Second Major.*

First Company, detached from the First Surry Regiment.

1 William McCraw, Capt.
2 John Shipp, 1st Lieut.
3 Bern. Franklin, 2d Lieut.
4 William Potter, Ensign.
5 Eleon'd. Moore, Cadet.
6 Baile' a'Johnston, Private,

7 Micajah Reaves,
8 Watson Holifield,
9 Richard Reaves,
10 Ezekiel Desern,
11 William Holder,
12 Charles Combs,
13 John Parish,
14 Charles Bryant,
15 David Gerwin,
16 Ralph Holifield,
17 Joseph Cartwright,
18 Joseph Muncas,
19 Seward McCraw,
20 Elijah Muncas,
21 Jesse Howard,
22 Solomon Griffith,
23 Benjamin Baker,
24 Isaac Pucket,
25 Martin Forkner,
26 Joshua Garrett,
27 Samuel Laurence,
28 William Smallwood,
29 John Griffith,
30 Samuel McCraw,

31 Calvin Robertson,
32 Henry Sparger,
33 Isaac Holbrooks,
34 Daniel Reece,
35 Lewis Raper,
36 Gentry Hodges,
37 William Hodges,
38 John Ryan,
39 Thomas Ketchum,
40 William Vest,
41 Thomas Bray,
42 Benjamin Cummin,
43 Dudley Reynolds,
44 Daniel Barker,
45 Thomas A. Ward,
46 Ephraim Stone,
47 Jonathan Reynols,
48 John Watson,
49 James Graves,
50 Moses Smith,
51 Peter Graves,
52 Richard White,
53 Robert Baber,
54 Conway Stone.

Second Company, detached from the Second Surry Regiment.

1 Samuel Speer, Captain.
2 Thos. D. Kelley, 1st Lieut.
3 Bowen Whitlock, Ensign.
4 John Kelly, jr., Cadet.
5 Wm. D. Kelley, Private,
6 Benjamin Howard,
7 Edmond Swenny,
8 William Frady,
9 William Spelman,

10 Allen Willard,
11 Asa Dinkins,
12 Isaac Jones,
13 Francis Moreland,
14 Samuel Goff,
15 Thomas Oliver,
16 Strangerman Johnston,
17 Abraham Wooten,
18 Joshua Angel,

19 David Anthony,
20 Jesse Folbet,
21 John Parks,
22 Thomas Osbourn,
23 Stephen Wood,
24 Solomon Johnston,
25 Joseph Phinney,
26 William Masters,
27 James Harris,
28 William Sparks,
29 Joel Patterson,
30 Daniel Teasly,
31 George Speer,
32 Robert Martin,
33 Robert Lyon,
34 Thomas Dyal,
35 James Lakey,
36 Archer Poindexter,
37 Joseph Lovill,
38 Edward Lovill,

39 John Logan,
40 Joshua Pumm,
41 William Pigg,
42 Jacob Shouse,
43 Joseph Hickman,
44 Ephraim Williams,
45 Jonathan Pendry,
46 John Martin,
47 Jesse Chinn,
48 Garret Mahaly,
49 James Pilcher,
50 William Brown,
51 Johnston Lindsay,
52 Willie Dickinson,
53 John McDonald,
54 Thomas Kell,
55 Richard Cook,
56 Jonathan Roses,
57 William Holloman,
58 John Sutliff.

Third Company, detached from the Wilkes Regiment.

1 Walter R. Lanoir, Capt.
2 Michael Swain, 1st Lieut.
3 Lewis Carlton, Ensign,
4 William Ferguson,
5 James Davis,
6 Thomas Lands,
7 Aaron Fox,
8 Jesse Cronch,
9 Thomas Carlton,
10 William Brookshire.
11 Smith Ferguson,
12 Joseph Howard,
13 Isaac Vanderpool,

14 David Robertson,
15 Clifton Keeton,
16 Charles Ragen,
17 Elijah Dyer,
18 Alexander Brown,
19 John Vannoy,
20 William Gullet,
21 William Goforth,
22 Francis Fox,
23 David Hickerson,
24 Ebenezer Castle,
25 John Lips,
26 David Laird,

27 Adam Kilby,
28 Joel Foster,
29 John N. Broyhill,
30 William Morgan,
31 John Hall,
32 Charles Main,
33 Joshua Morgan,
34 William Broyhill,
35 Joel Dyer,
36 William Kilby,
37 Abner Trebble,
38 Lewis Cash,
39 Martin Baker,
40 John Eversale,
41 William Bingham,

42 Laban Adams,
43 Aaron Wiatt,
44 Enoch Chapman,
45 Edmond Dorson,
46 Thomas Craton,
47 James Brown,
48 Stephen Roberts,
49 Joseph Teague,
50 John Carnest,
51 Thomas Crumpton,
52 Achillis Stipp,
53 William Alloway,
54 Jeremiah Hendrickson,
55 Richard Hawkins.

Fourth Company, detached from the Wilkes Regiment.

1 James Martin, Captain.
2 Moses East, Lieutenant.
3 James Benge, Ensign,
4 Benjamin Rose,
5 John Martin,
6 Sterling Rose,
7 Henry Welborn,
8 William Curby,
9 William Denny,
10 Thomas Ellis,
11 Edmund Bryan,
12 Isaac Martin,
13 John Green,
14 William Green,
15 Joseph Johnston,
16 Abel Nichilson,
17 William McBride,
18 James McBride,

19 Joseph Longbottom,
20 Ephraim Nichilson,
21 John Sale,
22 Hyram Ryan,
23 Barney Carter,
24 David Caperham,
25 John Cockerham,
26 Stephen Gentle,
27 Richmond Gordon,
28 John Shoemaker,
29 John Hawkins,
30 Isaac Adams,
31 Thomas Keelin,
32 Henry Trusty,
33 John Brooks,
34 Gordon Chavers,
35 Joseph James,
36 James Matthews,

37 Eli Brown,
38 William Underwood,
39 George Combs,
40 Benjamin Gamble,
41 George Laurence,
42 Henry Gamble,
43 Benjamin Adams,
44 John Adams,
45 James Tolby,
46 Thomas Roberts,
47 Willis Alexander,
48 John Brown,
49 John Blackburn,
50 Aaron McDaniel,
51 John Chustley,
52 Jeremiah Abshire,
53 John Abshire,
54 William Donally,
55 Colin Edwards,
56 George Brown.

Fifth Company, detached from the Ashe Regiment.

1 William Horton, Captain.
2 Squire Wilcoxen, Lieut.
3 Philip Baker, Ensign.
4 William Johnston,
5 John Kerby,
6 William Tolliver,
7 Stephen Crow,
8 Moses McBride,
9 David Maxfield,
10 James McMillan,
11 James Hart,
12 Jacob Stamper,
13 Alexander Cox,
14 John Price,
15 Elijah Smith,
16 William Ellison,
17 Edward Hart,
18 Thomas Collins,
19 Matthias Williams,
20 Archibald Blankinship,
21 William Baker,
22 George Crider,
23 Samuel Wilcoxen,
24 David Horton,
25 Joseph Green,
26 Lewis Tarckler,
27 James Fatam,
28 John Bear,
29 Henry Holsclaw,
30 George Brown,
31 Benjamin Chambers, Fifer

Sixth Company, detached from the First Lincoln Regimen

1 Edward Boyd, Captain.
2 Edwin S. Gingles, Lieut.
3 John Hill, Ensign.
4 Mason Harwell, 1st Sergt.
5 Josh. Abernathy, 2d Sergt.
6 David Linebarge, Cor'l.
7 John Club, Corporal,
8 Samuel Harwell,

9 Gardner Merys,
10 Levi Perkins,
11 Frederick Abernasty,
12 Thomas Long,
13 Michael Sides,
14 Henry Eddlemon,
15 Moses Abernathy,
16 Jacob Edman,
17 Joseph Burk,
18 Peter Evans,
19 George Club, jr.,
20 Ezekiel Abernathy,
21 James McGinnis,
22 Robert Ramsey,
23 Martin Gruson,
24 Robert McCullock,
25 Henry Holland,
26 Matthew Holland, jr.,
27 William Robison, jr.,
28 Robert Huggins, jr.,
29 James Rhodes,
30 David Rine, jr.,
31 John Ryne,
32 Joseph Senter,
33 Frederick Hovis,
34 Jacob Dutcherow,
35 Jonathan Nardike,
36 Nicholas Dillin,
37 John Friday,
38 Samuel Armstrong,
39 Matthew Armstrong,

40 John Neagle,
41 Alexander Irwin,
42 George Oliver,
43 William Oliver,
44 John Henderson,
45 William Hawkins,
46 John Linebarger,
47 Archibald Cathy,
48 Daniel Morrison,
49 Alexander Moore,
50 Adam Clominger, jr.,
51 Jonathan West,
52 George Hager,
53 William Stephenson,
54 Thomas Henry,
55 Andrew Forguson,
56 William Falls,
57 Samuel Carson,
58 John Hager,
59 Daniel Tucker,
60 Robert Beale,
61 Levi Sides,
62 William Hinkle,
63 William Hunt,
64 John Blalock,
65 John Little,
66 George Ferguson, Sergt.
67 Miles Farrer, Sergeant.
68 Sherod Little, Corporal.
69 John Ganny, Corporal.

Seventh Company, detached from the First Lincoln Regiment.

1 Henry Rudasil, Captain.
2 Robert Oats, Lieutenant.
3 Philip Hain, Ensign.
4 Moses Herring, 1st Sergt.

5 Peter Crites, 2d Sergt.
6 Chris. Lewis, 3d Sergt.
7 Wm. Fullbright, 4th Sergt.
8 Abraham Wiatt, 1st Cor'l.
9 Linas Sanford, 2d Cor'l.
10 David Cline, 3d Cor'l.
11 Samuel Edgin, 4th Cor'l.
12 John Master, Private,
13 John Tucker,
14 Jepeth Shaw,
15 James Clark,
16 Henry Barclay,
17 Jesse Wheeler,
18 John Ballard,
19 George Sifford,
20 Menucan Shelton,
21 George Freet,
22 William Sifford,
23 Isaac Flemming,
24 John Sifford,
25 Gatlip Sifford,
26 Adam Hoppis,
27 Martin Delinger,
28 Robert Williams,
29 William Lowe,
30 Iasiah Abernathy,
31 Drury Baggett,
32 Abram Baggett,
33 Absalom Bungarner,
34 George Moore,
35 William Walker,
36 Nicholas Laurence,
37 Thomas Ash,

38 Moses Bungarner,
39 Colbert Sherrell,
40 Isaac Robertson,
41 Jacob Burns,
42 John Caldwell,
43 Frederick Summey,
44 Jacob Fingo,
45 Elias Plot,
46 Henry Chipperd,
47 Christopher Hoffman,
48 Jacob Isaac,
49 Jacob Dunsill,
50 Solomon Cline,
51 Elijah Call,
52 John Wilson,
53 Alfred Moore,
54 Aaron Moore,
55 William Johnston,
56 Francis Asbury,
57 John Kistler,
58 James Martin,
59 Samuel Turner,
60 John Brim,
61 Thomas Hannon,
62 Edward Sneed,
63 William Bennett,
64 Jacob Miller,
65 Robert Wilson,
66 John Crago,
67 John Murphy,
68 James Lindsay,
69 Adam Speight,
70 Christy Speight.

Eighth Company, detached from the Second Lincoln Regiment.

1 George Hoffman, Capt.
2 David Bailey, Lieutenant.
3 Daniel Cline, Ensign,
4 John Jarratt, 1st Sergt.
5 Jacob Conner, 2d Sergt.
6 Thomas Bandy, 3d Sergt.
7 R. H. Simpson, 4th Sergt.
8 Philip Fry, 1st Corporal.
9 Thos. Sampson, 2d Cor'l.
10 John Norman, 3d Cor'l.
11 Chris. Acer, 4th Cor'l.
12 Daniel Shuford, jr.,
13 Daniel Whitener, jr.,
14 Adolph Fodz,
15 Michael Prolst,
16 David Bost,
17 John German,
18 Andrew Sleter,
19 Abram Kilyon,
20 Jacob Kink,
21 Daniel Peterson,
22 Abraham Sleter,
23 George Fisher,
24 Payton Vaughan,
25 Conrad Yoder,
26 George Mosteller,
27 Silas Wilson,
28 Jacob Thorne,
29 George McEntosh,
30 Thomas Huskey,
31 Reuben Copelin,
32 William Harlson,
33 Peter Harman,
34 Ephraim Davis,
35 James Patterson,
36 Samuel Gladdon,
37 Benjamin Waterson,
38 William Scoggin,
39 Solomon Harmon,
40 Abner Camp,
41 David Wier,
42 Perry G. Reynols,
43 Uell Reynolds,
44 John Rudaice,
45 John Turner,
46 Cyrus Peed,
47 Isaac Williams,
48 Benjamin Edwards,
49 Jacob Raugh,
50 Michael Hepner,
51 John Miller,
52 John Taylor,
53 William Caldwell,
54 William Hull,
55 William Bird,
56 William Carrol,
57 John Trout,
58 Peter Howzer,
59 Jacob Spengler,
60 James Center,
61 John Eders,
62 Wiley Harris,
63 John Harvener,
64 Robert Watts,
65 Joseph Kyson,
66 Thomas Laming,

67 Adam Husslater,
68 Feter Beem,
69 John Vickers,

70 Joseph Carpenter,
71 Peter Kiser.

Ninth Company, detached from the First Rutherford Regiment.

1 John Goodbread, Capt.
2 Robert Baber, Lieutenant.
3 John H. Crow, Ensign.
4 Michael Hudlow, 1st Sergt.
5 Jesse Milton, 2d Sergt.
6 Robert Porter, 3d Sergt.
7 Edward Elms, 4th Sergt.
8 Wm. McCurry, 1st Cor'l.
9 James Griffy, 2d Cor'l.
10 Littleton Parram, 3d Cor'l.
11 Chas. Chitwood, 4th Cor'l.
12 Samuel Campbell, Private.
13 Joseph Harmon,
14 Benjamin M. Gakey,
15 Leonard Painter,
16 Coleby Sutton,
17 William Wood,
18 Jeremiah Bennik,
19 Thomas Davis,
20 William Early,
21 Richard Fortune,
22 William Fortune,
23 Abner Green,
24 Henry Norbet,
25 Archibald Weeks,
26 Queen Hicks,
27 Daniel Hicks,

28 Christy Mooney,
29 Samuel Miltoe,
30 John Jones,
31 William Milton,
32 James Sargent,
33 James Thompson,
34 John Guffy,
35 John Walker,
36 Julias Logan,
37 William Carson,
38 James Dalton,
39 Joseph Hunter,
40 William Watson,
41 George Fluman,
42 William Freeman,
43 William Vickers,
44 William Adain,
45 Jonathan Hill,
46 Edward F. Fennington,
47 Peter Coon,
48 John Ownley,
49 William Fluman,
50 Thomas Williams,
51 Summons Bradley,
52 Terry Bradley,
53 Isaiah Wadkins,
54 Hiram Dunkin.

Tenth Company, detached from the Second Rutherford Regiment.

1 Abram Irvine, Captain.
2 John Craw, Lieutenant.
3 John Alexander, Ensign.
4 Isom Weather, 1st Sergt.
5 William Harder, 2d Sergt.
6 Abner Wessen, 3d Sergt.
7 John Williams, 4th Sergt.
8 James Lemons, 1st Cor'l.
9 Mark Harder, 2d Cor'l.
10 James Letever, 3d Cor'l.
11 Archibald Moore, 4th Cor'l.
12 Henry Johnston, Private.
13 Jacob Smith,
14 John Levan,
15 Hillery Scott,
16 Larkin Lea,
17 Richard Afria,
18 David Briars,
19 William Lea,
20 Richard Carver,
21 Charles West,
22 James Lea,
23 John Allison,
24 Jesse Huskey,
25 Robert Herren,
26 Hiram Hector,
27 James Thompson,
28 Wekins Nilman,
29 James Braley,
30 Isaac Brooks,
31 Samuel Scoggin,
32 John Gregory,
33 Joseph Smart,
34 Elijah Surrasy,
35 Levi Burn,
36 Robert Haney,
37 John Gibbs,
38 James Roach,
39 Aaron Bridges,
40 James Hamsick,
41 John Lea,
42 Lewis Blanton,
43 Samuel Humphries,
44 Byard McCraw,
45 Samuel Hamsick,
46 George Blanton,
47 Richard Bridges,
48 Charles Durham,
49 James Hall, Fifer.
50 Morris Quinn, Drummer.
51 John Blanton,
52 Francis Young,
53 Charles Scoggin.

Eleventh Company, detached from the Third Rutherford Regiment.

1 Major R. Alexander, Capt.
2 Christholm Daniel, Lieut.
3 Robert Marlan, Ensign.
4 Joseph Holbert, 1st Sergt..

5 John Price, 2d Sergt.
6 Ezekiel Waldrop, 3d Sergt.
7 Asa Hill, 4th Sergt.
8 Squire Cockeran, 1st Cor'l.
9 Wm. Redman, 2d Cor'l.
10 Thomas Cook, 3d Cor'l.
11 Jonathan Aldrige, 4th Cor'l.
12 James Cockeran, Private.
13 Joseph Robins,
14 Thomas Robins,
15 Jacob Cantrel,
16 John Martin,
17 George King,
18 William Owens,
19 Robert Suttle,
20 William McKennoy,
21 John Rivis,
11 ? John Davis,
12? James Wrier,
1 24 William Walker,
25 Henry Cockeran,
26 John Porter,
27 James M. Erwin,
28 Thomas Prater,

29 John Furlly,
30 John Anderson,
31 Chisolm Daniel,
32 James Early,
33 James Hood,
34 John Owens,
35 John Spencer,
36 John Grizzle,
37 Luke Wilson,
38 John Blackwell,
39 Raleigh Owens,
40 James Jackson,
41 Jeremiah Martin,
42 Patrick Scott,
43 Lemuel Milican,
44 Charles Wilson,
45 Solomon Blackwell,
46 David Dellbuck,
47 Daniel Foster,
48 George Logan,
49 Mathew Garrett,
50 John Forster,
51 John Hannon,
52 Robert Thompson.

Twelfth Company, detached from the Second Rutherford Regiment.

1 John C. Elliott, Capt.
2
3 Samuel Bridges, Ensign.
4 William Porter, 1st Sergt.
5 James Hunter, 2d Sergt.
6 James Purrucks, 3d Sergt.
7 John Dyer, 4th Sergt.
8 Joshua Hawkins, 1st Cor'l.

9 John Procter, 2d Cor'l.
10 William Daggett, 3d Cor'l.
11 Jacob Gage, 4th Cor'l.
12 William Wilson, Private.
13 John Waters,
14 Jesse Chitwood,
15 John Washburn,
16 Henry Lanson,

17 Samuel Gates,
18 James Parks,
19 Lewis Levity.
20 Cazor McCurry,
21 Jacob McCurry,
22 Nicholas Nancy,
23 Samuel Kirkland,
24 Robert Rickets,
25 Leroy Curruth,
26 William Holeyfield,
27 John McDonald,
28 Joseph Nichols,
29 Arthur Owenby,
30 James Anthony,
31 William Anthony,
32 Asa Loveless,
33 Marcy D. Holland,
34 James G. Beatty,

35 Samuel Downy,
36 Samuel M. Bryer,
37 Charles Y. Daggett,
38 Jonathan Harder,
39 Thomas Downy,
40 Jesse Hill,
41 John McFarland,
42 Robert Lirk,
43 Samuel Garland,
44 Henry Workman,
45 John Jarrels,
46 John Hoyle,
47 Thomas McReely,
48 Thomas Reader,
49 William Downs,
50 Joseph Willis,
51 James Newton,
52 Abner Wilson,

Thirteenth Company, detached from the Second and part of the First Burke Regiment.

1 Clinton Harthy, Captain,
2 Benjamin Parks, Lieut.,
3 Matthew Cox, Ensign,
4 Isaac Harris, Private,
5 John Waggoner,
6 John Hilemon,
7 Joseph Hilton,
8 William Fincannon,
9 Peter Constable,
10 Jacob Rample,
11 Alexander Moore,
12 Thomas Foster,
13 Elisha White,
14 Micajah Prine,
15 Leonard Keller,

16 Balum Ducary,
17 Abner Presnal,
18 Lewis Alman,
19 Reuben Henson,
20 Reuben White,
21 Thomas White,
22 John Wakefield,
23 Moses Jackson,
24 James Jackson,
25 Reuben Webb,
26 John Gibson,
27 Abner Staples,
28 John Staples,
29 William Farmer,
30 Samuel Gibson,

31 Thomas Green,
32 Joseph Green,
33 Thomas Sims,
34 Samuel Amburn,
35 William Amburn,
36 John Emmett,
37 Jacob Hise,
38 James Hust,
39 John Phillips,
40 James Penland,
41 Reuben Parks,
42 Ellis Marquis,
43 James Branch,
44 John Gipson,

45 Frederick Huffman,
46 Daniel Watman,
47 Daniel McFalls,
48 Abram Huffman,
49 Leonard Higdon,
50 William Poteet,
51 William Nell,
52 George Duckworth,
53 Jonathan Duckworth,
54 Thomas Colby,
55 Ephraim Evans,
56 John Deal,
57 Jacob Hips.

Fourteenth Company, detached from the Third and part of the First Burke Regiment.

1 Kenneth McKinsey, Capt.
2 Jesse Brevard, First Lieut.
3 William Mifee, Ensign.
4 John Perkins,
5 Jeremiah Boon,
6 William Kinkard,
7 John Boon,
8 Enoch England,
9 John Kinkard,
10 Athan McDowell,
11 James Davies,
12 Joseph Little,
13 Joseph Hood,
14 John McClure,
15 John Gribble,
16 Thomas Monteath,
17 Thomas Robertson,
18 Alexander Harris,

19 William Standford,
20 Alexander Glass,
21 John McDowell,
22 William Hicky,
23 James Warlow,
24 Benjamin Wise,
25 David Stroud,
26 Richard Bell,
27 Thomas Cripson,
28 Peter Stroud, jr.,
29 Peter Eplev,
30 Freeman Tomberlin,
31 Thomas Glass,
32 William Sanders,
33 John Oaks,
34 Daniel Stillwell,
35 Robert Childers,
36 Tillman Stillwell,

37 John Lowry,
38 Barnard Oaks,
39 Solomon Ellis,
40 George Triplett,
41 Joshua Jones,
42 William Triplett,
43 Solomon Wright,
44 Charles Medlock,

45 William Hill,
46 Charles Baley,
47 William Riddisk,
48 William Rickets,
49 James Hunhill,
50 Benjamin Allison,
51 Lemuel Paget,
52 Benjamin McDowell,

Fifteenth Company, detached from the First and Second Buncombe Regiments.

1 Thomas Rhodes, Captain.
2 Eli Merrell, Lieutenant.
3 Thomas Moore, Ensign.
4 James Kincade,
5 Francis Byers,
6 John Gargely,
7 William Wilson,
8 Benjamin Wilson,
9 Samuel J. Murry,
10 Thomas Justice,
11 Cornelius Caps,
12 Nathan Fletcher,
13 Edward Shipman,
14 Nimrod Merrell,
15 John Cancade,
16 William Murry,
17 William Janes,
18 Henry Cary,
19 Andrew Garron,
20 Joshua Owens,
21 Lewis Ward,
22 John Drake,
23 John Love,
24 James Case,

25 Reuben Step,
26 James Abel,
27 Sion Cook,
28 George Story,
29 Robert Byers,
30 John Story,
31 James Hickson,
32 Jonathan Cinard,
33 Matthew Patterson,
34 David Johnson,
35 Easly Dasson,
36 Thomas Kelley,
37 James Kitchen,
38 John Robertson,
39 Samuel Scott,
40 Benjamin Rickets,
41 George D. Davis,
42 Joel McKey,
43 Daniel Davin,
44 John Rutherford,
45 Albert Arsory,
46 William Spivey,
47 Sim Cannon,
48 Charles Hayes,

49 John Weaver, jr.,
50 John Plemmons,
51 John Frisby,
52 Joseph Black,
53 John Plemmons, jr.,
54 John Plemmons,
55 Andrew Plemmons,
56 Stephen Rogers,
57 Joseph Gudyer,
58 Nathaniel Person,
59 Elsey Reynolds,

60 Mitchell Alexander,
61 James Erwin,
62 Jonas Burns,
63 John Palmer,
64 John Harris,
65 Jesse Selah,
66 Jacob Dunket,
67 William Brown,
68 William Carpenter,
69 Peter Mason,
70 Pendleton Underwood,

Sixteenth Company, detached from the Haywood Regiment.

1 Joseph Hughey, Captain.
2 Robert Love, jr., Lieut.
3 John Anglin, Ensign.
4 Samuel Brittain,
5 James Avery,
6 David Vance, jr.,
7 John Killian,
8 Daniel Killian,
9 Azra Roberts,
10 John Dowell,
11 William L. Dalton,
12 John M. Patton,
13 George C. Alexander,
14 Lylas Ray,
15 James Rine,
16 James Welch,
17 William Welch,
18 Dell'd Love,
19 Charles Toler,
20 Marsh Coleman, jr.,
21 Henry Anderson,
22 Eli N. Henry,

23 Uriah Burns,
24 Hezekiah Burns,
25 J. Smith Armstrong,
26 John Bryson, jr.,
27 Joseph Morrow,
28 William Goodin,
29 Martin Hepley,
30 Phil Hyley,
31 Garret Gordon,
32 Thomas Hall,
33 Benjamin West,
34 Benjamin McMullen,
35 Benjamin Clark,
36 Josiah Crawford,
37 Enos McHenry,
38 John McHenry,
39 Price Adams,
40 William Davied,
41 David Rogers,
42 George Reed,
43 William Murry,
44 David Elders,

45 Henry Wild,
46 James Carson,
47 Daniel Giles,
48 John J. Wild,
49 John Anderson, jr.,
50 James Greenlee, jr.,
51 George Stanton,
52 John Griffith
53 Charles Hensley,
54 Ephraim Piercy,
55 John Baker,
56 James Edwards,
57 Robert Patterson,
58 John Edwards,
59 Joseph Shepherd,
60 Jesse Radford,
61 Niram Allen,
62 James Wood,
63 James Redman,
64 James Runnion,
65 Henry Keith,
66 Coleman Murry,
67 John Wild,
68 John Sams,
69 Phillip Wilson,
70 John Rice,
71 Isaac Rice,
72 Barney Landers,
73 James Thomas.

MUSTER ROLL OF THE CAVALRY.

DETACHED FROM THE MILITIA OF NORTH CAROLINA, IN PURSUANCE OF A REQUISITION FROM THE PRESIDENT OF THE UNITED STATES, BY VIRTUE OF AN ACT OF CONGRESS PASSED 10TH APRIL, 1812.

REGIMENT,

EDMUND JONES, *Lieutenant Colonel Commandant.*
ISHAM EDWARDS, *First Major.*
HENRY TAYLOR, *Second Major.*

First Company detached from the Fifth Brigade.

1 William G. Jones, Capt.
2 Wm. R. Bennett, 1st Lieut.
3 M. D. Jeffery, 2d Lieut.
4 Frederick Jones, Cornet.
5 Archibald Yarborough,
6 Robert Hill,

7 Samuel Thomas,
8 William Jenkins,
9 Robert Gill,
10 Parker Murphrey,
11 John Kelley,
12 Joshua Johnston,
13 James Cheaves,
14 Richard Hall,
15 Robert Gupton,
16 Benjamin Hertec,
17 Charles Hayes,
18 Thomas E. Hill,
19 Richardson Finch,
20 John F. Foster,
21 Mathew Struland,
22 Benjamin Carpenter,
23 Willie Williams,
24 Robert C. Hall,
25 Etheldred Pippin,
26 David Bowers,
27 Abner Cheaves,
28 Caffarld Harris,
29 Laban Webb,
30 Isaac House,
31 William Lancaster, jr.,
32 William H. Strother,
33 Allen Minnis,

34 William D. Freeman,
35 Jesse Pearce,
36 Joseph Ballard,
37 Jason Purvin,
38 John Skiles,
39 Arden Andrews,
40 John Barnhill,
41 William Cockburn,
42 Henry Wyne,
43 Collen Robeson,
44 Darling Cherry,
45 James Barner,
46 Benjamin Edmonds,
47 William M. West,
48 Iravin Jones,
49 Abner Read,
50 John B. Massey,
51 Frederick Campbell,
52 Robert B. Daniel,
53 William Eskins,
54 Pendleton B. Isbell,
55 Jared Weaver,
56 Hardy Newell,
57 Thomas Newell,
58 Absalom Brown,
59 Jesse Newell,
60 William F. Irrard.

Second Company, detached from the Sixteenth Brigade.

1 Thomas Cooke, Captain.
2 Leon'd. Cardwell, 1st Lieut.
3 Joseph Bowell, 2d Lieut.
4 Silas High, Cornet,
5 Wm. Mallery, 1st Sergt.
6 John Cheaves, 2d Sergt.

7 Hiram Taylor, 3d Sergt.
8 Robert Paine, 4th Sergt.
9 John O'Brian, 1st Cor'l.
10 Thos. Atkins, 2d Cor'l.
11 Groves Howard, 3d Cor'l.
12 James Jeffers, 4th or'l.

13 Nelson Thomason, trump.
14 Isaac Hirter, Dragoon,
15 Benjamin Thomason,
16 Pleasant Pearce,
17 George Stroud,
18 William Griffin,
19 Burford Twitty,
20 Jethro Lowry,
21 William Williams,
22 John Reaves,
23 Willis Newman,
24 Mathias Williams,
25 Daniel S. Barringer,
26 Anderson Hunter,
27 Green Alfred,
28 Robert H. Jackson,
29 John Baxter,
30 Thomas Matthis,
31 William Brown,
32 Hugh Cobb,
33 Alexander Gray,
34 Thomas Libscomb,
35 Samuel Mitchel,
36 Thomas Walton,
37 Samuel Day,
38 Benjamin Sneed,
39 John Daniel,
40 Charles Parrot.

Third Company, detached from the Sixth Brigade.

1 John Mebane, Captain.
2 James Forest, Lieut.
3 Hardy Ward, 2d Lieut.
4 Youn. McLastro, 1st Sergt.
5 Daniel Fossee, 2d Sergt.
6 Asin Moore, Dragoon,
7 David Craig,
8 Absalom Bulbec,
9 Charles Jones,
10 Jonathan Jones,
11 William McMillion,
12 Elam Hinton,
13 Noah Rhodes,
14 Samuel McBroom,
15 Joseph B. Shaw,
16 Elias Forte,
17 Thomas Hargis,
18 Alexander Mebane,
19 William Thompson,
20 David Patterson,
21 Samuel Nelson,
22 John Rogers,
23 Jacob Thomas,
24 William York,
25 Peter Croom,
26 William Elliott,
27 Tobias Moser,
28 Anarser Riddle,
29 John Spivey,
30 Anderson Williavy,
31 John W. Dismaks,
32 James Bell,
33 William Brinkley,
34 John Norwood,
35 Ferrington Burnett,
36 Patrick Pool,
37 John Smith,
38 Henry Whishenhunt.

Fourth Company, detached from the Eighth Brigade.

1 William Doak, Captain.
2 Sampson Smith, 1st Lieut.
3 John Stewart, 2d Lieut.
4 John Wharton, Cornet.
5 R. Woodburn, 1st Sergt.
6 Leaven Ross, 2d Sergt.
7 Francis Bell, 3d Sergt.
8 David Wiley, 4th Sergt.
9 Mark Gannon, 1st Cor'l.
10 Sample Garrigan, 2d Cor'l.
11 William Brown, 3d Cor'l.
12 Josiah Wiley, 4th Cor'l.
13 Peter Monet, Dragoon,
14 James Gillaspie,
15 Abdi Gillaspie,
16 Ralph Forbis,
17 Alexander Hanner,
18 Robert Gillaspie,
19 Abner Hannah,
20 Eli Hannah,
21 John Morrow,
22 Evan Wharton,
23 William Akin,
24 Findley Shaw,
25 Thomas Gilbreath,
26 Wenright Burns,
27 John Gillaspie,
28 Benjamin Alexander,
29 James Alexander,
30 John Harden,
31 Thomas W. Clands,
32 Levi Huston,
33 John Hannah,
34 James Hendrick,
35 George Sullman,
36 William Gannon,
37 James Gilbreath,
38 Charles Harden,
39 William Dyer,
40 John Alcorn,
41 William Gilbreath,
42 Isaac Wetherly,
43 Isaiah Wetherly,
44 James Russand,
45 Christopher Field,
46 Thomas McCullock,
47 Mathew Young,
48 Robert Johnston.

Fifth Company, detached from the Seventh Brigade.

1 Robert Lock, Captain,
2 John Smith, 1st Lieut.
3 Francis Penny, 2d Lieut.
4 John McCullock, Cornet.
5 John Brandon,
6 Joshua Gay,
7 John Pool, Sadler,
8 Thomas Smith,
9 George T. Smith,
10 George Lock,
11 John Locke,
12 Francis Lock,
13 J. Brandon, Fourth Creek.
14 David Stewart,

15 Henry Verval,
16 Christian Farr,
17 Harman Fisher,
18 Andrew Cook,
19 Henry Allimony,
20 Jacob Cauble,
21 Elias Caruthers,
22 William Henby,
23 Gassaway Gaither,
24 Scarlet Glasscock,
25 Jacob Kinkle,
26 Joseph Howard,
27 John Bailey,
28 Peter Rupard,
29 John Jones,
30 Daniel Bore,
31 John Hughs,
32 Richmond Hughs,
33 Jonathan Hunt,
34 Philip Craven,
35 Elijah Daniel,

36 Levi Reed,
37 Jonathan Hoge,
38 John Bodenhammer,
39 Killion Phelps,
40 James Flemming,
41 John Davidson,
42 John Falls,
43 John Kin,
44 Ross Nesbet,
45 Anguish McKinzie,
46 James Hughs,
47 John Crawford,
48 Howell Alby,
49 Ross McClenning,
50 Edward Mills,
51 Thomas Bell,
52 William Erwin,
53 Robert Johnston,
54 Thomas Sloan,
55 John Bell,
56 Tarlton Shoemaker.

Sixth Company, detached from the Eleventh Brigade.

1
2
3
4
5 Hugh H. McCane,
6 Joseph Robeson,
7 John Robison,
8 Solomon Gibbans,
9 John Shillington,
10 James Martin,
11 Henry Coruner,
12 John D. O. K. Pettes,

13 Alexander Ross,
14 William Duncan,
15 William Allison,
16 John Knox,
17 Jacob Barringer,
18 George Chits,
19 William Verner,
20 Zeblone Ford,
21 Robert Kirkpatrick,
22 Jeremiah Hood,
23 John Ford,
24 Joseph Johnston,

25 Nathan Orr,
26 James Plummer,
27 Isaac Price,
28 B. W. Darrison,
29 Thomas Duckworth,
30 Samuel Porter,
31 Mathew Houston,
32 Griffith Graham,

33 Thomas Blewet,
34 John Pemberton,
35 Thomas Pemberton,
36 Anguish Campbell,
37 William Burton,
38 John Asher,
39 Edmond Almond,
40 Barzum Kirk.

Seventh Company detached from the Tenth Brigade.

1 Henry Ramsour, Captain.
2 Wm. Green, 1st Lieut.
3 Jacob Summers, 2d Lieut.
4 John Zimmerman, Cornet.
5 John Falls, 1st Sergt.
6 John Slagle, 2d Sergt.
7 Henry Smith, 3d Sergt.
8 Moses Sides, 4th Sergt.
9 George Fry, Sadler,
10 Ezekiel Hazelett, Trum.
11 Elias Bost, Dragoon,
12 William Bost,
13 Jacob Smoyer,
14 Hiram Harbeson,
15 Alexander Nail,
16 Henry Smith,
17 Charles Reinhart,
18 Edward Sanders,
19 Mathew Haynes,
20 Absalom Taylor,
21 Allen Wetherly,

22 William Price,
23 John Henry,
24 Moses Heron,
25 John Rhine, jr.,
26 Edward Scarboro,
27 David Ramsour,
28 James Grist,
29 Richard Maze,
30 James Knox,
31 Samuel McMin,
32 John Wilkinson,
33 Alexander McCorcle,
34 John Cornelius,
35 Hardy Abernathy,
36 William Porter,
37 Frederick Kimmy,
38 Benjamin Suttle,
39 William Hannon,
40 Jeremiah Runyan,
41 Timothy Hanny,
42 Isaac Vanzant.

Eighth Company, detached from the Ninth Brigade.

1 Wm. P. Waugh, Captain.
2 John Jones, 1st Lieut.
3 John W. Gorden, 2d Lieut.
4 Samuel Parks, Cornet.
5 Nathaniel Gorden,
6 Alexander Nesbitt,
7 Hugh Jones,
8 Wiley G. Gorden,
9 John Reynolds,
10 Mechat McDowell,
11 Jesse Minton,
12 Andrew Shepherd,
13 Payten Gwyn,
14 Thomas A. Gorden,
15 David Waugh,
16 Braxton McLiven,
17 Ralph McGee,
18 James Huket,
19 John Finley,
20 John Johnston,
21 Lancaster Cunningham,
22 William F. Camble,
23 Little Hickason,
24 William Laws,
25 Abner Tribble,
26 Joel Vancy,
27 Joel Chandler,
28 Samuel Wellbourn,
29 John Hickeson,
30 John Pumphrey,
31 James M. Parks,
32 Charles Adams,
33 Henry Brown,
34 William Hudson,
35 Blewford McGee.

Ninth Company, detached from the Fifteenth Brigade.

1 Ezebulon Baird, Captain.
2 John Weaver, 1st Lieut.
3 Mathew Baird, 2d Lieut.
4 Wm. Alexander, Cornet.
5 Samuel Semple,
6 Samuel Hunter,
7 George Patton,
8 William Gillaspie,
9 David Gillaspie,
10 William Greenlee,
11 John Young,
12 Charles Carrell,
13 Nathaniel Culberson,
14 William Sedford,
15 Alexander Perkins,
16 Charles McDowell,
17 Obadiah H. Erwin,
18 Thomas Flemming,
19 John Harbison,
20 John Kinkaid,
21 Robert Cobb, Sergt.
22 Elisha Baird,
23 Joshua Conely,
24 Moses Cobb,

25 Elisha Dockry,
26 Henry McCall,
27 John Paxton.

MUSTER ROLL OF THE ARTILLERY,

DETACHED FROM THE MILITIA OF NORTH CAROLINA, IN PURSUANCE OF A REQUISITION OF THE PRESIDENT OF THE UNITED STATES BY VIRTUE OF AN ACT PASSED IN CONGRESS, 10TH APRIL, 1812.

First Company, detached from the Wake Regiment.

1 Elhannon Nutt, Captain.
2 Benj. Rogers, 1st Lieut.
3 Willis Whitaker, Ensign.
4 Nat. Whitaker, 1st Sergt.
5 Samuel Rogers, 2d Sergt.
6 Osborn Lockhart, 3d Sergt.
7 Jas. Nance, jr., 4th Sergt.
8 Robert Nutt, 1st Cor'l.
9 Mark Moore, 2d Cor'l.
10 Jesse Roads, 3d Cor'l.
11 F. Broadwell, 4th Cor'l.
12 John A. Smith, Drummer.
13 Turner McInvail, Fifer.
14 Wilie Nichols,
15 Alsey Rockett,
16 Jones Fowler,
17 Durham Hall,
18 William Rigsby,
19 Robert Hall,
20 Wiley Freeman,
21 Brittain Boykin,
22 David Jones,
23 Oram Muller,
24 Jacob Williams,
25 John Ames, jr.,
26 Alfred Acock,
27 Hardy Dean, jr.,
28 Oram Tamon,
29 Miles Allen,
30 Edward Moore,
31 Alsey Nichols,
32 Reason Rabourn,
33 Kade Alfred,
34 Micajah Stricklin,
35 Cader Bunn,
36 Israel Privett,
37 James Chamblee,
38 Elijah Todd,
39 Jeptha Massey,
40 Micajah Jordan,
41 William Griffin,
42 Littleton Ivey,
43 Solomon Hartsfield,
44 Samuel Thompson,

45 Charles Sandiford,
46 Miles Scarbrough,
47 James Bell,
48 James Peace,
49 Bailey Alfred,
50 Gilbert Alfred,
51 Kinchen Medlin,
52 James Lewis, jr.,
53 Joshua Beasley,
54 Daniel Beasley,
55 Jacob Utley,
56 Lemuel Jones,
57 Robert Edwards,
58 Michael Duskins, jr.,
59 Howard Pool,
60 John Hutchins, jr.,
61 Gillis Brown,
62 John Hull,
63 Taban Armstead,
64 Arthur Reaves,
65 Peter Amget,
66 William Holand,
67 Noel Norris,
68 Isma Killum,
69 Anthony Pilkinton,
70 Miller Sexton,

71 Giles J. Bledsoe,
72 Darling Jones,
73 John Band,
74 John Watson,
75 Wiley Wemack,
76 Tyrel Parish,
77 Alvin Utley,
78 Whitmill Hunter,
79 Frederick Spain,
80 Jesse Powell,
81 Isham Holding,
82 Jesse Turner,
83 Robertson Ward,
84 George Kith,
85 Donas Yeargan,
86 Aaron Shiner,
87 David Geer,
88 Richard Ferguson,
89 Richard White,
90 James Hicks,
91 Elijah Kimbrough,
92 David Read,
93 Harbut Hobby,
94 Williams Ladd,
95 John Holloway, jr.,
96 Thomas Parham.

Second Company, detached from the Edgecombe Regiment.

1 John Thomas, Captain.
2 Lat. Vins, 1st Lieut.
3 Thomas Amosin, 2d Lieut.
4 John Bridges, Ensign.
5 Theo. Thomas, 1st Sergt.
6 Benj. Sharp, 2d Sergt.
7 Wm. O. Carter, 3d Sergt.

8 Wm. Williams, 4th Sergt.
9 H. C. Knight, 1st Cor'l.
10 James Pender, 2d Cor'l.
11 Ithiel Eason, 3d Cor'l.
12 William White, 4th Cor'l.
13 James Cobb, Drummer.
14 May Moore, Fifer.

15 John Barrow,
16 Jesse C. Knight,
17 Levi Long,
18 Robert Long,
19 John Stallings,
20 Elijah Williams,
21 Henry Walter,
22 James Permerter,
23 Elisha Fellon,
24 Benjamin Varnel,
25 John Taylor,
26 Reddin Thigpen,
27 William Gay,
28 Thomas Moore,
29 Dempsey Hicks,
30 Abram Coles,
31 David Wollard,
32 Martin B. Liles,
33 Hansford Burress,
34 Hardy Simpson,
35 James Moore,
36 Ephraim Wooten,
37 John Peele,
38 Lemuel Lancaster,
39 William Williams, sr.,
40 Edward Sherod,
41 Daniel Land,
42 John Thomas,
43 Thomas Williams,
44 David Thomas,

45 Jethro Weaver,
46 Stephen Bullock,
47 John Brantly,
48 Achles Barnes,
49 Dixon Summuns,
50 Isaac Daniel,
51 James Daniel,
52 John Johnston,
53 William Johnston,
54 Asahel Bateman,
55 Ashael Farmer,
56 Jokn Farmer,
57 Reddick Barnes,
58 John Barnes,
59 Haman Mann,
60 Enos Barnes,
61 Jesse Parker,
62 John B. Cobb,
63 Barnwill Moore,
64 Bryant Shoots,
65 Jesse Hedgepeth,
66 Silas Mitchel,
67 Thomas Whitly,
68 Rickmon Cobb,
69 Benjamin Sumerlin,
70 Isaac Hobbs,
71 Timothy Harris,
72 Enoch Robertson,
73 Moses Moore,

Third Company, detached from the Bertie Regiment.

1 Joseph H. Bryan, Capt.
2 Augustin Pugh, Lieut.
3 Lodswick Pruden, Ensign.
4 William McGruder,
5 Isaac Wilson,
6 Hardy Hunter,

7 Anthony Wiggins,
8 Benjamin Brogdon,
9 Washington Turner,
10 John A. Cordle,
11 Rheuben Wilkes,
12 David Harrell,
13 Fred Wimberly,
14 John Wilkes,
15 Henry Wilkes,
16 Jesse Powell,
17 John Ruffin,
18 Thomas Bickell.
19 Turner McGlawhon,
20 Edward Turner,
21 Elijah C. Bryan.
22 John B. Everitt,
23 John Minor,
24 John Stewart, jr.,
25 Richard L. Bowers,
26 John Brickell,
27 Linus Leonard,
28 Shade Britt,
29 John Brantly,
30 William Brickell,
31 Cader Bunch,
32 Samuel Hobbs,
33 Edward B. Baker,
34 John Allen,
35 Edward Gill,
36 Edmond Fleetwood, jr.,
37 Frederick Miller,
38 Reuben Lawrence,
39 Wil Wilkins,
40 Asa Radett,
41 Levi Todd,
42 Joshua P. Brantly,

43 James Boswell,
44 Asa Gregory,
45 John Ramsey,
46 Josiah Miller,
47 John Rhodes,
48 Haller Calway,
49 Richard Bagwell,
50 William H. Green,
51 Nathaniel Culeper,
52 Benjamin Winburn,
53 James Simonds,
54 Benjamin James,
55 Thomas Corbett,
56 William Gardner,
57 David Garrett,
58 Ryan Jonagon,
59 Abner Aaron, jr.,
60 Samuel Martin,
61 Elisha Pritchard,
62 Cader Mitchel,
63 Jacob Pruden,
64 Levi Outlaw,
65 David Fleetwood,
66 Neal Nicholas,
67 James Carley,
68 Thomas Hogard,
69 Lawrence Cook,
70 William Roll,
71 Jesse Garrett,
72 George Wilson,
73 Cader Hunter,
74 Dred Evans,
75 Silas Wilson,
76 Thomas Sorrell,
77 William Brogdon,
78 William Hunter,

79 Stephen Hymon,
80 James Ryman,
81 John West,
82 Hardy Clements,
83 Benjamin Rogers,
84 William Robertson,
85 Malacha Green,
86 Isaac Wiggins,
87 William Higgs,
88 James Wilkes,
89 Augt. Callum,
90 West Tines,
91 David Folk,
92 Redden Rutland,
93 George Core,

94 Johnston Rutland,
95 Simeon Harrell,
96 Joseph Harrell,
97 W. M. Bishop,
98 David Outlaw,
99 John Waltan,
100 Nathl. Wattoman,
101 William Holloman,
102 John Holly,
103 Moses Freeman,
104 George Ward,
105 Cader White,
106 Hardy White,
107 Miles Rollins,
108 William Evans.

Fourth Company, detached from the Carteret Regiments.

1 Jacob Henry, Captain.
2 William Jasper, 1st Lieut.
3 Samuel Leffers, 2d Lieut.
4 David Wallace, Ensign.
5 Thomas Howland,
6 John Rigs,
7 Elijah Canaday,
8 John Linch,
9 Joseph Fulford, jr.,
10 Anthony Davis,
11 George Gibble,
12 Timothy Small,
13 James Johnston,
14 John Simmons,
15 Zacheus Green,
16 Archibald Green,
17 Abram Wilder,
18 John Sanders,

19 Elias Meadors,
20 Nevil Russell,
21 Elijah Gardner,
22 Thomas Willis,
23 John Bell,
24 Benjamin Willis,
25 Loftin Quin,
26 Francis Gardner,
27 William Lewis,
28 Joseph Salter,
29 Walace Salter,
30 Cason Willis,
31 Jacob Smith,
32 James Dixon,
33 William Gaskill,
34 David Ireland,
35 George Golding,
36 John Lewis,

37 Caleb Wade,
38 Eliza Wade,
39 John Wharton,
40 Clifton Fulford,
41 Benjamin Guthrie,

42 George Price,
43 Beliher Hakee,
44 Elijah Guthrie,
45 Zachariah Willis,

Fifth Company, detached from the Brunswick Regiment.

3 John Sullivan, 2d Lieut.
4 David Tolson,
5 Richard Harris,
6 Burnel Cason,
7 John Cherr,
8 William Pound,
9 Joel Robins,
10 Allegood Suggs,
11 Eldred Tellers,
12 William Key,
13 William Hankens,
14 Randal Hewet,
15 John Clemons,
16 Levi Swain,
17 Absalom Beasley,
18 William Bennett,
19 Josiah Little,

20 Coleman Runnels,
21 Benjamin Sellers,
22 Samuel Harris,
23 Arthur Pinner,
24 Josiah Cox,
25 Alexander Campbell,
26 Moses King,
27 James Ellis,
28 Niram Skipper,
29 Jonathan Rothwell,
30 Joseph Walters,
31 Thomas Vines,
32 Jonathan Keater,
33 Benjamin Purrell,
34 John Spencer,
35 Daniel Bennett,
36 William Gilbert.

MUSTER ROLL OF THE RIFLEMEN,

DETACHED FROM THE MILITIA OF NORTH CAROLINA, IN PURSUANCE OF A REQUISITION OF THE PRESIDENT OF THE UNITED STATES, BY VIRTUE OF AN ACT OF CONGRESS, PASSED 10TH APRIL, 1812.

First Company, detached from the Cumberland Regiment.

1 William Loyd, Captain,
2 Robert Carver, 1st Lieut.
3 George Kenedy, 2d Lieut.
4 Richardson Watson, En.
5 Jas. Holmes, 1st Sergt.
6 John Rhea, 2d Sergt.
7 Jesse Townsend, 3d Sergt.
8 John Dixon, jr.,
9 Isaac Howard,
10 Menas Howard,
11 Allen Brown,
12 Egbird Hall,
13 Isham Carver,
14 William Gyton,
15 Elijah Ward,
16 John Campbell,
17 Isaiah Toler,
18 Samuel Taylor,
19 Daniel Pharis,
20 Josiah Culberson,
21 Frederick Brewer,
22 Aaron Smith,
23 James C. Myrick,
24 Jesse Ritter,
25 Julius Brewer,
26 John Corkuran,
27 Mitchel Rowland,
28 John Milton,
29 Gideon Moore,
30 Louis Williamson,
31 Louis Russell,
32 Thomas D. King,
33 Hardy Chesnut,
34 Willie Dodd,
35 Jesse Oats, 4th Sergt.
36 Richard Clinton,
37 Joshua Chesnut,
38 William Blackman,
39 Nathan King,
40 Louis F. Peck,
41 Daniel Cogdell,
42 John Turner, jr.,
43 Travers Beddue,
44 Archibald McMillan,
45 Stephen Hester,
46 David Thomas,
47 John Robertson,
48 James Jackson,
49 Cornelius Kellyham,
50 Arthur Hardy,
51 David M. Kemp,
52 William Lewis,

53 Warren Baldwin,
54 John Bright,
55 William Huff,

56 Jonathan Cribb,
57 John Graham,
58 Thomas Carteret.

Seventh Company, detached from the Fourteenth Brigade.

1 Nell Buie, Captain,
2 William Leod,
3 James McFarland,
4 Malcom Gills,
5 Neil Curry,
6 Alexander McKay,
7 Alexander McDonald,
8 Malcom Yates,
9 Malcom Curry,
10 John Rainwater,
11 Elisha Gibson,
12 John Gillis,
13 Hugh Gillis,
14 Dugald McDuffy,
15 Moses Parker,
16 John Little,
17 John McDuffy,
18 John Turrege,
19 Stephen Dees,
20 Levy Dees,

21 Daniel McEathan,
22 William McNeil,
23 Duncan Mathews,
24 Alex. McNabb,
25 Daniel Calbroth,
26 Dugald Stewart,
27 Hugh Curry,
28 Hector Bethune,
29 Archibald Curry,
30 Neil McNeil,
31 Archibald McNeil,
32 Duncan McGregar,
33 Daniel Smith,
34 Peter Livington,
35 John Sinclair,
36 John Wilkinson,
37 Peter McArthur,
38 Duncan McMillan,
39 James Watson,
40 Neil Ferguson.

Tenth Company, detached from the Ninth Brigade.

1 Gideon Lewis, Captain.
2. Elijah Wilcoxen,
3 Jonathan Taylor,
4 Matthias Langly,
5 Fulty Miller,
6 Isaiah Miller,
7 Elias Robeson,

8 Theophilus Baldwin,
9 David Bogan,
10 Larkin Bunyard,
11 Fulty Miller,
12 John Ray,
13 James Kethborn,
14 Rich'd. Allen, jr., 1st Lieut.

15 Jacob Pilear,
16 John Foss,
17 John Sparks, jr.,
18 Francis Kurby,
19 Jacob Hoots,
20 Solomon Sparks,
21 Isaac Stover,
22 Jeremiah Johnston,
23 John N. Green,
24 John Chapman,
25 James Robinet,
26 James Franklin, 2d Lieut.
27 John Shipp, Ensign,
28 William Oglesby, Cadet,
29 Bartlet Hanmock,
30 John Snow,
31 Miley Cave,
32 Thomas Cox,
33 Thomas Oglesby,
34 William Potter,
35 Ephraim Witcher,
36 Levi Snow,
37 William Hammonds,
38 Bernard Franklin.

Fourth Company, detached from the Seventh Brigade.

1 Francis Young, Captain.
2 Samuel Young,
3 William McOnnel,
4 Richard Harris,
5 Solomon Ellis,
6 William Tomlinson,
7 John Young,
8 John Dobson,
9 John Green,
10 William Murdy,
11 Fans Sharp,
12 Solomon Jacobs,
13 Robert Callahan,
14 Thomas Francis,
15 John Yeark,
16 James Beil,
17 Enos Campbell,
18 Erasmus Lazenby,
19 Ezekiel Pearce,
20 George Summers,
21 Daniel Brown, Lieut.
22 Daniel Starns,
23 Benjamin Agender,
24 Jacob Trees,
25 Henry Eller,
26 David Butner,
27 John Rainy,
28 Joseph Graham,
29 David Masters,
30 Henry Berger,
31 Isaac Cummins,
32 Peter Mourey,
33 Jacob L. Peterson,
34 Peter Agender,
35 John Hartman,
36 John Rose,
37 Edward Burgess,
38 William Glasscock,
39 Jacob Booe,
40 Jacob Helfer,
41 Daniel Booe,
42 Joshua Brinigan,

43 Philip Baker,
44 Georges Graves,
45 Jacob Call,
46 Zedekiah Jarvis,
47 Jacob Hoover,
48 David Larkabee,
49 George Bodenhammer,

50 Thomas Newcomb,
51 George Miller,
52 John Michael,
53 John Long, jr.,
54 Andrew Yoakley,
55 Jacob Sink.

Fifth Company, detached from the Second Rutherford Regiment, Tenth Brigade.

1 John C. Elliott, Captain.
2 Wm. Porter, 1st Sergt.
3 Samuel Bridges, Ensign.
4
5 James Hunter, 2d Sergt.
6 James Parish, 3d Sergt.
7 John Dyer, 4th Sergt.
8 Joshua Hawkins, 1st Cor'l.
9 John Proctor, 2d Cor'l.
10 William Daggett, 3d Cor'l.
11 Jacob Gage, 4th Cor'l.
12 William Wilson,
13 John Waters,
14 Jesse Chitwood,
15 John Washburn,
16 Henry Lanon,
17 Samuel Gates,
18 James Parks,
19 Lewis Levity,
20 Cazor W. Curry,
21 Jacob McCurry,
22 Nicholas Nancy,
23 Samuel Kirkland,
24 Robert Rickets,
25 Leroy Curretch,
26 William Holyfield,

27 John McDonald,
28 Joseph Nichols,
29 Arthur Owerly,
30 James Anthony,
31 William Anthony,
32 Asa Labeless,
33 Marcus D'Holland,
34 James G. Beaty,
35 Samuel Downy,
36 Samuel McBroyer,
37 Charles Y. Dogget,
38 Jonathan Harder,
39 Thomas Downy,
40 Jesse Hill,
41 John McFarland,
42 Robert Link,
43 Samuel Garland,
44 Henry Workman,
45 John Jarrels,
46 John Hoyle,
47 Thomas McReely,
48 Thomas Reader,
49 William Downs,
50 Joseph Willis,
51 James Newton,
52 Abner Wilson.

15 Jacob P.
16 John F
17 John S *ompany, detached from the Eleventh Brigade.*
18 Franci Long,
2 Robert Farr,
3 Samuel McCurdy,
4 Eli Newell,
5 Peter J. Bane,
6 George Sifford,
7 Jacob Cruise,
8 Francis Newel,
9 John W. Davis,
10 Jacob Stough,
11 William Gray,
12 Charles Juhn,
13 Francis McClosky,
14 Henry Fisher,
15 Isaac Helms,
16 Aley McCorkle,
17 Robert Givens,
18 Andrew Walker,
19 William Campbell,
20 John Campbell,
21 Henry Lewis,
22 John Price,
23 James Todd,
24 James Thompson,
25 Robert Robinson,
26 Milton Harris,
27 Cyrus Harris,
28 Solomon Ballard,
29 Charles Cupples,
30 Thomas Frasure,
31 James Haywood,
32 Will Johnston,
33 James Lesbury,
34 Benjamin Williams,
35 John Layton,
36 Laban Carter,
37 Zachariah Walker,
38 John Hasley,
39 Henry Goodman,
40 John Reddell,
41 Isom Williams,
42 Adam Shular,
43 John Ball,
44 Jesse Gallimore,
45 Robert C. Davis,
46 David Davenport,
47 John Milsaps,
48 John Loftin,
49 Solomon Heath,
50 Jacob Myers.

MUSTER ROLL

OF THE DETACHED MILITIA, ORGANIZED IN AUGUST, 1814.

General Officers designated to command in this Detachment of Militia:

MONTFORD STOKES, *Major General.*
JEREMIAH SLADE,
JESSE A. PEARSON,   } *Brigadier Generals.*

The first regiment to be composed of the counties of Chowan, Currituck, Camden, Pasquotank, Perquimans, Gates, Hertford Bertie, Northampton, Halifax, Warren, and Nash.
Officers.—Duncan McDonald, Lieutenant Colonel, Commandant; Andrew Joyner, Lieutenant Colonel; Joseph F. Dickerson, First Major; John C. Green, Second Major.

Second Regiment of Washington, Tyrell, Hyde, Beaufort, Craven, Carteret, Jones, Lenoir, Greene, Pitt, Martin, Edgecombe and Wayne.
Officers.—Simon Bruton, Lieutenant Colonel Commandant; Nathan Tisdale, Lieutenant Colonel; Thomas H. Blount, First Major; James W. Clark, Second Major.

Third regiment of Onslow, New Hanover, Bladen, Brunswick, Columbus, Duplin, Sampson, Robeson, Cumberland, Moore, Richmond and Anson.
Officers.—Maurice Moore, Lieutenant Colonel Commandant; Richard Nixon, Lieutenant Colonel; Archibald McNeil, First Major; Edward B. Dudley, Second Major.

Fourth regiment of Wake, Johnston, Franklin, Granville, Person, Orange and Chatham.
Officers.—Richard Atkerson, Lieutenant Colonel Commandant; Mourice Smith, Lieutenant Colonel; John C. Wyatt, First Major; Benjamin Chambers, Second Major.

Fifth regiment of Caswell, Guilford, Rockingham, Stokes, Surry, Wilkes, Ashe and Randolph.
Officers.—Alexander Murphy, Lieutenant Colonel Commandant; Samuel Hunter, Lieutenant Colonel; James Campbell, First Major; Joseph Winston, jr., Second Major.

Sixth Regiment of Rowan, Montgomery, Mecklenburg, Cabarrus and Iredell.
Officers.—Richard Allison, Lieutenant Colonel Commandant; John H. Freeling, First Major; Amos Sharpe, Second Major.

Seventh regiment of Lincoln, Rutherford, Burke, Buncombe and Haywood.
Officers.—Andrew Irwin, Lieutenant Colonel Commandant; William Cathey, First Major; Nathan A. McDowell, Second Major.

FIRST REGIMENT.—CHOWAN COUNTY.

1 James Iredell, Captain.
2 Joseph Manning, 1st Lieut.
3 J. M. Roberts, 2d Lieut.
4 Myles Wilder, Ensign.
5 John D. Castillow,
6 John Bond, sr.,
7 Charles Simpson,
8 Jones Parish,
9 James Hinsley,
10 Edwin Bond,
11 Hardy Morgan,
12 John Evans,
13 Richard Paxton,
14 Nathaniel Miller,
15 Sampson Wilder,
16 Thomas Mires,
17 James R. Creecy,
18 Martin Noxon,
19 Edmond Hoskins,
20 Clement H. Blount,

21 Samuel Charlton,
22 Michael Hendrick,
23 Benjamin Whidler,
24 William Nickolls,
25 Jackson S. Hoyle,
26 Obediah Roberts,
27 Jonathan Parks,
28 Henry Evans,
29 Isaac Boice,
30 Charleston Ward,
31 Joseph Winslow,
32 William Jordan,
33 Josiah Ward,
34 Thomas Smith, sr.,
35 Michena Trulove,
36 John Wilder,
37 Thomas Rhea,
38 Alfred M. Gatlin,
39 George Waff,
40 William Cheshire,
41 George Mewbern,
42 Edmond Bunch,
43 John Ashley,
44 William Todd,
45 John Boyce,
46 John Rhody,
47 Joseph Small, jr.,
48 Jesse Mitchel,
49 Stacy Floyd,
50 William Ashley,
51 John Reddic,
52 Jethro Woodard,
53 Alexander Parish,
54 Julius Deale.

CURRITUCK COUNTY.

1 William Bray, Captain,
2 John Baxter, 1st Lieut.
3 Phillip Dozier, 2d Lieut.
4 Thomas Summon Ensign.
5 William Etheridge,
6 Lemuel Ferebee,
7 Samuel Gregory,
8 Malachi Holstead,
9 Charles Seears,
10 Tully Dozier,
11 Samuel Glasgow,
12 Peter Ferebee,
13 William Spence,
14 Iles Collins,
15 Arthur Heath,
16 Wilson Nash,
17 Anthony Simmons,
18 Caleb Woodard,
19 Martin McBride,
20 Dempsey Gregory,
21 Willoughby Boswood,
22 Jordan Dozier,
23 Jasper Dozier,
24 Grandy Barnard,
25 William Dozier,
26 Willoughby Barnard,
27 William Ferebee,
28 William Guilford,
29 John Baxter,
30 Wallis Hutchins,
31 Hillary Finters,
32 Jeremiah Mercer, jr.,

33 Nnoch Whithurst,
34 Samuel Whithurst,
35 Josiah Etheridge,
36 Hillary Fanchier,
37 John C. Glasgow,
38 Cornelius Mercer,
39 Branson Bell,
40 William Messenger,
41 Peter Parr,
42 Peter Gregory,
43 James Parr,
44 Samuel Nicholson,
45 Levi Etheridge,
46 Arthur Spence,
47 William Hanners,
48 John Gregory,
49 Jacob Aydelotte,
50 Frederick Northern,
51 Ralph P. Beeling,
52 James Northern,
53 Charles Sawyer,
54 Jesse Robinson,
55 John Morse,
56 John Bunnell,
57 Joseph Sawyer,
58 John Floro,
59 John Brickhouse,
60 James Bunnell,
61 Aaron Floro,
62 Henry Bright,
63 Willoughby Whally,
64 William Etheridge,
65 Charles Perkins,
66 James Brabble,
67 John W. Hughs,
68 William Brumsey,

69 James White,
70 Jesse McClannan,
71 John Lee,
72 Enoch Lee,
73 Joseph Tatum,
74 Tatum Brabble,
75 Jesse Balance,
76 John Brabble,
77 Bartholomew Thompson,
78 Isaac Snowden,
79 Dempsey Doxey,
80 Matthias Bell,
81 George Cason,
82 Daniel Tatum,
83 Maxey Tatum,
84 John Caps,
85 John Brabble, jr.,
86 Thomas Balance,
87 James Poyner,
88 Dempsey Douglass,
89 Isaac Roberts,
90 James Fentus,
91 John Baxter,
92 Alexander White,
93 George Perkins,
94 James Snowden,
95 Samuel Payner,
96 Peter Barco,
97 Thomas Etheridge,
98 Francis Camp,
99 Spencer Oneal,
100 Reuben Taylor,
101 John Forbes,
102 Thomas Roberts,
103 Mitchell Simmons,
104 Joseph Baxter, jr.,

105 Moses Cox,
106 Amos Davis,
107 James Lee,
108 John Wilson,
109 Willis Ballentine,

110 William Cilgrow,
111 Henry Williamson,
112 Nicholas Ellison,
113 Stephen Etheridge.

CAMDEN COUNTY.

1 Jas. S. Garlington, Capt.
2 Archibald Sawyer, Lieut.
3 John H. Wright, Ensign.
4 John A. Brockett,
5 William Mercer,
6 John Jerrell,
7 Thomas Berry,
8 Nathan Harrison,
9 John Pue,
10 Malachi Collins,
11 Frederick Gregory,
12 James Owens,
13 Edward Cerlin,
14 Cader Wright,
15 Dempsey Collins,
16 Malachi Knight,
17 Charles Wright,
18 Asa Cartwright,
19 Wilson Coats,
20 Miles Mercer,
21 Thomas Surry,
22 William Garrett,
23 Thomas Bray,
24 Adam Baum,
25 Bradly Smith,
26 Reuben Gibson,
27 Job Gregory,
28 William Collin,

29 Elijah Staples,
30 Simeon Jones,
31 Ferebee Sanderlin,
32 Silas Forbes,
33 Joseph Bell,
34 Seth Wright,
35 Isaac Burges,
36 Joab Bell,
37 John Jones,
38 Frederick Daily,
39 James Sawyer,
40 Frederick Kanady,
41 Samuel Godfrew,
42 Jonathan Gregory,
43 Abner Cooper,
44 William Dowtey,
45 Dempsey Squiers,
46 Nathan Gregory,
47 Miles Williams,
48 James Beales,
49 Henry H. Wright,
50 Samuel Needham,
51 Zephaniah Sawyer,
52 Freeman Sawyer,
53 John Godfrey,
54 Josiah Sanderlin,
55 Jeremiah Jones,
56 James Godfrey,

57 Benjamin Douge,
58 Densey Dunkin,
59 Caleb Forbes,
60 Peter Pugh,
61 Joseph Love,
62 Waxsey Sawyer,
63 Jesse Douge,
64 Hiram Godfrey,
65 James McHarney,
66 Jesse Temple,
67 Dempsey Riggs,
68 Silas Riggs,
69 Dempsey Forbes,
70 Isaac Harrison.
71 Cornelius Wright,
72 Berket Beales,
73 Joseph Seamon,
74 Levi Wright,
75 William Kanady,
76 Abraham Cartwright,
77 Joseph Barco,
78 Samuel Gregory,
79 Dempsey Douge,
80 Edmond Gregory,
81 Lot Needham,
82 Samuel Jarvis,
83 Amos Pue.

PASQUOTANK COUNTY.

1 Carter Bernard, Captain,
2 Abraham Simons, Lieut.
3 Miles Jones, Ensign.
4 William Gammon,
5 Henry Keaton,
6 James Sawyer,
7 James Turner,
8 Jesse Maddux,
9 Thomas Lowry,
10 John Lester,
11 Thomas Markum,
12 Joshua Trewblood,
13 Alfred Turner,
14 John White,
15 Richard Clayton,
16 Miles Brothers,
17 Caleb Brothers,
18 Robert Cartwright,
19 David Davis,
20 Malachi Davis,
21 Thomas Palin,
22 Cyprian Chopard,
23 Jesse Walden,
24 Keder Morgan,
25 Richard Madrew,
26 William Casey,
27 James Cartwright,
28 Thomas Pritchard,
29 Harvey Harris,
30 James Jackson,
31 Thomas Cartwright,
32 William Morris,
33 Isaac Williams,
34 Kader Perry,
35 Hezekiah Jackson,
36 James Munden,
37 Charles Roberts,
38 Nathan Small,

39 Daniel White,
40 Caleb Bundy,
41 William Munden,
42 Daniel Spence,
43 Thomas Burnham,
44 Evergain Carver,
45 William Cartwright,
46 Joseph Haireld,
47 John Hallstead,
48 Harvey Stokely,
49 Robert Sawyer,
50 Henry Temple,
51 James Williams,
52 John Williams,
53 Peleg Prichard,
54 David Frew,
55 Johnson Davis,
56 William Smithson,

57 Isaac Sawyer,
58 Stephen Richardson,
59 Adam Stafford,
60 Grandy Pritchard,
61 Stephen Hooker,
62 Thomas Madrew, jr.,
63 Jesse Gray,
64 William Allen,
65 Thomas McKey,
66 W. Jackson, (son of Thos.);
67 Jaboz Bright,
68 J. Brothers, (son of Jos.),
69 Joshua Pool,
70 William Albertson,
71 William Bumbough,
72 Daniel Bray,
73 Henry Pendleton.

PERQUIMANS COUNTY.

1 Wm. R. Sutton, Captain.
2 Alfred Moore, Lieutenant.
3 John Branch, Ensign.
4 Benjamin Smith,
5 Charles Elliott,
6 Caleb Chappel,
7 Joseph Roberts,
8 Joseph Elliott,
9 Jesse Elliott,
10 John White,
11 Foster Elliott,
12 Henry Smith,
13 John Rogerson, jr.,
14 Hugh Morgan,
15 Joseph W. Weeks,

16 Barnabas Ward,
17 Francis Godfrey,
18 Harrison Turner,
19 James Tweedy,
20 Purry Weeks,
21 Thomas Feveash,
22 John Jackson, jr.,
23 Nathaniel Cole,
24 Robert Harrison,
25 John Madre,
26 Charles Hall,
27 John Bunch,
28 Joseph Jordan,
29 James Thach,
30 Willis Butter,

31 John Wingate,
32 William Thach,
33 William Tailor,
34 William Thorn,
35 Charles W. Skinner,
36 Seth Hendricks,
37 Thomas Hasket,
38 Mexum Newby,
39 Josiah Smith,
40 John Woodley,
41 George Low,
42 William Bagley,
43 Hezekiah Savage,
44 William Gregory,
45 Willis Morgan,
46 John Hasket,
47 Nathan Bagley,

48 Joseph Cooper,
49 Dempsey Webb,
50 John White, (of John,)
51 John Sampson,
52 James Perry,
53 Moses Boyce,
54 William Walton,
55 Asa Pelon,
56 Samuel Barclift, sr.,
57 Robert Reed,
58 William Humphries,
59 John Stanton,
60 James Needham,
61 James Tatlock,
62 John Stephenson,
63 James Gipson.

GATES COUNTY.

1 Henry Pugh, Captain.
2 Isaac K. Hunter, Lieut.
3 George Kittrell, Ensign,
4 John Gordon, 1st Sergt.
5 Wm. Kittrell, 2d Sergt.
6 John Barnes, 3d Sergt.
7 Robt. Powell, 4th Sergt.
8 Jonas Franklin, 1st Cor'l.
9 Whitmill Hill, 2d Cor'l.
10 Joseph Harrell, 3d Cor'l.
11 Jethro Brinkley, 4th Cor'l.
12 William White, Private.
13 Elijah Lyons,
14 Amos Hobbs,
15 William Hofler,
16 Jesse Hyett,

17 Anson Williams,
18 Joseph Derden,
19 James Eure,
20 Timothy Spivey,
21 Solomon Eason,
22 William Pearce,
23 William Blanchard,
24 Seth Blanchard,
25 Edward Briggs,
26 Samuel Green,
27 Robert Simons,
28 Miles Knight,
29 Richard Farlass,
30 Francis M. Foster,
31 Edward Daughtie,
32 Henry Holt,

33 Samuel Smith,
34 Frederick Williams,
35 Kindred Parker,
36 Kinchen Taylor,
37 Benjamin Eure,
38 Elisha Umphlet,
39 Thomas Cullins,
40 William Crofford,
41 Lewis Lee,
42 Elisha Pyland,
43 Jesse Parker,
44 James Williams,
45 Miles Williams,
46 John Evens,
47 Jethro Reddick,
48 Shedric Pyland,
49 Watson Hilley,
50 William Pyland,
51 Dempsey Hall,
52 James Lapland,
53 Kader Briggs,

54 Reuben Miller,
55 James Jones, (of John.,)
56 Jesse Mathias,
57 Noah Speight,
58 Joshua Small,
59 Robert Parker,
60 Harmon Hayes,
61 Robert Wilson,
62 Hardy Williams,
63 John Polson,
64 David Brown,
65 John Shearod,
66 Elisha Duke,
67 James Parker,
68 Henry Crafford,
69 Jacob Ealey,
70 Joshua Lang,
71 William March,
72 John March,
73 William Spivey.

HERTFORD COUNTY.

1 Irvin Jinkins, Captain.
2 Benjamin Hill, Lieut.
3 Henry G. Darden, Ensign.
4 Benj. Brown, Drummer.
5 Silas Shewcraft, Fifer.
6 William Brown,
7 James Johnston,
8 Willie Willoughbee,
9 Luke Hare,
10 John Brown,
11 Burrell Eure,
12 Jacob Overton,

13 Elisha Overton,
14 Jeremiah Aikin,
15 William Wynns,
16 Wm. W. Whitfield,
17 Jeremiah D. Aikin,
18 James Reiberry, jr.
19 Allen Moore,
20 William Downing,
21 James Barns,
22 Willie Cullan,
23 Jesse Harrison,
24 William Sessoms,

25 George Hollomon, jr.,
26 Justin Hollomon,
27 Samuel Britton,
28 Jethro Sowell,
29 Aaron Hare,
30 Isaac Baker,
31 David Welch, jr.,
32 William Sewell,
33 Thomas Elerton,
34 Benjamin Hocall,
35 George H. Bond,
36 Isaac Taylor,
37 William Purnell,
38 William Yeats,
39 Samuel Parker,
40 William Peaster,
41 Benjamin Wynns,
42 Samuel Ely,
43 Eli Harrell,
44 Boan Driver,
45 John Dickinson,
46 Thomas Early,
47 John P. Hare,
48 Stephen Howell,
49 John A. Anderson,
50 Benjamin Blan,

51 Sterling Francis,
52 Arthur Vick,
53 George Whitley,
54 John Scall,
55 David William,
56 James Skinner,
57 Henry Brantley,
58 Daniel Williams,
59 James Worrell,
60 Thomas Faircloth,
61 Benjamin Williams,
62 Lemuel Sanders,
63 Gray Mabane,
64 John Vinson,
65 John Vaughan,
66 Jonas Clitton,
67 William Rodgers,
68 Nelson Joyner,
69 William Andrews,
70 Robert Montgomery,
71 William Parker,
72 Mathias Cook,
73 Hilary Vaughn,
74 Joel Grizzard,
75 Hardy M. Banks.

BERTIE COUNTY.

1 Jona. H. Jacocks, Capt.
2 Powell Harrel, Lieut.
3 James Wilson, jr., Ensign.
4 Thomas Morgan, Private.
5 Miles Gilliam,
6 William C. Terrell,
7 William M. Darlett,

8 Simon A. Bryant,
9 William B. Mastin,
10 Joseph Blount,
11 Gaven Hogg,
12 William P. King,
13 Lewis Wimberly,
14 Levi Kenaday,

15 Thomas Liversage,
16 James Douglas,
17 William W. Johnson,
18 Kenneth Clark,
19 Cullen Shoolders,
20 Thomas Ruffin,
21 William R. W. Bozman,
22 Hatter Calloway,
23 Asa Gregory,
24 Aquilla Harden,
25 Josiah Reddit,
26 William Simons,
27 Jasper Ward,
28 William Castellow,
29 Trustum Capehart,
30 Thomas L. West,
31 Curry Butler,
32 Josiah Bird,
33 Benjamin Baker,
34 Benjamin Bowen,
35 John Bowen,
36 Levi Jennings,
37 John P. Butler,
38 Silas Butler,
39 Reuben Barns,
40 Nehemiah Bunch,
41 Cullen Bazimore,
42 William K. Miller,
43 Stephen Bazimore,
44 James Cherry, jr.,
45 Ralph Outlaw,
46 Lodowick Jenkins,
47 Elisha Cook,
48 James Early,
49 James Williford,
50 Isaac Early,

51 Willie Jenkins,
52 John Cobb,
53 Lawrence Mizells,
54 John Lassiter,
55 Joshua Harrell,
56 Thomas Harrell,
57 Josiah Davidson,
58 Isaac White,
59 Peter White,
60 Zachariah Ellison,
61 George Mizells,
62 Charles Miller,
63 Meredith Harrell,
64 Benjamin Williams,
65 George White,
66 James Mizell,
67 Whitmell White,
68 Joshua Hale,
69 Charnley C. Dundalow,
70 Noah Outlaw,
71 Elisha Hoggard,
72 David White,
73 Lewis Miller,
74 King Mitchel,
75 William Griffin,
76 Hatton Fleetwood,
77 John Hunter,
78 Timothy Mizells,
79 Seth Morgan,
80 Michael Mardre,
81 Henry Tood,
82 Luke Smithwick,
83 John Watson,
84 Jeremiah Legett,
85 James Baswell,
86 Hardy Clements,

87 Leven McTuller,
88 Jonathan Zaloc,
89 David Calloway,
90 John Mhoon,
91 John Boyd,
92 Henry Lee,
93 Henry Harrell,
94 John Murdough,
95 Dancy Harrell,

96 Whitmell Ruffin,
97 Moses Purvis,
98 Jesse Brown,
99 Jason Minton,
100 John Higgs,
101 Kinchen Wilks,
102 Cullen Grimmer,
103 James Hoggard,

NORTHAMPTON COUNTY.

1 John F. Walker, Captain.
2 Darius Parker, 1st Lieut.
3 Solomon B. Goodson, 2d do.
4 Sterling Finnie, 3d Lieut.
5 John C. Wood, Ensign.
6 Henry Adams, Private.
7 Burges Burkett,
8 Lemuel Burkett,
9 Robert Caum,
10 Bennet Boon,
11 Brittain Brittle,
12 John T. Benns,
13 William Boon,
14 Elijah Brewer,
15 John Cornwell,
16 James Day,
17 Goodwin Daniel,
18 David C. Darden,
19 Britain Doles,
20 Thomas Deloach,
21 William Draper,
22 Lewis Davie,
23 Jesse Deloach,
24 Pink Edwards,

25 Thomas Ellis,
26 Williamson Edwards,
27 Ricks Eliott,
28 John Edwards,
29 Sterling Faison,
30 William Futrell,
31 Enos Futrell,
32 Winborne Futrell,
33 Claiborne Griffin,
34 Edward Gatlin,
35 Joseph Griffin,
36 Armstead Grizzard,
37 William Gay,
38 Green Hart,
39 William Harriss,
40 Gideon Harriss,
41 Elias Harriss,
42 William Hicks,
43 Henry Hailey,
44 Henry Hart,
45 John Holmes,
46 James Hill,
47 Jeremiah Horton,
48 Moore Higgs,

49 William Ingram,
50 John Jenkins,
51 John Johnson,
52 John Jordan, Sen.,
53 Elias Johnson,
54 Robert Johnson,
55 Nathaniel Ingram,
56 Benjamin Jenkins,
57 Jesse Jones,
58 George Key,
59 Robert Little,
60 Edwin Liles,
61 Henry Leek,
62 Lemuel Lane,
63 Benjamin Lawrence,
64 Joshua Morgan,
65 John Maughon,
66 Jesse Morgan,
67 Wilson Mongar,
68 Bartlett McDonald,
69 Samuel Norwood,
70 William Naresworthy,
71 Burwell Norwood,
72 Everett Oliver,
73 Samuel Patterson,
74 William Pledger,
75 George W. Pledger,
76 Barnaby Pope,
77 Joel Peele,

78 Jesse Philips,
79 Philip Poyland,
80 James Pierce,
81 Robert Roe,
82 Thomas Richards,
83 Willis Roane,
84 Boswell Smith,
85 John B. Stanback,
86 Robert Snipes,
87 William Short,
88 Benjamin Strickling,
89 Matthew Spivey,
90 Benjamin Sweter,
91 Henry Sweter,
92 Britain Smith,
93 James Summer,
94 John Thompson,
95 Edmond Wilson,
96 James Wheeler,
97 Joseph T. Wornam,
98 Sion Wheeler,
99 Simeon Wood,
100 Samuel Warren,
101 Abram Wall,
102 Lemuel Winborne,
103 Lemuel Warr,
104 John E. Wallace.
105 John Wade, (const.)

HALIFAX COUNTY, FIRST REGIMENT.

1 William Price, first lieut.
2 William Brinkley Ensign,
3 John Allen,
4 Ludwell Allen,

5 German Baker,
6 William Curliles,
7 Anderson Clardy,
8 John Crawly,

9

9 William Campbell,
10 Stephen Eubank,
11 John Fulgem,
12 Nathaniel Gilliam,
13 Alfred Harwell,
14 Jesse Harlow,
15 Robert Hynes,
16 Orren Harris,
17 Hugh Hatheway,
18 Hall Hudson,
19 Joseph C. Justiss,
20 Willis Johnston,
21 Henry Jones,
22 Willis Johnston,
23 Samuel King,
24 William Keeter,
25 Gregory Moore,
26 Henry Morris,
27 Willie Matthews,
28 Eli Marshall,
29 Eaton Morris,
30 Elijah Nevill,
31 William Onions,
32 James Powell, jr.,
33 Benjamin Partin,
34 Isham Perdue,
35 John Pitts,
36 Irby Powell,
37 Edmond Powers,
38 Allen Rainey,
39 Edward Robinson,
40 Jacob Sykes,
41 Caleb Smith,
42 Lodiman Shelton,
43 Isham Sykes,
44 James Shaw,
45 Battie Smith,
46 Peter Smith,
47 Daniel L. Sturdivant,
48 Joel Smith, jr.,
49 Joseph A. Sturdivant,
50 Laban Vinson,
51 Warren Vinson,
52 Richard Vick,
53 Lewis Willis,
54 Samuel Weldon,
55 Sharp Wright,
56 James Wood,
57 Joseph Williams,
58 Thomas Weldon,
59 Guilford Williams,
60 Washington Yarborough.

HALIFAX COUNTY, SECOND REGIMENT.

1 Jeptha A. Barns, Capt.
2 John Peebles, 1st Lieut.
3 John Bradford, 2d Lieut.
4 William Brinkley, Ensign.
5 Thomas Cochran,
6 Micajah Alsobrook,
7 Benjamin Vick,
8 Abud Gray,
9 Samuel Murder,
10 Henry Harris,
11 Benjamin Jones,
12 James Liscomb,
13 Turner Brewer,
14 John Sills,

15 Joel Carlisle,
16 John Roan,
17 Mills Parker,
18 Jesse Curling,
19 Josiah Fort,
20 Wilson Brantly,
21 William Brantly,
22 David Brantly,
23 William T. Bryant,
24 Thomas Drew,
25 John Dawson,
26 Benjamin Paull,
27 Cordy Drew,
28 Ira Coffield,
29 Edmund Wiggins,
30 Whitmell Braswell,
31 General Dawson,
32 Marmaduke Braswell,
33 Aquilla Lock,
34 Dempsey P. Hillman,
35 Jesse Hayes,
36 Nathaniel Mullen,
37 Valentine Minton,
38 Edward II. Davis,
39 James Northcut,
40 Thomas Gall,
41 Thomas Jolly,
42 Richard Doggett,
43 Henry Doggett,
44 Thomas Lowe,
45 Joseph Randolph,
46 James Turner,
47 Peter Brunt,
48 Herbert Warner,
49 Thomas Merrit,
50 Landin Smith,
51 John Archer,
52 Ralph Skinner,
53 James Bachelor,
54 Mathew Holtfoot,
55 Daniel Glover,
56 Augustin Willis,
57 Elisha Euse,
58 Samuel Davis,
59 Joshua Manning,
60 Blake Davis,
61 Peyton R. Tunstall,
62 James Young,
63 Dempsey Pittman.

WARREN COUNTY.

1 Amos P. Sledge, Lieut.
2 John Munholland, Ensign.
3 James Powell, 1st Sergt.
4 John Alleh, 2d Sergt.
5 Wilmot Egerton, 3d Sergt.
6 William Powell, 4th Sergt.
7 James Tolley, 1st Cor'l.
8 Owen F. Myrick, 2d Cor'l.
9 Henry Person, 3d Cor'l.
10 Dr. G Robberson, 4th Cor.
11 Allen Wren,
12 Bird Ellington,
13 Cudberth Neal,
14 Charles Stewart,
15 Claton Lambert,
16 Daniel A. Perdue,

17 Drury Thompson,
18 Daniel White,
19 Elish Sherren,
20 Edward Patillo,
21 George Hazlewood,
22 Hardaway Davis,
23 Henry James,
24 James Edwards,
25 Joseph Whaer,
26 Joshua Harper,
27 James Alston,
28 James Thomas,
29 James C. Bennet,
30 James Smith,
31 Joel Tolley,
32 Joel Ellington,
33 Jiles Carter,
34 Jeptha Caps,
35 Ira Allen,
36 John Hawks,
37 John Lancaster,
38 Kinchen Williamson,
39 Lemuel Mitchell,
40 Lewis Sherren,

41 Littleton B. Roberson,
42 Lewis Ellis,
43 Lunceford Baker,
44 Michael Bell,
45 Miles Ellis,
46 Obediah Ellis,
47 Philemon Perdue,
48 Peter Randolph,
49 Richard Allen,
50 Ransome Acock,
51 Richard Davis,
52 Ransome Worrell,
53 Richard Brook,
54 Samuel Dowton,
55 Thomas Newsman,
56 Thomas Walker,
57 Thomas Harton,
58 Thomas Davis,
59 Thomas Tolley,
60 William Oliver,
61 Willis Person,
62 William Sherren,
63 William Breedlove.

NASH COUNTY.

1 Isaac Watkins, Captain.
2 Joseph Vick, Lieutenant.
3 Willie Rick, Ensign,
4 Henry Hedgepeth,
5 Joseph Griffen,
6 James Beckworth,
7 Elijah Whelas,
8 William Walker,
9 Solomon Thomas,

10 Thomas Cobb,
11 Holliday Hedgepeth,
12 Nelson Bowie,
13 William Langley,
14 Lewis Tucker,
15 Robert Crickmore,
16 William Ballard,
17 Asberry Lindsey,
18 Briant Lewis,

19 Willis Hammons,
20 Allen Brantley,
21 Hopni Pucket,
22 John Perry,
23 John Rice,
24 Joseph Bissit,
25 Reuben Strickland,
26 William Colston.
27 William Bunn,
28 Whitmell Ricks,
29 Samuel Vick,
30 James W. Daniel,
31 Henry Bunn,
32 Valentine Chapman,
33 Thomas Valentine,
34 Duncan Ricks,
35 Oran D. Powell,
36 Thomas Pott,
37 Bennet Mason,
38 James Manning,
39 John Williams,
40 Frederick Parish,
41 Henry Blount,
42 Tompkins Rose,
43 Thomas Aven,
44 Enoch Flood,
45 Samuel Williams,
46 Samuel S. Lampkin,
47 Valentine Perkinson,
48 Edward Strickland,
49 David Hunt,
50 Major Potter,
51 German Mann,

52 Claibourn Mann,
53 Peter Prigen,
54 Irwin Eatman,
55 Elisha Tisdal,
56 Eli Never,
57 Everret Morriss,
58 Griffin Lewis,
59 Irvin Boykin,
60 James Duck,
61 Lee Horn,
62 Thomas Landers,
63 Thomas Williamson,
64 William Landers,
65 Amden Horn,
66 William Braswell,
67 Sion Beckworth,
68 Arch. G. Whitfield,
69 John Harris,
70 Alfred Strickland,
71 Edwin Harris,
72 Thomas White,
73 Jesse Thorp,
74 James Hunter,
75 Reddick Massengill,
76 Joab Tucker,
77 Wright Bachelor,
78 Cornelus Taylor,
79 Boen Wren,
80 Joseph Brown,
81 William Bilbee,
82 Joseph Bachelor,
83 Wilson Bachelor.

SECOND REGIMENT.

WASHINGTON COUNTY.

1
2
3 David Airs,
4 Joseph H. Adams,
5 Joshua Alexander,
6 Anthony Alexander,
7 Andrew Bateman,
8 Evin Bateman,
9 James Blount, [3d son of S.
10 Isaac Brown,
11 Reuben Carnel,
12 Robert McClary,
13 Richard Corprew,
14 Elijah Etherige,
15 Robert Everitt,
16 Solomon Armstrong,
17 Aaron Fagan,
18 James Forlaw,
19 Jacob N. Gordon,
20 Josiah Haughton,
21 Daniel Barns,
22 Edward Hollis,
23 George Harrison,
24 John Jethro,
25 Harman Legett,
26 Downing Leary,
27 Joshua Long,
28 Charles Wiley,
29 Aquilla Norman,
30 Frederick Oliver,
31 William Readit,
32 Evin Phelps,
33 Hezekiah Phelps,
34 Willibough Phelps,
35 Edward J. Ransom,
36 John M. Roulhac,
37 Roger Snell,
38 Stephen Swain,
39 William H. Star,
40 James Walker, sr.,
41 Martin Walker,
42 Joshua Young.

TYRRELL CFUNTY.

1 Richard Hawett, Captain.
2 Benjamin Clayton, Ensign.
3 Jeremiah Giles,
4 Daniel Ensley,
5 Eli Woodley,
6 Henry Mariner,
7 Abel Cahoon,
8 Talket Davenport.
9 Samuel Davenport,
10 Ebenezer Pettigrew,
11 Charles Phelps,
12 Uzziah Spruell,
13 Willis Sawyer,
14 Edward Man,

15 Lewis Mydgett,
16 Benjamin Mydgett,
17 Major Brickhouse,
18 Gardener Alexander,
19 Richard Brickhouse,
20 Elikim Swain,
21 John Cooper,
22 Matthew Brickhouse,
23 Henry Norman,
24 Darius Phelps,
25 Seth Sanders,
26 Silas Etherige,
27 Peter Wynn,
28 Spence Hooker,
29 Joseph Pledger,
30 David Alexander,
31 Joshua Swain,
32 Zadock Hassel,
33 William Ranton,

34 Thomas Sweedy,
35 Isaac Liverman,
36 James McKinney,
37 Joseph Swain,
38 William Edwards,
39 Charles Johnson,
40 Josiah Jermanny,
41 Carney Spinner,
42 Henry Baker,
43 Tilby Bilangey,
44 John Cahoon, (of John,)
45 Benjamin Cooper,
46 Thomas Clayton,
47 Willis Liverman,
48 Hardy Powers,
49 Ebenezer Smith,
50 Miles Sawyer,
51 James Cahoon, (of John,)

HYDE COUNTY.

1 Seth B. Jordan, Captain.
2 Wyriott Windley, Lieut.
3 Christopher Gaskins, En.
4 David Paine,
5 Asa Oneal,
6 Benjamin Turner,
7 Henry Clark,
8 Matthew English,
9 William Meekins,
10 Sparrow Midgett,
11 Josiah Knox,
12 Stephen Owens,
13 Samuel Selby,
14 Daniel Seabrook,

15 William B. Spencer,
16 Benjamin Brinn,
17 John Swindell,
18 Thomas Mason,
19 Samuel Williamson,
20 Edward Rose,
21 Uriah Lewis,
22 Elias Mooney,
23 Thomas Moore,
24 Wilson Sawyer,
25 Clement Daniels,
26 Thomas Daniels,
27 Zedekiah Swindell,
28 Frisby Spencer,

29 Morris Daniels,
30 Henry Delow,
31 Alexander Cohoon,
32 Israel Henry,
33 Robert Hopkins,
34 Samuel Gibbs, sr.,
35 Selby Spencer,
36 Thomas Sanderson,
37 Jeremiah Hall,
38 Stephen Gibbs,
39 Washington Gibbs,
40 William Cohoon,
41 Thomas Gurganus,
42 Zachariah Wilkinson,
43 Zachariah Bishop,
44 John Allen,
45 Mark Smedick,
46 Martin Davis,
47 Henry Hobbs,
48 William Eborn,
49 Robert Barnett,
50 John Shavener,
51 Mounceu Peckham,
52 Henry Blount,
53 Enoch Robins,
54 Zachariah Kipps,
55 Richard Jordan,
56 Thomas Moore,
57 William Hooten,
58 Lewis Blount,
59 Nathan Harvey,
60 Moses Windley,
61 John James,
62 William Barrow,
63 William Fetterton,
64 Richard Sadler,
65 Robert Harris,
66 Bartee Gibbs,
67 David Gibbs,
68 Josiah Harris,
69 John Silverthorn,
70 William Easter, sr.,
71 Solomon Easter,
72 Sheldon Tooley,
73 John Dixon,
74 Thomas Mason,
75 John Gaylard,
76 William Easter, jr.,
77 Franklin Dixon,
78 Valentine Slade,
79 Jeremiah Tooley,
80 Timothy Parmarle,
81 Hosea Tyson,
82 James Loyd.

BEAUFORT COUNTY.

1 John Cox, Captain.
2 Henry Williams, 1st Lieut.
3 Samuel Taylor, 2d Lieut.
4 Wilson B. Hodges, Ensign.
5 Achilles Hawkins,
6 Richard Mastin,
7 Jesse Godley,
8 William S. Holmes,
9 Allen Grist,
10 William McDonald,
11 Charles Holland,
12 Jesse Swonner,

13 James Sworner,
14 Christ. Crandell,
15 Benjamin Legget,
16 Joseph Legget,
17 John Brown,
18 David Latham,
19 Major Ball,
20 Eden Beacham,
21 James Gorden,
22 Joel Dickenson,
23 Isaac Peacock,
24 Peter Demill,
25 William D. Barr,
26 Michael Hanrahan,
27 James Kelly,
28 Hugh McCullough,
29 William Shaw,
30 Solah Hammon,
31 Levin Wallace,
32 Willie Bagner,
33 Alfred Bagner,
34 Benjamin Braddy,
35 John Wollard,
36 Jacob Allegood,
37 James B. Ellison,
38 Littleton Hawkins,
39 Nathan Cutler,
40 Slamil Bagner,
41 Thomas Hawkins,
42 Isaac Chauncey,
43 Irra Paul,
44 John Seaward,
45 John Pilley,
46 Jacob Cordin,
47 Israel Windley,
48 J. Gardner,

49 Thomas Floyd,
50 William Fortisque,
51 John Whitley,
52 Aaron Gurganus,
53 Jacob Wilkinson,
54 John Kelley,
55 Jeremiah Garrot,
56 William Sleatey,
57 James Harris,
58 George Harris,
59 James Waters,
60 Dempsey Martin,
61 Elisha Harris,
62 Shadric Downs,
63 Noah Spear,
64 John G. Hill,
65 Joseph Millar,
66 Thomas Morris,
67 William E. Edwards,
68 William N. Edwards,
69 Willie Hill,
70 William Telliton,
71 Richard Blacklidge,
72 Israel Harching,
73 Uriah Slade,
74 John Evitt,
75 Daniel Warren,
76 Hardy Rue, jr.,
77 Lott Evitt,
78 William Dixon,
79 Thomas Robason,
80 Hilery Whitchurst,
81 William Hudnal,
82 Will. Bond,
83 Jesse Puiser,
84 John Danals,

85 Zadock Ives,
86 David Camper,
87 Frederick Watson,
88 Luke Lenton,
89 Zedekiah Mirow,
90 Burage Linton,
91 Jeremiah Slade,
92 Nathaniel Woodard,
93 James Jones,
94 Thomas Cox,
95 William Springle,
96 Joshua Moore,
97 Price Wm. Lewis,
98 Solomon Brag,
99 Archibald Wilcox,
100 William Walker,
101 William Thomason,
102 John Roll,
103 William Hollowell,
104 John Dowty.

CRAVEN COUNTY.

1 Minor Huntington, Capt.
2 John S. Smith, 1st Lieut.
3 Isaac Hellen, 2d Lieut.
4 Uriah Sandy, 3d Lieut.
5 John Forlaw, Ensign.
6 M. H. Stephens, 1st Sergt.
7 Abner Heartley, 2d Sergt.
8 Lewis Griffen, 3d Sergt.
9 Isaac Patrick, 4th Sergt.
10 Harvey Morris, 1st Cor'l.
11 Mason Ives, 2d Cor'l.
12 Wm. Caruthers, 3d Cor'l.
13 Nathaniel Clark, 4th Cor'l.
14 Moses Prescott,
15 Will. Whitford,
16 James Daniels,
17 Jesse Collins,
18 Joseph Stephens,
19 Jesse Hampton,
20 David B. Gibson,
21 Michael Fisher,
22 John Shipp,
23 Kinchen Canady,
24 George Lane,
25 Jesse Weatherington,
26 Samuel Avery,
27 Amos Hudler,
28 William Sanders,
29 Jacob Dudley,
30 Levin Dunn,
31 George Lewis,
32 Linkfield Perkins,
33 Robert Barns,
34 Stephen Hawkins,
35 Elisha Arnold,
36 Edmund Heath,
37 Henry Shute,
38 Isaac White,
39 John Arnold,
40 Frederick Heath,
41 William West,
42 Cason Fell,
43 Elijah Wheedleton,
44 William Spikes,
45 James Edwards,
46 Moses Caton,

47 Jos. S. Brinson,
48 Rollin Dixon,
49 Jordan Butler,
50 John Clark,
51 Joseph Bryan,
52 Lewis Warren,
53 Stephen Chapman,
54 Will. Griffin,
55 Levi Griffin,
56 Jesse Griffin,
57 Daniel Daughety,
58 Elijah Randal,
59 Louis Cox,
60 William King,
61 Zach Barrot,
62 Shad Holloway,
63 Allen Smith,
64 Ervin Taunt,
65 Ennis Cooper,
66 William Hall,
67 William Mills,
68 Reding Harrison,
69 John Kirk,
70 Levi Gallin,
71 John Taylor,
72 John Sparrow,
73 John Griffin,
74 John S. Brown,
75 John Jones,
76 Nathaniel Lewis,
77 Elijah Dunn,
78 Evan Jones,
79 Andrew Morgan,
80 Thomas Hall,
81 Lazarous Ipock,
82 John Ipock,

83 John Kemp,
84 Aaron Eventon,
85 Abner Gatlin,
86 Henry Ipock,
87 Thomas Carraway,
88 Parks Ryal,
89 James Masters,
90 John Pittman,
91 Job Smith,
92 Richard Parsons,
93 John Holley,
94 Jepthy Simpson,
95 Duran Ives,
96 Isaac Reed,
97 Frederick Folson,
98 Peter Parris,
99 William S. Brinson,
100 Robert Phillips,
101 Elijah Ives,
102 William Harper,
103 Thomas King,
104 Jesse Lawson,
105 James Vendrick, jr.,
106 Ezekiel Simpkins,
107 John Woods,
108 William Williams,
109 Cornelius Dixon,
110 Samuel Collins,
111 Thomas Hamilton,
112 Lewis Dawson,
113 Murphy Trott,
114 John Smith,
115 Joshua Mitchell,
116 Elijah V. Pittman,
117 Benjamin Marriner,
118 John Herrington,

85 Zadock
86 David ᵃˢ McKelroy, 122 Francis Beasley,
87 Fre? ᵒᵐᵃˢ Pittman, 123 Reuben Prentiss.
88 J William Muse,
8?

CARTERET COUNTY.

1 Nathaniel Pinkham, Capt. 31 Samuel Gardener,
2 D. A. Wallace, 1st Lieut. 32 James Piver,
3 Thomas Martial, 2d Lieut. 33 David Gould,
4 James Chadwick, 3d Lieut. 34 Joseph Morton,
5 Jacob Paquanett, Ensign. 35 Counsel Fealds,
6 John Paquanett, 1st Sergt. 36 Thomas Louis,
7 Jesse Prescott, 2d Sergt. 37 Archibald Louis,
8 Alexander Hamilton, 38 John S. Davis,
9 Samuel Sanders, 39 Zephaniah Howland,
10 Uriah Suggs, 40 Washington Willis,
11 Thomas Meadows, 41 Newel Bell,
12 Hardy Lane, 42 William Morton,
13 Wilboga Prescott, 43 William Pigett,
14 Fama Gaskett, 44 Williams Brooks,
15 John Simmons, 45 Joseph Willis,
16 Allen Robinson, 46 Uriah Gillikan,
17 Samuel Piver, 47 George Gillikan,
18 Daniel Dickerson, 48 Richard Arthur,
19 Barton Hendesty, 49 George Linguish,
20 James E. Gibble, 50 Isaac Wade,
21 Joseph Hall, 51 Martin Chadwick,
22 Samuel Guthree, 52 William Holland,
23 Samuel Buckman, 53 David Gabriel,
24 John Martial, 54 Joseph Willis,
25 Logan Key, 55 Thomas Nelson,
26 Zemeriah Harris, 56 Abisha Nelson,
27 Jesse Haskett, 57 Littleton Willis,
28 John Weaks, 58 David Gaskitt,
29 Thomas Elliott, 59 David Hamilton,
30 Josiah Harris, 60 Henry Saulter,

61 William Smith,
62 Joseph Tulcher,
63 David Mason,

64 James Styson,
65 Reubin Willis.

JONES COUNTY.

1 Sears Bryan, 1st Lieut.
2 Jonathan Wood, Ensign.
3 Jonathan Kay,
4 James Mades,
5 Aaron Eubanks,
6 John Dudley,
7 James Frazer,
8 Theolifus Odium,
9 William Foskey,
10 Amos Sanderson,
11 James Griffith,
12 Joshua Millar,
13 Joseph Wallis,
14 Josiah Taylor,
15 Benjamin McKinney,
16 James Monford, sr.,
17 Frederic J. Becton,
18 John Wilcox,
19 James Reynolds,
20 Robert Reynolds,
21 Thomas Mackney,
22 Jonathan Lee,
23 Thomas McQuillan,
24 Alfred Harget,
25 Ivey Anders,
26 Daniel Mallard,

27 Adam Anders,
28 Shadrich Mallard,
29 Joseph Killingsworth,
30 Benjamin D. Gray,
31 John Overton,
32 Ariel Jones,
33 Daniel Smith,
34 Hezekiah Alphin,
35 John Shelfer,
36 Lewis Kinsey,
37 William Garman,
38 William Wilcox,
39 John Gilbert,
40 K. McDaniel, (son of R.)
41 William Harget,
42 James Monford, jr.,
43 Alfred McDaniel,
44 Daniel Stanley,
45 John Harrington,
46 John McDaniel,
47 James Oliver,
48 Jesse Alphin,
49 Abner Harrison,
50 Samuel Dillahunta,
51 Durant Green,
52 Peter Harget.

LENOIR COUNTY.

1 Joshua Mosley, Captain.
2 Rich'd. Aldridge, 3d Lieut.
3 Thomas Aldridge,
4 William Benton,
5 Silas Bowen,
6 Lewis O'Bryan,
7 Bartholamy Cauley,
8 John Slismore,
9 Jesse Slismore,
10 William F. Davis,
11 Reading K. Davis,
12 David Evans,
13 John Evans,
14 Major Fields,
15 Zachariah Gray,
16 David Griffin,
17 Samuel Hines,
18 Rigdon Henry,
19 William Hood,
20 David Hartsfield,
21 Burwell Herring,
22 Kenon Hudlow,
23 Josiah Horton,
24 Isam Jackson,
25 Isaiah Johnston,
26 Isham Lassiter,
27 Herod Lovit,
28 Thomas Midlin,
29 Kenon Meloney,
30 William Moore.
31 William Mosely,
32 Walker Moore,
33 Radner Moore,
34 William Potter,
35 John Phillips,
36 Moses Pool,
37 Farniford Pool,
38 William Pearson,
39 Abraham Peacock,
40 Bryan Pate,
41 Thomas Rows,
42 Edward Smith,
43 William Sutton,
44 Patrick Sparrow,
45 John Tilman,
46 Arthur Tull,
47 Jeremiah Waters,
48 John Westbrook,
49 Garrot Williams,
50 Thomas Witherington,
51 William Vause,
52 Briton King.

GREEN COUNTY.

1 Henry Miller, 1st Lieut.
2 James Eastwood, 2d Lieut.
3 Joseph Harrel, Ensign.
4 John Gardner,
5 John Andrews,
6 Mark Taylor,
7 Jonathan Parker,
8 James Wasden,
9 Aven Lane,
10 Willis Newsom,

11 John Goff,
12 Henry David,
13 Joel Mears,
14 Gardner Jones,
15 Silas Lassiter,
16 Abraham Grizzard,
17 William Britt,
18 William Barrow,
19 Joseph Williams,
20 Beverly Belsher,
21 John Murrah,
22 Haswell Hay,
23 Woody Belsher,
24 James Rogers,
25 Charles Tindall,
26 Samuel Harrel,
27 Benjamin Hardy,
28 Lemuel Hardy,
29 David Shirley,
30 Henry Moring,
31 Nicholas Smith,
32 Samuel Forrest,
33 John Potter,
34 Allen Stanul,
35 Simon Jones,
36 William Harper,
37 William Farmer,
38 Owen Lockhart,
39 Abram Joyner,
40 William Turnage,
41 Jesse Cunninggem,
42 Stuart Summerlin,
43 Augustin Moore,
44 James Hill,
45 Spears Denny,
46 Micajah Kenaday,
47 James Edmonson,
48 Fountain Ward,
49 Nehemiah Garras,
50 Timothy Roddick,
51 Stephen Tison,
52 James Ranch,
53 Noah Dunn.

PITT COUNTY.

1 George Eason, Captain.
2 Summer Adams, 1st Lieut.
3 Sam'l. Albritton, 2d Lieut.
4 Gideon Brindon, 3d Lieut.
5 William Briley, Ensign.
6 John Stocks,
7 Burrel Bell,
8 John Moye,
9 Jacob Rogers,
10 Samuel Truss,
11 James Johnston,
12 David Hathway,
13 Kedar Randolph,
14 William Whitchurst,
15 Turner House,
16 Jacob Moore,
17 William Nichols,
18 Reuben Gardener,
19 Isaac Gardener,
20 William Quinley,
21 Stephen Quinley,
22 Hardy Trip,

23 Jonathan Pelt,
24 James Bell,
25 Jesse Cherry,
26 Thomas Adams,
27 John Duvol,
28 John Eason,
29 William Mills,
30. Daniel Duvol,
31 James Bryant,
32 Caleb Nelson,
33 Bryant Grimes,
34 Jordan Nelson,
35 Joseph Boyd,
36 Naisby Mills,
37 Naboth Nelson,
38 Noah Adams,
39 John Arnold,
40 William Boyd,
41 William Barber,
42 Moses Herrington,
43 Arthur Magleham,
44 Franklin Moye,
45 Gilford Broom,
46 Isaac Turner,
47 Joab Smith,
48 Noah Harriss,
49 Worley White,
50 Ervan Dudley,
51 Erandal Little,
52 Hugh Telfair,
53 Joseph Griffin,
54 Samuel Moore,
55 Silvenus Harris,
56 Willie Daniel,
57 James Buch,
58 Amos Joyner,

59 Icabod Moore,
60 Willis Hodges,
61 Sparkman Smith,
62 Abner Askew,
63 Absalom Page,
64 Thomas Flanigen,
65 David Leget,
66 Willis Flemming,
67 Mansel Flake,
68 Miles Spier,
69 Allen Moore,
70 John Harriss,
71 Charles Tison,
72 William Bird,
73 William Norriss,
74 James Grist,
75 John Willoughby,
76 John Wallace,
77 Joseph Judkins,
78 John Smith,
79 Richard Gammon.
80 Bryant Corbet,
81 Richmon Cobb,
82 William Braddy,
83 John Teal, jr.,
84 Samuel Williams,
85 Elisha Braddy,
86 Frederick Barfield,
87 Micajah Teal,
88 Allen Mayo,
89 William Thomas,
90 Benjamin Bell,
91 Simpson Meeks,
92 Frederick Sommerlin,
93 John Thomas,
94 Alvin Mayo,

95 Elisha Taylor,
96 William Downs,
97 Henry Jolley,
98 Henry Moore,
99 Solomon Harriss,
100 Richard Carson,
101 Amos Pelet,
102 John Cox,
103 James Wilson,
104 Henry Cannon,
105 William Emery,

106 Edmond Evans,
107 James Whitehead,
108 William Brooks,
109 Hugh Pritchett,
110 John Barnhill,
111 Willie Gurganus,
112 Henry Barnhill,
113 Edward Acrey,
114 Jonathan Briley,
115 John Bullock,

MARTIN COUNTY.

1
2
3 Lemuel Ballard,
4 Obediah Bullock,
5 James Belflower,
6 Barnaby Brown,
7 Redding Brown,
8 Zachariah Browney,
9 Hardie Cobb,
10 Littleberry Carlisle,
11 Harred Craft,
12 Jesse Cow, jr.,
13 Jonathan Callaway,
14 John Douglas,
15 Wright Evans,
16 Michael Ellis,
17 Jesse Griffin,
18 Edward Griffin,
19 Joshua Griffin,
20 John Haislip,
21 Branson Haislip,
22 William Hassel,

23 Joshua Hodge,
24 Edward Hardison,
25 Jesse Harrel,
26 Benjamin Hallsey,
27 Theophilus Jenkins,
28 Lemuel James,
29 Lovett, Lanier,
30 Josephus Moore,
31 Ith Medford,
32 Marcum Manning,
33 Mathew Pickelson,
34 Simon Perry,
35 John Petty,
36 William Pennywell,
37 Hardy B. Price,
38 John Quin,
39 William Roebuck,
40 Reddick Rawls,
41 Abraham Rawls,
42 Joshua Robinson, jr.,
43 Josiah Rogerson,
44 Bond Stawls,

45 Joel Smithwick,
46 Reuben Salenger,
47 William Swain,
48 James Swain,

49 Samuel Spruel,
50 David Wynns,
51 Henry Wynns,
52 George Wynns.

EDGECOMBE COUNTY.—FIRST REGIMENT.

1
2
3 Abraham Taylor,
4 Amos Walston,
5 Allin Balton,
6 Brient Evens,
7 Benjamin Larder,
8 Benjamin Granthon,
9 Bryant Little,
10 Bryant Stallons,
11 Burwell Page,
12 Culin Andrews,
13 Dempsey Owens,
14 Dempsey Gardner,
15 Edwin Sherwood,
16 Edward Amison,
17 Eanos Askin,
18 Elisha Jones,
19 Ephraim Wooton,
20 George Moore,
21 George H. Killibrew,
22 Henry Waller,
23 Henry Wooten,
24 Isaac Scarborough,
25 James Harman,
26 Hilliard Thomas,
27 Jonathan Thomas,
28 Jordan Bruce,
29 Jacob Barnes,

30 Jonas Williford,
31 Joshua Taylor, jr.,
32 Joseph Farmer,
33 Jacob Sims,
34 John Evins,
35 John Sharpe,
36 Joseph Pittman,
37 James Tart,
38 Jeremiah Horne,
39 Joseph Ruffin,
40 John Holomon,
41 John Thespin,
42 Joshua Killibrue,
43 Joseph Page, jr.,
44 James Ambrose,
45 John Dowdin,
46 Joseph Ansley,
47 James Norvil,
48 Jessy Morris,
49 Lawrence Page,
50 Lewis Peele,
51 Marshal White,
52 Martin B. Morne,
53 Mills Harvil,
54 Moses Moore,
55 Perry White,
56 Hobbert Coleman,
57 Robert Long,
58 Richard Singleton,

59 Samuel R. Jenkins,
60 Thomas Dixon,
61 Thomas Morris,
62 Thomas Barrow,
63 Uriah Stallings,

64 William Dixon,
65 Whitmel C Bullock,
66 Wilham Webb,
67 William Singleton.

EDGECOMBE COUNTY—SECOND REGIMENT.

1
2
3 William P. Coleburn,
4 William Savage,
5 Maurice Redmond,
6 John Parker,
7 Stephen West,
8 Robert Broadstreet,
9 James Griffis,
10 Berry Brown,
11 Lott Killibrew.
12 Laden Abrahams,
13 Luke Nowells,
14 Daniel Conner,
15 James Cobb,
16 John Anderson,
17 John Moon,
18 John Knight,
19 Drury Mayo,
20 Charles Knight, jr.,
21 Hardy Harrill,
22 Geraldus Batts,
23 Littlebury Edwards,
24 David Pender,
25 Thomas Hayner,
26 James Everitt,
27 William Bayton,
28 James Taylor,

29 James Rainer,
30 Reading Crisp,
31 Moulden Loops,
32 Jesse Turner,
33 Michael Horn,
34 J. Jolly Horn,
35 James Williams,
36 Nincen Vaughn,
37 Elijah Jackson,
38 Robert Barnes,
39 John Hines,
40 Joseph Stallions,
41 John Penney,
42 David Lain,
43 James Foreman,
44 John Garrock,
45 Jason Matthews,
46 William Armstrong,
47 John Sarsnot,
48 James Mayo,
49 Kenneth Coopper,
50 Lewis Purvis, jr.,
51 Stancel Hoard,
52 Thomas Wiggins, jr.,
53 William Exum,
54 James Petman,
55 Thomas Jones,
56 Book Dickson,

57 Levi Denton,
58 John Lain,
59 Joseph Sessums,
60 Spier Bradley,
61 Stephen White,
62 Archibald Pope,

63 Reuben Taylor,
64 John Spyva,
65 Thomas Strickland,
66 William Kea,
67 Joseph Loyd.

WAYNE COUNTY.

1 John Flowers, Captain.
2 Hillary Hook, 1st Lieut.
3 Major Blont, 2d Lieut.
4 David Thompson, 3d Lieut.
5 Willis Hall, Ensign,
6 Henry Roberts,
7 Burwell Martin,
8 Jeremiah Smith,
9 John Wasdon,
10 Thomas Beard,
11 Pearce Brogden,
12 Kenrard Holland,
13 Matthew Gennet,
14 Bryan Bradberry,
15 Joseph Smith,
16 Jesse Taylor,
17 Caleb Howell,
18 Edward York,
19 Anson Gurly,
20 Raiford Wiggs,
21 Lewis Forehand,
22 John Hardy,
23 Jethro Barns,
24 Simon Barns,
25 Hermant Hooks,
26 Joseph Ware,
27 Miles Lamb,

28 William Bass,
29 Cornelius Durden,
30 Levi Winflet,
31 Ransom Comanch,
32 Samuel Barns,
33 Elisha Devoun,
34 Bryan Bass,
35 John Mitchell,
36 Lewis Powell,
37 Joel Ellis,
38 Noah Bass,
39 Johnston Corbet,
40 Michael Watson,
41 John Skipper,
42 Ephraim Grant,
43 Kelly Creamer,
44 Joseph Smith,
45 Samuel Pope,
46 Richard Langston,
47 Miles Rodford,
48 Thomas Grant,
49 Richard Ivy,
50 James McCullin,
51 Jesse Warturs,
52 Bryan Rhodes,
53 Bryan Pipkin.
54 Arthur Pearce,

55 James Britt,
56 Henry Cannon,
57 William Atwill,
58 Rolen Coley,
59 Williams Bundy,
60 Joshua Fletcher,
61 William Ham,
62 Taylor Smith,
63 Henry Britt,
64 Henry Ham,
65 Wm. Landcaster,
66 William Lasser,
67 Isaac Hill,
68 Henry Boget,
69 Everit Thompson,
70 Bryan Thompson,
71 Richard Worrel,
72 Wiley Peacock,
73 Handy Alfred,
74 Jesse Worrel,
75 Matthew Bradford,
76 John Thompson,
77 James Futcret,
78 Jeremiah Bunton,
79 James Bartlet,
80 John Elventon,

81 Richard Wodel,
82 Noah Peacock,
83 Henry Hare,
84 Elisha Cook,
85 Nathan Bremon,
86 William Deal,
87 Simon Peacock,
88 Thomas Outland,
89 Arthur Bogan,
90 John Heath,
91 James Bridger,
92 Matthew Grace,
93 Joseph Herring,
94 James Tindal,
95 John Harrass,
96 William Kelly,
97 Richard Carey,
98 John Cox,
99 Richard Kelly,
100 Jesse Peacock,
101 Rheuben Mitch,
102 John Bizzel,
103 Sion Granthon,
104 William Dunn,
105 Jacob Sims.

ONSLOW COUNTY—THIRD REGIMENT.

1 William Mitchell Captain.
2 Titus Howard, 1st Lieut.
3 Hardy Pitts, 2d Lieut.
4 Lewis Oliver, 3d Lieut.
5 Hilory Hennerson, En.
6 Lott Huffman,
7 George Williams,

8 James Mills,
9 William Calvet,
10 Henry Foster,
11 Henry Hyde,
12 James Strange,
13 Charles Cox,
14 James Harvey,

15 Jesse Wilder,
16 Thomas Hawkins,
17 Absalom Barber,
18 Stephen Calvet,
19 John Brown,
20 Hillkiah Horn,
21 Nathan Futral,
22 Rigdon Whaley,
23 Peter Ambrose,
24 Edmund Littleton,
25 William Parker,
26 John Ellis,
27 Isaac Simpson,
28 Reuben Melton,
29 James Barrow,
30 Josiah Hawkins,
31 Everitt Simmons,
32 Edward Kellam,
33 Charles Thompson,
34 Benjamin Littleton,
35 John Murrel,
36 John Edmondson,
37 Dexter Farnel,
38 Hawkins Marshall,
39 Kilby Henderson,
40 John Enbanks,
41 Otway Hawkins,
42 Purnal Haskins,
43 Robert Caston,
44 John Marshall,
45 John Morton,
46 Enock Haskins,
47 John Gibson, jr.,
48 Ezekiel Enbanks,
49 Brice Fields,
50 Henry Wells,

51 Elijah Enbanks, jr.,
52 Bryan Barber,
53 John Gilbert,
54 Jos. Collins, jr.,
55 William Gibson, jr.,
56 William Carraway,
57 John Garrett,
58 Richard Simmons,
59 Alexander Gray,
60 Edmund Milson,
61 Solomon Davis,
62 Josiah Ward,
63 Elijah Taylor,
64 William Bell,
65 Charles Scott,
66 James Hurst,
67 Jesse Hardison,
68 John Edens,
69 Samuel Nicholas,
70 Peter Venters,
71 Leckariah Evins,
72 Laben Justice,
73 Simon Hobbs,
74 Whitlift Casten,
75 Frederick Mills,
76 John Shepard,
77 James Lloyd,
78 Lewis Thompson,
79 Thomas King,
80 Jesse Fryer,
81 John Higgs,
82 George Hinkley,
83 William Sammons,
84 John Goints,
85 David Horn,
86 Henry Milton,

87 Edward W. Shiver,
88 Hosiah Clark,
89 Josiah Fayles,
90 Moses Jinkins,
91 James Baker,
92 Ohed Eason,
93 William A. Pearce,
94 James Oman,
95 Daniel Mashborn,
96 Henry Howard,

97 William Orme,
98 Thomas Fryer,
99 John Bell,
100 Samuel Howard,
101 John Jones,
102 David Riggs,
103 James Caston,
104 Jackariah Jackson,
105 Amos Goints.

NEW HANOVER COUNTY.

1 M. W. Campbell, Captain.
2 James Nixon, Lieut.
3 Joel E. Larkins, Lieut.
4 William Lewis, Ensign.
5 William McCurdy,
6 Stephen Notton,
7 Richard Saunders,
8 James Larkins,
9 Robert Rankin,
10 Reuben Loving,
11 John Walker,
12 Joseph Jones,
13 William S. Nickols,
14 Donald R. McLeod,
15 Jesse Scarborough,
16 Jonathan J. Long,
17 Moses Sholders,
18 William Taylor,
19 Aaron Alexander,
20 Woodman S. Ledbury,
21 Joshua McClammy,
22 David Eddons,
23 Buckner Stokely,

24 Jacob Pickett,
25 Jeremiah Nickols,
26 Thomas Coston,
27 William Nixon,
28 Robert Nickols,
29 Henry King,
30 John James,
31 Edmond Hansley,
32 John Riley,
33 James Ratcliff,
34 William Revenbark,
35 John Wood,
36 William George,
37 Daniel George,
38 Richard Millar,
39 Joseph Mumford,
40 Robert Larkins,
41 John Parker,
42 John Beesley,
43 Solomon Beesley,
44 John Moore,
45 John Highsmith,
46 Anthony Williamson,

47 Hugh Lamb,
48 Nickolas Boon,
49 Berd Boon,
50 Samuel Gerganious,
51 William Gerganious,
52 James Malfrass,
53 John Register,
54 James Bonham,
55 David Bonham,
56 James Busby,
57 Obed Smith,
58 Dempsey Powell,
59 Francis Devane,
60 William Corbet,
61 George Corbet,
62 James Lee,
63 Duncan Sellars,
64 Timothy Johnson,
65 John Airs,
66 Ross Cogdell,
67 James Roe,
68 Fredric Simpson,
69 Luton Orr,
70 John Black,
71 Benjamin Moore,
72 William Malpass,
73 George Moore,
74 John B. Bourdeaux,
75 Benjamin Due,

76 John Bainhill,
77 Timothy Rooks,
78 Joseph Rooks,
79 Benjamin Mott,
80 Morris Bishop,
81 William Adkins,
82 Daniel Adkinson,
83 Fredric Gerganions,
84 Thomas Bishop, jr.,
85 William Robeson,
86 Ensign Hinklin,
87 Joseph Farrow,
88 William Goodman,
89 Benjamin Rockell,
90 Jacob Castill,
91 Altred Wadkins,
92 Lawrence Mason,
93 Henry Dickson,
94 James Evans,
95 Daniel Bucher,
96 Gilbert New,
97 Hardy Bowen,
98 Samuel Straughan,
99 Duncan Henderson,
100 Daniel Henderson,
101 John Taylor,
102 Matthew Johnston,
103 David Paget,
104 Isaac Taylor.

BLADEN COUNTY.

1 John Sellars, Captain.
2 John Andrees, 1st Lieut.
3 John Andres,
4 Matthew Sikes,

5 James Sikes,
6 Nathaniel Sutton,
7 David Sikes,
8 Aaron Larkins,

9 Peter Cromartee,
10 Beatty Sikes,
11 Ever McMillan,
12 Nehemiah Done,
13 Charles Oliver,
14 Elisha Baker,
15 James Benson,
16 Matthew Benson,
17 Elijah Smith,
18 James Counsel,
19 Alfred Sikes,
20 William Jones,
21 Cornelius Ray,
22 Samuel Smith,
23 William Anderson,
24 Philemon S. Hodges,
25 Philip Cheshire,
26 James Singletary,
27 Morgan Allan,
28 John Beard,
29 Aaron Plummer,
30 Samuel Cain,
31 Neil McArthur,
32 Colin Monroe,
33 Joseph Allan,
34 Neil Clark, jr.,
35 David Perry,
36 John Robeson,
37 Simon Smith,
38 Duncan Clark, jr.,
39 Angus Clark,
40 Willis Hudson,
41 David Russ,
42 John Mulford,
43 Ever McMillan,
44 Sion Callum,

45 William White,
46 Benjamin Singletary,
47 William Wood,
48 George Russ,
49 Willis Singletary,
50 Zadock Hillbourne,
51 Samuel Pool,
52 Henry Hillbourn,
53 Abraham Blackwell,
54 Jesse Jones,
55 William Jones,
56 William Bobeson,
57 Absalom Mairs,
58 William McEwen,
59 William Mooney,
60 Archibald Robeson,
61 John Bluie,
62 John Lisley,
63 Randolph McMillan,
64 James Rising,
65 William Lewis,
66 Daniel McEwen,
67 Samuel Singletary,
68 John Hair,
69 Jonathan Lock,
70 Edward Plummer,
71 Brayton Singletary,
72 John Martin,
73 Alexander Watson,
74 Richard Taylor,
75 Jacob Long, -
76 Thomas Bedsold,
77 Henry Bullard,
78 Thomas Davis,
79 Lewis Suggs,
80 John McDonald,

81 Shadrack Wethersby,
82 William Smith,
83 John New,
84 Travis Bedsold,
85 Daniel Sellars,
86 William Simmons,
87 Duke Edge,
88 John Smith,
89 Arthur Smith,
90 John Edwards,
91 John Davis,
92 Daniel Melvin,
93

BRUNSWICK COUNTY.

1 John Bryan, 1st Lieut.
2 Thos. Flowers, 2d Lieut.
3 Moses Bruton,
4 John Liles,
5 William Sellers,
6 George Oliphant,
7 James Keath,
8 George Keath,
9 Bennet Flowers,
10 William Taylor,
11 Samuel Tharp,
12 Samuel Hill,
13 Meady Osby,
14 Henry Raiby,
15 Peter Staraland,
16 James Highsmith,
17 John Barns,
18 Henry Stanaland,
19 William Gause,
20 Bryan Gause,
21 Elisha Sellers,
22 John Ward.

COLUMBUS COUNTY.

1 Caleb Stephens, Captain.
2 Josiah Powell, Ensign,
3 William Bryan, Private,
4 Armilain Bryan,
5 Meskick Wilson,
6 Duthan Hammons,
7 Demsey Worrell,
8 William Register,
9 Jonathan Dial,
10 Robert Ward,
11 James Campbell,
12 Andrew Coleman,
13 Henry Coleman,
14 John Campbell,
15 William Faulk,
16 Asa Coleman,
17 Elisha Nickols,
18 John Gore,
19 Levi Stephens,
20 Malachiah Hews,
21 Hinnant Faulk,
22 Joseph Gore,
23 Needham Fairfax,
24 Jonathan Beech,

25 William Flinn,
26 Nathaniel Ward,
27 William Stubbs,
28 Henry Johnston,
29 George Stubbs,
30 James Lasser,
31 John Barefoot,
32 John Lasser,
33 Arthur Mooney,
34 Isaac Dage,
35 John Wilson, jr.,
36 Thomas Faulk,
37 John Billberry,
38 Shadrick Wilson, [enlisted,]
39 Amos King,
40 William Hook,
41 Goldsberry Boswell,
42 Reuben Stephens,
43 Gilbert McKeithan,
44 Eli Nobles,
45 William Mooney,
46 John Addison,
47 James Jones,
48 William Little,
49 Curtis Fields,
50 Henry Billbiuny,
51 Lewis Price,
52 J. Wilson, [en. in U. S. A.],
53 Austin Innman,
54 John Faulks.

DUPLIN COUNTY.

1 John E. Hussey, Captain.
2 Amos J. Walker, 1st Lieut.
3 Abraham Glisson, 2d Lieut.
4 John Swinson, 3d Lieut.
5 John T. Grady, Ensign,
6 Charles Bowan,
7 William Streets,
8 David Teachey,
9 Jonathan Allen,
10 Caldwell Thalley,
11 George Mallard,
12 Isaac Allen,
13 James Norriss,
14 John F. Bowey,
15 Lemuel Thigper,
16 Tobias Fountain,
17 William Fountain,
18 James Scarborough,
19 James Borey,
20 Felic Hancock,
21 Nathan Murray,
22 Henry Hollingsworth,
23 Noah Lanier,
24 John Bishop,
25 Caleb Ostien,
26 Owen Bishop,
27 Joseph Brooks,
28 John Farrier,
29 William Sandler,
30 Daniel Kenady,
31 David Farrier,
32 William Nuthercut, jr.,
33 Benjamin Pearce,
34 William Farrier,
35 Joseph Brooks, sr.,
36 Jonas Jones,

37 Fathan Kennady,
38 Reding Smith,
39 Thomas Davis,
40 Jesse Grimes,
41 Theophilus Williams,
42 James Stuart,
43 Richard Matthews,
44 Michael Matthews,
45 Enock Quin,
46 William Macner,
47 Felix Sullivan,
48 Stephen H. Glisson,
46 William Hardison,
50 Henry Deal,
51 Benjamin Herring,
52 Theophilus Blount,
53 John Beardan,
54 William Connerly,
55 Henry Moore,
56 Lemuel Guy,
57 Isaac Gore,
58 John Pollock,
59 Archibald McCaleb,
60 Benjamin Rivenbark,
61 John Bennet,
62 Solomon Kenady,
63 Joel Burnham,
64 Daniel Parker,
65 John Barfield,
66 Bennet Millard,
67 Lewis Rouse,
68 Daniel Jones,
69 Dickson Sullivan.
70 Henry Sommerlin,
71 Thomas Jones,

72 Daniel Swinson,
73 Thomas Brock,
74 John Swinson,
75 Reading Bowden,
76 Joseph Sollace,
77 Jesse Brock,
78 Henry Boyt,
79 James Wade,
80 Moses Bourdeaux,
81 Elam Lea,
82 Allen Jones,
83 John Hines,
84 David Floan,
85 Alexander Heath,
86 David Brock,
87 James Morris,
88 John Miller, jr.,
89 Jacob Mallard,
90 Samuel Chambers,
91 George Cummings,
92 Patrick Ezell,
93 Nicholas Rogers,
94 Isaac Taylor,
95 Samuel Grier,
96 Nathan Jones,
97 William White,
98 Isaac Wilson,
99 Byrd Williams,
100 John Oneal,
101 Stephen Noles,
102 Joseph Waller,
103 Jacob Taylor,
104 Elijah Jones,
105 Daniel Cannon.

SAMPSON COUNTY.

1 Payton R. Parker, Capt.
2 Thos. Sutton, 1st Lieut.
3 Ira Tucker, 2d Lieut.
4 Burrel Register, Ensign.
5 James Pennington,
6 John Brewer,
7 Zackariah Parker,
8 Thomas James,
9 Cornelius McKay,
10 John Cook, jr.,
11 Levi S Mars,
12 Joshua S. Mars,
13 Zepheniah Parker,
14 Felix Merritt,
15 Levi Register,
16 Manassah Williams,
17 Lewis Williams,
18 Michael Shurly,
19 Aaron Marlin,
20 Lowamy Flowers,
21 Whitfield Sutton,
22 Wiley Merrit,
23 Philip Flowers,
24 Wm. Hope,
25 Gabriel Peterson,
26 Wm. Stephens,
27 William Robinson, jr.,
28 George Robinson, jr.,
29 William Edge,
30 Allen Jones,
31 Needham Watkins,
32 James Chesnut,
33 Joseph Chesnut,
34 Joseph Kelly,
35 John Boon,
36 Abraham Joiner,
37 Robert Wilkins,
38 James Hall,
39 Cornelius Autrey,
40 Ezekiel Owens,
41 Sherrod Simmons,
42 John Faircloth,
43 Isom Faircloth,
44 Raphial Faircloth,
45 Curtis Nillens,
46 Juni Pope,
47 Thomas Owens,
48 John McLewinnen,
49 Jesse Carr,
50 Thomas Britt,
51 Stephen Pope,
52 Jonathan Carrold,
53 John W. Turner,
54 Martin Hare,
55 Thomas Howard,
56 Nathan Williams,
57 Nathan Strickland,
58 William Stewart,
59 Tobias McGee,
60 James Faircloth,
61 Martin Strickland,
62 Matthew Porter,
63 Elbert Strickland,
64 Henry Hall,
65 Drew Daughtrey,
66 William Goodwin,
67 Hardy Daughtrey,
68 David Strickland,

69 Jonas Quimby,
70 Michael Hobbs,
71 Henry Woods,
72 John Royals Owmson,
73 Robert Dardin,
74 Nias Waters,
75 Uriah Westbrook,
76 Green Hill,
77 Jordan Coats,
78 Barney Blackman,
79 Young Wood,
80 John Tallow,
81 John Tart,
82 David Rainer,
83 James Wilson,
84 Felix Bass,
85 William Williford,
86 James Anderson,

87 Hardy Warrick,
88 Duncan Peterson,
89 Joseph Lorraman,
90 Clemm Sales,
91 Robert Wilson,
92 Malcom McCorquadale,
93 David Dudley,
94 Hugh McQueen,
95 Neil Stewart,
96 Lurrel Mobley,
97 James Rench,
98 John Hare,
99 James Rainer,
100 Ervin Jackson,
101 William Chesnut,
102 John Royal (Isom's son.)
103 Bailey Chesnut,
104 Owen Page,

ROBESON COUNTY—FIRST REGIMENT.

1 John McPhattair, Captain.
2 Duncan Murphy, 1st Lieut.
3 James McRee, 2d Lieut.
4 Jacob Little, 3d Lieutenant.
5 John McPhaul, Ensign.
6 Archibald McIntyre,
7 Stephen Cumboe,
8 Neil McMillan,
9 Jesse Manuel,
10 Jesse Pittman,
11 Dempsey Powell,
12 Aaron Braswell,
13 William Shipwash,
14 Elias Bullard,
15 Richard Bullard,

16 Anderson Taylor,
17 Henry Trawick,
18 James Brassie,
19 Charles Williams,
20 John McNeil,
21 John McDonald,
22 John Walker,
23 James Watson,
24 Peter Nicholson,
25 Peter Munroe,
26 Malcom McEachern,
27 Duncan McEachern,
28 Lanchlin McLanchlin,
29 Stephen Powell,
30 Henry Bullock,

31 Sterling Powell,
32 Stephen Ammons,
33 Lalathel Pippin,
34 Willis Jones,
35 Richard Watson,
36 Richard Small,
37 John Townsend,
38 Burwell Britt,
39 Stephen Land,
40 John Philips,
41 James Wilcox,
42 Benjamin Lovet,
43 William Histers,
44 Zachariah Pate,
45 Reuben Musslewhite,
46 Charles Pate,
47 Michael Baxley,
48 Joel Stephens,

49 John Hammons,
50 Cade Barfield,
51 Albertain Barnes,
52 Erick Legget,
53 Asa Daniel,
54 James Taylor,
55 Burwell Lee,
56 Giles Herring,
57 Elijah Pittman,
58 Needham Barfield,
59 John Parnell,
60 John Powers,
61 Moab Willis,
62 Paul Allen,
63 Thomas Wilson,
64 James Bourne,
65 Hardy Cox.

ROBESON COUNTY—SECOND REGIMENT.

1
2
3 Willis Baslay,
4 Neill Thompson,
5 Malcolm McRainey,
6 Edward Malloy,
7 Robert McAlpin,
8 James McMillan,
9 John McMillan,
10 Neel McKennon,
11 John Davis,
12 Daniel Stewart,
13 Daniel McAlpin,
14 Hugh Carmickdet,

15 Hugh Mathews,
16 John Shaw, jun.,
17 Daniel Ruthoen,
18 Elijah Wilks,
19 Duncan Smith,
20 Hugh McKenzie,
21 John McKay,
22 Neill Wilkinson,
23 Alex McNeill,
24 Alex Johnson,
25 Archibald McNeel,
26 Angus McAlpin,
27 Gadi Strickland,
28 James Furguson, jun.,

29 Malcolm McAlpin,
30 Neil McNeill,
31 Daniel Buie,
32 Marsh Barlow,
33 Hugh McKay,
34 Daniel McNeill,
35 Hugh McPherson,

36 John Smith,
37 John Powell,
38 John Currie,
39 John Farrell,
40 Malcolm Smith,
41 Malcolm McLeod,
42 Peter McEacheron.

CUMBERLAND COUNTY—SECOND REGIMENT.

1 John Burt, Captain,
2 John Armstrong, 1st lieut.
3 Murdoch Ochiltree, 2d do.
4 Neil McArthur,
5 James Cameron,
6 Wm. Kennaday,
7 Archibald Patterson,
8 Malcolm Clark,
9 Duncan McLean,
10 Archibald McGregor,
11 Murdock McLeod,
12 John Morrison,
13 Hugh McLean,
14 James Hucksby,
15 James Ferguson,
16 Ica Parker,
17 Lewis Walker,
18 John Dollihit,
19 Young Blanchet,
20 Jones Stephen,
21 John Knight,
22 James Stewart,
23 Asey Pearson,
24 Asa Matthews,
25 Durham Aven,
26 Elijah Spencer,
27 Henry Urquhart,

28 John Eley,
29 James Christian,
30 Tapley Johnston,
31 William Watson,
32 Duncan McDongald,
33 Hardy Parker,
34 Duncan Dorman,
35 Wm. Smith,
36 James Campbell,
37 Neil McAllister,
38 James Dean,
39 Alex McAllister,
40 John Evans,
41 James Kellin,
42 Allen Godwin,
43 David Balentine,
44 Daniel McLeod,
45 George Learcey,
46 John Avery,
47 John Johnston,
48 Jonathan Smith,
49 Levi Ennes,
50 Lemi Scarcy,
51 Norman Urquhart,
52 Norman Urquhart,
53 Sam'l Card.

MOORE COUNTY.

1 Wm. Dowd, Captain.
2 John Oats, 1st Lieut.
3 Alex McNeill, 2d Lieut.
4 John Stuart, Ensign,
5 Archibald Graham,
6 John Blackman,
7 Kenneth Black,
8 Ezra Russel,
9 Martin Eagle,
10 Wm. Barrot,
11 John Moore, Drummer.
12 Merriman Ball, Fifer.
13 James Spicer,
14 Daniel Kelley,
15 John McBeth,
16 Benjamin Siler,
17 Abner Hawser,
18 Alex. Curry,
19 James Curry,
20 Peter Kelly,
21 Burwell Maples,
22 James Ringstaff,
23 John Hancock,
24 Henry Phillips,
25 Hugh Kelly,
26 Thomas Muse,
27 Joseph Johnston,
28 Henry Stuts,
29 Malcom McCrommon,
30 Duncan McLanchlin,
31 Kindrick Brickhead,
32 William Jinkins,
33 John MacDonald,
34 George Ritter,
35 Neil Black,
36 George Fry,
37 John Rouse,
38 John McLane,
39 Duncan McInnish,
40 Angus McNeill,
41 Peter Blue,
42 Neil McMillan,
43 Malcom Buchan,
44 John Black,
45 Neil Sulivant,
46 Joseph Robeson,
47 John Morris, +
48 Martin Thomas,
49 John MacIver, jun.,
50 James Walker,
51 Duncan Baker,
52 Edward Walker,
53 Robert McIver,
54 Malcom MacFarland,
55 Martin Dye,
56 Bartholomew Dunn,
57 Wm. Smith, jun.,
58 John Gibson,
59 Thomas Dunn,
60 John Smith,
61 William Britt,
62 Angus McKennon,
63 Wm Jones,
64 Daniel Buchan,
65 Thomas Keyson,
66 Alexander MacLane,
67 John Nicholson,
68 Dahald Campbell,

69 Allen McLeod,
70 Wm. Milton,
71 Daniel Buie,
72 Duncan Thompson,
73 Duncan McDuffee,
74 Wm. Brown,
75 Gardener Rowling,
76 Joseph Owens,

77 Wm. Smith,
78 John Dunlop,
79 Wm. Brewer, jun.,
80 Kindrick Williamson,
81 Jacob Ormand,
82 Moses Myrick,
83 Isaac Teaque,
84 Robert Brady.

RICHMOND COUNTY.

1 Pleasen M. Mask, Captain,
2 Henry Thomas, 1st Lieut.
3 John MacKinnon, 2d Lieut.
4 John Carmichael, 3d Lieut.
5 Shelsby Cobman, Ensign,
6 Thomas H. Lewis,
7 David D. Tedder,
8 John Steele,
9 John Buck,
10 John Kelly,
11 Absolem Wall,
12 James Gorden,
13 William Robeson,
14 Joseph Dark,
15 Daniel Smith,
16 Thomas Cope,
17 William Long,
18 Isham Shepard,
19 Thomas Shepard,
20 Culiver Britt,
21 Daniel Laslie,
22 Israel Luced,
23 Moses Overstreet,
24 Daniel McLeod,
25 Lewis Thomas,

26 William Scott,
27 Burrel Graham,
28 Stephen Herring,
29 Benjamin Scott,
30 Nehemiah Hadder,
31 John Pate,
32 Archibald Macgee,
33 Silas Norton,
34 Benjamin Watkins,
35 Richard Welsh,
36 John Webb, jun.,
37 Jacob Lampley,
38 Alexander Oliver,
39 Moses Watkins,
40 Thomas Serjiner,
41 Daniel Munroe,
42 Malcom Morrison,
43 John Quick,
44 Neill Laslie,
45 Alexander McCall,
46 Alexander Martin,
47 Archibald McCattum, jun
48 John MacDonald,
49 Dugal MacDuffie,
50 Archibald Graham, jun.,

51 John Leech,
52 Dugal Leech,
53 John Morrison,
54 John McQuain,
55 Miles K. Well,
56 Norman Campbell,
57 Alex Cunningham,
58 Noah Sanderford,
59 Vincent Rainwater,
60 Roland Hammons,
61 John Powell,
62 Eli MacDonald,
63 John MacInnis,

64 Gooden Capell,
65 Huncan MacRae,
66 Alfred Balding,
67 George Dawkins,
68 Duncan Cunningham,
69 Alexander Gordon,
70 Landerford Loving,
71 Briant Loving,
72 Archibald McCabler,
73 Alex Cunningham,
74 John Stewart,
75 Isham Scott.

ANSON COUNTY—FIRST REGIMENT.

1 Benjamin A. Laniere, Capt.
2 Thomas Godfrey, 1st Lieut.
3 Gideon Threadgill, 2d Lieut.
4 John Lockhart, 3d Lieut.
5   , Ensign,
6 Nathaniel Hales,
7 John Legoe,
8 Micajah Dawkins,
9 James Runnols,
10 Joshua Legoe,
11 Hugh Monroe,
12 John Martin,
13 John F. Russell,
14 Theophilus Hopgood,
15 Joseph Parish,
16 Ezekiel Wynn,
17 Abner Beverly,
18 Emanuel Courtney,
19 Henry Gullidge,
20 Leroy Pounds,

21 Isaac Boggaw,
22 Thomas Ward,
23 William Davis,
24 William Taylor,
25 Philip Gathings,
26 William Howell,
27 John Howell,
28 John Patterson,
29 Daniel McKay,
30 Willis Struter,
31 William Dilport,
32 James Short,
33 John Hopkins,
34 John Hinson, jun.,
35 John Harrington,
36 Daniel May,
37 Daniel MacRae,
38 John Punkett,
39 John Launcan,
40 Daniel Murphy,

41 Elias Best,
42 Charles Gathings,
43 William Johnson,
44 Axum Turner,
45 Burwell Messer,
46 Freeman Winkfield,
47 Jeremiah Messer,
48 Jacob Pope,
49 Peyton Lunsford,
50 Richard McBride,
51 Shadrick Brazil,
52 Wright Lee,
53 John Lockhart,
54 John Gewin,
55 John Ingram,
56 Thomas Smith,
57 Wm. Vandiford,
58 Angus Murchison,
59 Joel Hamn,
60 John Morel,
61 William Wallace,
62 Jonathan Boggan,
63 Jesse McLindon,
64 Jesse Little,
65 Wm. Bailey, jun.,
66 Colin Evans,
67 John Cochran,
68 Ashur Myres,
69 William Rivers,
70 William McDonald,
71 Needham Eddins,
72 Enock Little,
73 Levi Medor,
74 John H. Gormen,
75 Isaac Morce.

ANSON COUNTY—SECOND REGIMENT.

1 Obadiah Curbee, Captain,
2 Solomon Trull, 1st Lieut.
3 James White, 2d Lieut.
4 Stephen Rushing, 3d Lieut.
5 Hardy Harton, Ensign,
6 Abraham Griffin,
7 Saunders Taylor,
8 John Parker,
9 William Trull.
10 William Gurly,
11 Solomon Tragall,
12 Thomas Trull,
13 Joel Williams,
14 Charlton Joiner,
15 Enoch Griffin,
16 Moses Pearce,
17 Horanio Rosser,
18 Reuben White,
19 Thomas Jones,
20 John Meggs,
21 John Jones,
22 Asa Pearce,
23 John Lassiter,
24 John Davis,
25 Jesse Green,
26 John Wm. Thomas,
27 Philip Hagler,
28 David Tomerlin,
29 Nathaniel Bibby,
30 William Shelby,

31 David Medcalf,
32 Joseph Price,
33 Jordan Drake,
34 Joshua Hudson,
35 Wyatt Nance,
36 William Hatcher,
37 James Bawcom,
38 Jephtha Beverly,
39 James Dunn,
40 Hansel Horn,
41 George Hobbs,
42 Isaac Williams,
43 John Hyatt,
44 James Hill,
45 George Nash,
46 Willis Williams,
47 David Allen,
48 John Wilkerson,

49 William Morgan,
50 Elijah Cook,
51 John Holifield,
52 Joel Meador,
53 George Duran,
54 Thomas Moss,
55 Isham Harrell,
56 David Prince,
57 Robert Leonard,
58 George Williams,
59 Elijah Carthedge,
60 Wm. McMillan,
61 Jeremiah Anderson,
62 John Jones,
63 Charles Trull,
64 Stephen Williams,
65 David Brumblow.

FOURTH REGIMENT.

WAKE COUNTY—FIRST REGIMENT.

1 John Bell, Captain,
2 William Battle, Lieut.,
3 Zenas O'Kelly, Ensign,
4 Joel H. Lane,
5 Wm. W. Mason,
6 William Wiggins,
7 Dennis Wilson,
8 William M. White,
9 Charles Gilliam,
10 Thomas Hill,
11 Thos. R. Cooke,
12 John Vandigriff,
13 John Terry,

14 Hardy Dodd,
15 Charles Stewart,
16 Newton Wood,
17 Benjamin Brantly,
18 Charles Johnson,
19 Williams Damsell,
20 James Reddish,
21 John Luced,
22 John Smith,
23 John Andrews,
24 John Cooke,
25 Isham McGee,
26 Wm. Buffalo,

27 Thomas Neal,
28 Lewis Bunn,
29 Harris Liles,
30 Robert Hicks,
31 Bennet Brown,
32 Reuben Mitchell,
33 Thomas Williams,
34 Micajah Wall,
35 Charles Horton,
36 William Learcey,
37 Berry Ambrous
38 John Butter,
39 Hardy Peane,
40 William Boyakin,
41 Budd Bagwell,
42 Dickson Jordan,
43 Burwell Fowler,
44 William Hopkins,
45 Mark Cole,
46 Reddick Massey,
47 Jedemiah Pulley,
48 John Jones,
49 Isaac Massey,
50 Benjamin Marriott,
51 William Reddish,
52 Jerrod Chamblee,
53 Budd Bunn,
54 Wm. Philips,
55 John Perry,
56 Henry Culpepper,
57 Robert B. Williams,
58 Seth Jones,
59 Hinton Pugh,
60 John Leopard,
61 Elie Alford,
62 Samuel Landiford,

63 Bennet Perry,
64 William Clark,
65 William Reaves,
66 Thomas Garrett,
67 Shadrack Bolar,
68 Josiah Battle,
69 Brittain Acock,
70 Thomas Alston,
71 David Williams,
72 Simon Williams,
73 Peter Porter,
74 James Williams,
75 Samuel Sugg,
76 Acril Myatt,
77 Ephraim Messer,
78 Wm. Rand,
79 Wm. Roads,
80 Hardy McGuffe,
81 Willie Pollard,
82 Wm. Canwadd,
83 Samuel Slaughter,
84 Jacob Baltin,
85 Henry Smith,
86 Osborne Jordan,
87 Bryan Ferrill,
88 Hardy Lewis,
89 Ansel Price,
90 Brittain Deloch,
91 Bennet Bawcom,
92 David Hutchins,
93 William Todd,
94 Jesse Hason,
95 John Traywick,
96 Simon Stephens,
97 Joseph Shaw,
98 Johnson Britt,

99 Samuel Jones,
100 David Slawson,
101 Allen Parker,

102 William King,
103 Thomas Spiar.

WAKE COUNTY—SECOND REGIMENT.

1 John Green, Captain,
2 Willis Whitaker, 1st Lieut.
3 Joseph Barbee, 2d Lieut.
4 Jephthah Tyrrell, 3d Lieut.
5 John W. Lee, Ensign,
6 Alexander Smith,
7 Allen Jones,
8 Aaron Matthis,
9 Alsey Yates,
10 Anda Burges,
11 Asa Blake,
12 Abner Green,
13 Anthony Bledsoe,
14 Alfred Wilkins,
15 Absalom Hayes,
16 Aquilla Hubbard,
17 Bradford Jones,
18 Burwell Brown,
19 Britain Smith,
20 Benjamin Ashworth,
21 Britain Mills,
22 Benjamin Davis,
23 Christopher Woodard,
24 Christopher Spier,
25 Daniel Jackson,
26 Daniel Matthis,
27 Dawson Adkinson,
28 Eldah Brown,
29 Edward Bledsoe,
30 Ewell Watts,

31 Francis Jones,
32 Gideon Vaughn,
33 Green Hill,
34 Hillsman King,
35 Henry Haley,
36 Hillsman Parish,
37 Hinten Courtis,
38 Henry Moore,
39 Harwell Sims,
40 James King,
41 John Tedrick,
42 Jacob Vandigriff,
43 Isham Olive,
44 Joseph H. Hill,
45 Joseph Woodard,
46 John W. Lee,
47 John Crocker,
48 John Peddy,
49 John Betts,
50 John Fadgett,
51 John Surls,
52 Jacob Sorrel,
53 John Luallen,
54 James Walker,
55 Johnston Loyd,
56 John Carpenter,
57 John Moore,
58 John Jarrel,
59 James Thompson,
60 Jonathan Hall,

61 James Estes,
62 John Geer,
63 John Holloway,
64 John Ward,
65 Isham Goodwin,
66 John Marshall,
67 James Rigsby,
68 John Edwards,
69 Kinchen Griffin,
70 Laban Jones,
71 Martin Mann,
72 Mordecai Joplin,
73 Matthews Goodwin,
74 Major Bradley,
75 Nash Standley,
76 Neal Womble,
77 Peyton Norris,
78 Robert Ray,
79 Robert Glenn,
80 Stephen King,
81 Samuel Narris,
82 Sion Untly,
83 Stephen Seagroves,
84 Seth Sexton,
85 Stephen Pearson,
86 Samuel Reaves,
87 Timothy W. Jones,
88 Thomas Dennis,
89 Thomas Edwards,
90 Thomas Laffoon,
91 Wm. Evans, jun.,
92 William Silvey,
93 Westley Jones,
94 William Woodard,
95 William Braker,
96 William Eves,
97 William Yates,
98 Ridley Jones,
99 William King.
100 Walter Marshal,
101 William Harris,
102 Willie Harrison,
103 Woodson Allen,
104 William Marshall,
105 Young Allen, jun.,

JOHNSON COUNTY.

1 Harry Bryan, Captain,
2 Thos. J. Walton, 1st Lieut.
3 David Bryan, 2d Lieut.
4 Hardy Pool, Ensign,
5 Hartwell Ivey, 1st Sergt.
6 Young Allen, 2d Sergeant
7 David Bridgers, 3d Sergt.
8 Godfrey Stannsill 4th Sergt.
9 Rice Price, Fifer
10 Futrill Cockrett, Drummer
11 Ambrose Ingram,
12 William Johnson,
13 Averytt Holston,
14 Nelson Andrews,
15 Burwell Blackburn,
16 Thomas Price,
17 Allen Watson,
18 Martin Price,
19 James Smith,
20 Bridgers Porch,

21 John Brown,
22 William Pullen,
23 Larkin Smith,
24 Joel H. Atkinson.
25 Dixon Philips,
26 William Willons,
27 John Patterson, jun.,
28 John Evans,
29 Henry Capps,
30 William Braddy, jun.,
31 William Edwards,
32 Noel West,
33 John Hobby,
34 Hartwell Ivey,
35 William Jones,
36 James Ivey,
37 Elisha Stanley,
38 Benjamin Stephens,
39 James Dozier,
40 John Woodall,
41 Moses Johnson,
42 Alexander Woodall,
43 Sion Hill,
44 Samuel Wilder, jun.,
45 John Nawl,
46 Eunuch Whitley,
47 James Hinton,
48 Theophilus Biddingfield,
49 John Cooper,
50 John Pullen,
51 Wm. Cockrill,
52 Isaac Keen,
53 Stephen Williamson,
54 William Watson,
55 Edmond Balance,
56 Arthur Pearce,

57 Stephen Lasser,
58 John Lamb,
59 Silas Horn,
60 Nathan Morris,
61 Samuel Mitchiner,
62 Wm. Thompson,
63 Wm. Farrow,
64 Asa Learcey,
65 Osborn Howell,
66 John Powell,
67 Samuel Learcey,
68 Nathaniel Hood,
69 Lewis Tiner,
70 Irvin Price, jun.,
71 George Bayett,
72 Micajah Oneal,
73 Jacob Peacock.
74 Willie Price,
75 John Eatman,
76 Stephen Oneal,
77 Stephen Price,
78 Willie Hall,
79 John Stansill, jun.,
80 Jonathan Austin,
81 Nathaniel Jones,
82 Alexander Franklin,
83 Jacob Vincent,
84 Zadock Gower,
85 Willis Hayes,
86 Benjamin Stephenson,
87 William Stephenson,
88 Wm. Snipes,
89 Thomas Frail,
90 Jonathan Baker,
91 Willie Junigan,
92 Nathan Almond,

93 John Jordan,
94 Joseph Bryan,
95 Edward Stevens,
96 James Brown,
97 Lewis Smith,
98 William Noals,
99 John Warwick,
100 John Kelly, jun.,
101 John Turner, jun.,
102 Abner Smith,
103 Jesse Ellington,
104 Theophilus Pool,
105 Reddin Johnson,
106 Isaac Pinney,
107 Alsey Busby,
108 Elisha Reding,
109 James Pool,
110 Willie Jones.

FRANKLIN COUNTY.

1 Jones Cook, Captain,
2 Sherrod Sanders, Lieut.
3 Benjamin Carpenter, Ens.
4 Hicks Wynne,
5 Nathan Patterson,
6 Jeremiah Solomon,
7 John B. Debnam,
8 Richard Caisar,
9 Micajah T. Cotten,
10 Samuel Johnson,
11 William Asque,
12 James Langon,
13 Peter Denton,
14 William Denton,
15 Solomon Perry,
16 MacKollach Stone,
17 Thomas Gay,
18 Charles Hines,
19 Willis Peale,
20 Arthur Fassel,
21 Charles Coppage,
22 John Nelms,
23 Jones Walker,
24 Jesse Winston,
25 Robert Robertson,
26 Nathaniel Nicholson,
27 William Duke,
28 Ransom Brogdon,
29 William Browning,
30 Reuben Neale,
31 David Cook,
32 Benjamin Priddie,
33 John Arnolds,
34 Benjamin Thomas,
35 Joseph Bledsoe,
36 George Bledsoe,
37 William Murphree,
38 Patrick Bledsoe,
39 Miles King,
40 Thomas Driver,
41 James Upchurch,
42 William Owens,
43 John Bell,
44 Isaac Griffin,
45 Banister Peppin,
46 Berkely Upchurch,
47 Richard Spivey,
48 Wm. T. Hollingsworth,

49 Elisha Sandeford,
50 William Phelps,
51 James Medlin,
52 William Sanders,
53 James Cooley,
54 John Harris,
55 Jos. Young,
56 Jacob Alford,
57 Henry Harris,
58 Nathaniel Williams,
59 John Denglas,
60 Isaac House,
61 John B. Bobbit,
62 John Dickson,
63 James H. Murry,
64 James Graham,
65 Sugar McLemore,
66 James Moore,
67 Wm. Loyd,
68 John Merrit,
69 Wm. Pulliam,
70 Thomas Wise,
71 James Wiggins,

72 Joseph Pleasant,
73 Joseph Heltan,
74 John Fuller,
75 John Hornsby,
76 Malachi Simmons,
77 Jeremiah Cook,
78 James C. Jones,
79 Caswell Finch,
80 Josiah Jackson,
81 Dickson Cour,
82 Oram Jackson,
83 Peyton Tunstall,
84 John Gill,
85 Turner Gupton,
86 James Nelms,
87 Jacob Gupton,
88 John Cook,
89 Joel Parish,
90 Benjamin Hamm,
91 Willie Alford,
92 John Farmer,
93 Bobert Cary.

GRANVILLE COUNTY—FIRST REGIMENT.

1 Willis Johnson, Captain,
2 Wm. Nailing, Lieutenant,
3 William Mann, Ensign,
4 Absalom Parish,
5 Lemuel Kittrell,
6 Micajah Harris,
7 John Inscore,
8 Anthony Moore,
9 Malachiah Frazer,
10 Edward Sutton,

11 Richard Harris,
12 Harrel Wiggins,
13 John Wiggins,
14 James Conway,
15 Beriman Ham,
16 Wm. W. Reavis,
17 Alfred Hicks,
18 Joshua Archer,
19 Edward Bryant,
20 James Bryant,

21 David McGlanklin,
22 William Warrels,
23 Reuben Harris,
24 Egrippy Nance,
25 Gideon H. Macon,
26 Thomas White,
27 James Tate,
28 John Floyd,
29 Green B. Walker,
30 Dick H. Dalby,
31 Zachariah Lyon,
32 James Bowers,
33 Taswell Spain,
34 Littleton Spain,
35 Alexander Walters,
36 Nathaniel M. Taylor,
37 James Suite,
38 Joseph Hister,
39 Wm. Brogdon,
40 Leonard Bullock,
41 John Haley,
42 James Arnold,
43 Ezekiel Wheeler,
44 Gideon Davis,
45 Edward Chappel,
46 Joseph Lysle,
47 Burges Walls,

48 John Stephenson,
49 Samuel Forsythe,
50 Archibald Mitchell,
51 Wm. McFarland,
52 Micajah Dally,
53 Thomas Forsythe,
54 Jeremiah King,
55 John Adams,
56 William Adams,
57 John Fuller,
58 Abner Fletcher,
59 Hezekiah Jones,
60 James Allison,
61 Gilliam McGehe,
62 James Cook,
63 Gilford Ball,
64 Washington Womouth,
65 Dempsey Brown,
66 Willie Jones,
67 Winkfield Morgan,
68 Gideon Gill,
69 Isham Huskey,
70 Barnet Jester,
71 John W. Finch,
72 William Hiflin,
73 James B. Eustis.

GRANVILLE COUNTY—SECOND REGIMENT.

1
2 .
3
4 George Parker,
5 John P. Beasley,
6 Matthew Chandler,

7 Robert Blackwell,
8 Anderson Satterwhite,
9 William Amos,
10 John Whitamore, .
11 Francis Oliver,
12 Robert Hester,

13 James Smith,
14 George Lumpkin,
15 Joseph Ames,
16 Graves Hart,
17 Robert Knott,
18 James Falconer,
19 John Finch,
20 Bird Lofter,
21 Robert Lewis,
22 Samuel Lewis,
23 Bussee Lewis,
24 Charles Yancey,
25 Samuel Daniel,
26 John Royster,
27 John J. Inge,
28 Wm. Martin,
29 James Lewis, jun.,
30 Richard Brown,
31 Willis Hanks,
32 Thomas Grissom,
33 Thomas Terry,
34 Nathaniel Roberson,
35 John Hanks,
36 John Dorch,
37 Laban Grissom,
38 John Cretcher,
39 Archibald Gordon, jun.,
40 Allen Jones,
41 Wm. Longmire, jun.,
42 William Frazier,
43 Larkin Curren,

44 Thomas Morris,
45 John Lander,
46 Alfred Hester,
47 Richard Lemay,
48 Samuel Ussery,
49 Thomas Rice,
50 Evan Raglin,
51 Richard Ball,
52 Abner Hicks,
53 James K. Clark,
54 Pumphrett Gooch,
55 Abraham Eastwood,
56 Simon Clements,
57 John Hopkins,
58 Riley Meadows,
59 Elkanah Lyon,
60 John Dodson,
61 Young Montague,
62 Bennet Foster,
63 Ephraim Frazier,
64 Thomas Hunt,
65 John Cobs,
66 Anthony Wood,
67 John Duncan,
68 Woodson Washington,
69 Daniel Tucker,
70 John Bowls,
71 Jordan Bowls,
72 Thomas Hayes,
73 Benjamin Hester,

PERSON COUNTY.

1 John Bradshaw, Captain,
2 William Bagley, 1st Lieut.
3 Bradshaw Fuller, 2d Lieut.
4 Jeremiah Dixon, Ensign,

5 John Scoggin,
6 Morgan Fitts,
7 Elijah O'Briant,
8 Robert Carter,
9 Samuel Wheeler,
10 John Russel,
11 Downey Wade,
12 John Riggs,
13 Samuel Burke,
14 Richard Broach,
15 Robert Jones,
16 Churchwell Jones,
17 Anderson Jones,
18 James Jones,
19 Mark Glenn,
20 Daniel Meadows,
21 Richard Farrer,
22 Samuel Maugrum,
23 Riley Suit,
24 Caswell Vaughan,
25 Jeremiah Roberts,
26 Wm. Cates,
27 Seth Coleman,
28 James Cozort,
29 Daniel Hicks,
30 Ambrose Day,
31 Ambrose Dary,
32 Archibald Day,
33 Grant Allen,
34 James Hay,
35 John Parrot,
36 Wyatt Painter,
37 Wm. Bumpass,
38 Thomas Gill,
39 Wm. Elliot,
40 Josiah Oliver,

41 Gilliam Mitchell,
42 Peter Warren,
43 Pleasant Hall,
44 John Harralson,
45 Archibald Harralson,
46 Wm. Martin,
47 George Berry,
48 Edward Johnston,
49 James Johnston,
50 Richard Jones,
51 David Bell,
52 James Bradshaw,
53 Henry Worsham,
54 Henry Lipscomb,
55 James Dollerhide,
56 Vincent Bradshaw,
57 Vincent Lea,
58 McFarland Oakley,
59 Samuel Winstead,
60 Wm. Royster,
61 Reuben Lea,
62 Wm. Southward,
63 Richard Harris, sen.,
64 Drury A. Pulliam,
65 Thomas Marit,
66 Joseph M. Stanfield,
67 Ransom Austin,
68 John Brooks,
69 Samuel Bull,
70 Drury Pulliam,
71 Daniel Rease,
72 John Jas. Brooks,
73 Allen Green,
74 Henry Bailey,
75 John Buckanan,
76 Daniel Walker,

77 Thos. Townsend,
78 Wm. Buckanan,
79 Wyatt Ford,
80 John Wilkerson,

81 Hastin Blalock,
82 Wm. Mann,
83 Wm. Hill,
84 Benjamin Sampson.

ORANGE COUNTY.—FIRST REGIMENT.

1 John Young, Captain,
2 Arthur Bobbit, Lieut.
3 Isaiah Davis, Ensign,
4 James Linsey,
5 Elijah Hunt,
6 Alfred McDaniel,
7 John Cummins,
8 Thos. Ward,
9 Wm. Ringstaff,
10 James Guttis,
11 John Crabtree,
12 Wm. Wilson,
13 Lemuel Carrol,
14 Green Williams,
15 Joseph Proctor,
16 Levy Cole,
17 Timothy Cate,
18 Isaac Wood,
19 Archibald Carrington,
20 Thomas Cate,
21 Wm. Carrington,
22 Zilmon Allison,
23 Jos. McCullock,
24 John L. Woods,
25 Jesse Clark,
26 John Jordan,
27 David Ray,
28 Green Richards,
29 James Lindsey,

30 Wm. Herndon,
31 Edmond Linch,
32 John Browning,
33 John Carden,
34 Bartlet Hinchey,
35 May Desern,
36 John Scarlett,
37 John Hutchins,
38 James Raney,
39 Daniel Boothe,
40 George Nickolas,
41 Wm. Woods,
42 Hugh Riggs,
43 John Woods,
44 Bradley Collins,
45 Robert Turrentine,
46 Jesse McGee,
47 Carter Garrard,
48 Wilie Sweaney,
49 Mark Oakley,
50 Harrison Parker,
51 George Moore,
52 John Taylor,
53 Willis Roberts,
54 Amos Nickolas,
55 John Garrard,
56 Arthur Stephens,
57 Charles Roberts,
58 Ephraim Carrington,

59 Thornton McFarland,
60 James Stagg,
61 John Roberts,
62 James Parish,
63 Levi Owens,
64 John Tilly.
65 Robert Clinton,
66 Wiley Glenn,
67 Canady Horton,
68 Joshua Horton,
69 Westley Rhodes,
70 Lewis Hutchins,
71 Moses Dorset,
72 Delamy Chizenhall,
73 Daniel Holden,
74 James Browning,
75 Laney Chizenhall,
76 Samuel Strayhorn,
77 Anderson Whithead,
78 Benjamin Haswell,
79 Newcomb Thompson,
80 Pleasant Herndon,
81 James Whithead,

82 Edward McDade,
83 Thomas Ruffin,
84 James Thompson,
85 Morris Henderson,
86 Thomas Walker,
87 David Strain,
88 Thomas Gattis,
89 Joseph Dawson,
90 Bennet Pattin,
91 Patterson Yeargin,
92 Wm. Kirkland,
93 Lewis Pattin,
94 Andrew McCauley,
95 James Woods,
96 Willis Marcomb,
97 Drury Leigh,
98 John Browning,
99 Asa Brown,
100 Thos. Luter.
101 James Shepard,
102 Daniel Holden,
103 Willie Marcomb.

ORANGE COUNTY—SECOND REGIMENT.

1 David Tate, Captain,
2 Joseph Allison, Lieut.
3 Egbert Shepard,
4 Wm. Mabane,
5 George Mebane,
6 Henry Mulhollan,
7 Allan Mebane,
8 Thomas Tinnon,
9 Burk Walker,
10 Robert Smith,

11 Robert Shanklin,
12 Samuel Gilston,
13 Alex. Criswell,
14 Thomas Finnen,
15 Thomas Woods,
16 Hunter McCulloch,
17 Will Campbell,
18 Joseph Smith,
19 Larkin Sanders,
20 Thos. McClushy,

21 John Bain,
22 Walter Murray,
23 John Wilson,
24 Wesley Carson,
25 Walker Pickett,
26 James Davis,
27 Robert Dickee,
28 Barnabas Perry,
29 William Wilson,
30 William Price,
31 George Jordan,
32 Frederick Bason,
33 Sterling Price,
34 Alex Lasly,
35 John Woody,
36 James Grimes,
37 Wm. Clendinen,
38 Wm. Stewart,
39 Elisha Pickart,
40 John Thomas [Miller]
41 James Pindar,
42 James Thompson, jun.,
43 Thomas Rhadshaw, sr.,
44 Simon Buckum,
45 Matthew Tutral,
46 David Ray,
47 Jesse Ray,
48 Samuel Kirkpatrick,
49 Berry Duke,
50 Stephen Glass,
51 Alex Patten,
52 James Webb,
53 Erasmus Compton,
54 Leroy Acros,
55 Alfred Compton,
56 Jeremiah Compton,
57 Robert Faucett,
58 Eli Faucett,
59 Anderson Faucett,
60 Thos. Millington,
61 Andrew Murray,
62 Peter Belvin,
63 Joshua Ward,
64 Thomas Ward,
65 Richard Hayes,
66 Jesse Pickart,
67 Thos. Durham,
68 Benj. Cruchfield,
69 Richard Cate,
70 Richmond Workman,
71 Green O. Daniel,
72 James Minnis,
73 Wm. Workman,
74 Alex NayBo,
75 Alex NayUts,
76 Reuben Owens,
77 Thos. Moore,
78 Thos. Durham,
79 Thos. Williams,
80 James Weaver,
81 Wm. Beaver,
82 George Haywood,
83 James Crabtree,
84 Wm. Caven,
85 Wm. Ivey,
86 James Miles,
87 Wm. Brewer,
88 Thos. Cate,
89 Anderson Blackwood,
90 Benj. Bridges,

91 Jasper Glawson,
92 John Fowler, Drummer,
93 John Webb, Fifer.

ORANGE COUNTY—THIRD REGIMENT.

1 James Grahams, Captain,
2 Wm. Holt, Lieut.
3 Absalom Harvey, Ensign,
4 Henry Holt,
5 Thos. Powell,
6 David Parks,
7 Isaac Rainey,
8 Jacob Whitsell,
9 Richard Wilkins,
10 Jeremiah Grant [s. of John]
11 James Faddis,
12 Jacob Albright,
13 Charles Webster,
14 Alex McDaniel,
15 Joseph Albright,
16 John McDaniel,
17 George Ephland,
18 Wm. Hashford,
19 Wm. Caps,
20 Joseph Smith,
21 Nickolas Troxler,
22 John Troxler,
23 John Coe,
24 James Wilson,
25 Barney Troxler,
26 Oliver Powell,
27 Anderson Thompson,
28 Simpson Harris,
29 Avery Coe,
30 Daniel Theek,
31 George Spoon,
32 Frederick Moser,
33 John Wells,
34 John Kimbro,
35 Stephen Wells,
36 Wm. Thompson,
37 John Ray,
38 Philip Rose,
39 Ezekiah Hendley,
40 George Martinn,
41 Robert Fausett,
42 Wm. Cooke,
43 Thos. Rumbley,
44 Wm. Jones,
45 Joseph West,
46 Nathaniel Jones,
47 Robert Lackey,
48 Joseph Hughes,
49 George McCulley,
50 Andrew McCulley,
51 Edmund Branock,
52 Alfred Moore,
53 Wm. Dickey,
54 James Jackson,
55 James Busick,
56 James Burnet,
57 Levi Kilton,
58 James McPherson,
59 Jos. Marshall,
60 Wm. Carter,
61 Richard Cambel,
62 Timothy Weaver,

63 George Stafford,
64 Caleb Busick,
65 Boston Tiley,
66 James Melvan,
67 Daniel Johnston,
68 Jacob Huffins,

69 Stephen Willis,
70 Zackeriah Philips,
71 John Cooke,
72 Matthew Cotner,
73 Jacob Cockcleress,

CHATHAM COUNTY.

1 Aaron Evans, Captain,
2 Richard C. Cotten, Lieut.,
3 Isaac Headen, Ensign,
4 Mial Ramsey, 1st Serg't,
5 John Taylor, 2d Serg't,
6 Wm. Underwood, 3d Serg't
7 Wm. Duty, 4th Serg.t,
8 Thomas Craver, 1st Corp'l,
9 Stephen Cruchfield, 2d do
10 Asa Stone, 3d Corporal,
11 Rufus McMasters, 4th Cor'l
12 Alex Boyd, Drummer,
13 Henry Harris,
14 George Harman,
15 Ira Rosson,
16 Thos. Beal,
17 Thos. Clark,
18 David Blalock,
19
20 Jephthy Fooshee,
21 Reuben May,
22 Allen Goodwin,
23 Bennona Rossen,
24 Jonathan Lindley,
25 John Lewis,
26 Jos. Blaylock,
27 Peter Quakenbush,

28 George Rodgers,
29 Wm. Lea,
30 Sam'l Jackson,
31 John Powell,
32 Edward Caudle,
33 Nathaniel Roberson,
34 Richard Cates,
35 James Crow,
36 Hasten Poe,
37 Jos. Wilkerson,
38 John Glass,
39 John Fields,
40 Jos. Glass,
41 Jonathan Green,
42 Jonathan Miles,
43 Tabner Beal,
44 Wm. Tilman,
45 James Jones,
46 Joel Edwards,
47 Jesse Bray,
48 Samuel Elkins,
49 James Limbory,
50 John Moorey,
51 Eli Bone,
52 John Purvis,
53 John Mann,
54 John Brown,

55 John Brigat,
56 Asa Gunter,
57 Alex Lassiter,
58 Wm. Thomas,
59 Jourdan Davis,
60 Archibald Little,
61 John McIver,
62 Thomas Bland,
63 Burwell Williams,
64 John Clegg,
65 Whitmil Little,
66 James Ward,
67 Charles Johnston,
68 Abner Minter,
69 Wm. Lassater,
70 George Drake,
71 Alfred Buckanan,
72 Robert Wicker,
73 Wm. Hinton,
74 Benj. Tedder,
75 Stephen Loot,
76 Wm. Smith,
77 Harman Cox,
78 Jos. Pearson,
79 Benj. Philips,
80 Jesse Hicks,
81 Claiborn Deaton,
82 Gambol Powers,
83 Daniel Brown,
84 Tyson Womble,
85 Jesse Highland,
86 Aaron McMasters,
87 Wm. Perry,
88 Isaac Philips,
89 Isaac Harrington,
90 Jos. May,

91 Ephraim Oldham,
92 Henry Fields,
93 John Gilman,
94 Peter Smith,
95 James Burns, jun.,
96 Wm. Smith,
97 Joseph Holliday,
98 Reuben Reeves,
99 Jos. Whitehead,
100 Elisha Harris,
101 Frederick Philips,
102 Henry Smith,
103 Daniel Smith,
104 Rufus MacMasters,
105 Nickolas Fox, sen.,
106 David Vestal, sen.,
107 Jesse Nelson,
108 Nathaniel Whitehead,
109 Amos Ward,
110 Joseph Allen,
111 James Smith,
112 John Norwood,
113 Hiram Burns [112]
114 John Wesly Bynum, Lieut
115 John Cocke, Ensign,
116 John Smith, 1st Serg't,
117 Avent Cotten,
118 James Thomas,
119 Rora Womack,
120 John Bowers,
121 Thos. Williams,
122 Joseph Mims,
123 Richard Holt,
124 Ransom Byrum,
125 John Bishop,
126 Henry Williams,

127 James Boling,
128 Thomas Garner,
129 Allen Riddle,
130 Guilford Garner,
131 Green Straughan,
132 Samuel Brewer,
133 Elbert Williams,
134 Watson Mitchell,
135 Henry Wilson,
136 Wm. Pennington,
137 Thos. M. Sturdivant,
138 Samuel Wilson,
139 Elijah Willis,
140 Wilson Willis,
141 John Parker,
142 Britain Hatley,
143 Elijah Bell,
144 Jacob Womble,
145 Allen Parker,
146 John Clark,
147 Ruffin Upchurch,
148 Allen Rhodes,
149 Nickolas Long,
150 Robert Council,
151 Britain Harwood,
152 John A. Mason,
153 Thomas Oliver,
154 Presley Moore,
155 James C. Barbee,

FIFTH REGIMENT.

CASWELL COUNTY.

1 James Holder, Captain,
2 John Johnston, Lieutenant,
3 John Roan, Ensign,
4 Francis H. Burton,
5 Wm. Eddins,
6 James Darby,
7 Drucis Briggs,
8 Wm. P. Jackson,
9 Thos. Dameron,
10 Adam Stafford,
11 John Tirrill,
12 Spencer Ball,
13 Wm. Nelms,
14 Harbert Samuel,
15 Archibald Samuel,
16 Edward Kersey,
17 James Gordon,
18 Samuel Johnston,
19 Timothy Warren,
20 John Hodge,
21 Wm. Johnston,
22 Jas. Johnston [son of Jas.]
23 Alex Jackson,
24 Charles Connally,
25 Giddal Gillaspie,
26 Thos. Evans,
27 James White,
28 John Gunn,
29 James Ingram,
30 Thos. Pittard,
31 Birditt Escridge,
32 Dempsey Sargent,

33 Abraham Price,
34 James Florence,
35 Wm. Murry,
36 Absalom Burton,
37 Christopher Matthews,
38 John Love,
39 Wm. Tolloch,
40 Eli Stafford,
41 James McCain,
42 Noel Burton,
43 John Farley,
44 Newman Durham,
45 David Ball,
46 Bird Wisdom,
47 Virgil M. Rainey,
48 James Swann,
49 Laban Farland,
59 Wm. Tirrell,
51 Williamson Moore,
52 Lewis Tirrell,
53 Paul Tirrel,
54 Henry Wilson,
55 Major Stanfield,
56 Henry Mahoon,
57 Robert Malone,
58 John N. Fuller,
59 Peter P. Stublefield,
60 Levi Simpson,
61 Thos. Brinsfield,
62 Philip Eubank,
63 Richard Gates,
64 James Balridge,
65 Benj. B. Nelson,
66 Luke Sanders,
67 John Norris,
68 Thos. Hobbs,

69 Matthew Walker,
70 Wiley Mason,
71 James Nighton,
72 Jos. Swann,
73 James H. Pass,
74 Wm. W. Price,
75 John Thompson,
76 Robt. Ware,
77 Thos. Penix,
78 Joseph Burroughs,
79 Thomas Swann,
80 David Farley,
81 Nathaniel Lea,
82 Christopher Dameron,
83 John Wray,
84 James Thompson,
85 Lewis Samuel,
86 Abraham Montgomery,
87 John Montgomery,
88 Rowzee Samuel,
89 Wm. Randolph,
90 George Finlay,
91 Thos. Turner,
92 Isaac Patterson,
93 Edley Campbell,
94 Wm. Fullington,
95 Christopher Spencer,
96 Jos. Swann, jun.,
97 Robert Yealock,
98 John Covington,
99 John Mansfield,
100 Gabriel B. Lee,
101 John Woods,
102 Nickolas Thompson,
103 Anderson Smith,
104 Stephen Stuart,

105 John Stuart,
106 Sandy Smith,
107 Wm. Culberson,
108 John Fitch,
109 James Johnston,
110 Jesse Corbith,
111 David Culberson,
112 David Mitchell,
113 Oney Randolph,
114 Robert Randolph,

115 James Underwood,
116 Wm. Jones,
117 Edw. Moore,
118 Johnson Brooks,
119 Edward Wattington,
120 James Rozwell,
121 Henry Willis,
122 Edward Jones,
123 James Holdesnes,
124 George Brooks, jun.,

GUILFORD COUNTY.—FIRST REGIMENT.

1 Robert McEuiston, Captain,
2 Moses Owen, 1st Lieut.
3 Wm. McBride, 2d Lieut.
4 Jesser McCurston, Ensign,
5 John Grogan,
6 Levi Fosbers,
7 Samuel Hillmon,
8 James Donnel,
9 John McCurston,
10 John McCain,
11 Wm. Adams,
12 John Hoskins,
13 Amos Page,
14 Nathan Lester,
15 Caleb Hillmon,
16 Wm. McCuiston,
17 Samuel Kellum,
18 Jos. Hoskins,
19 James Lap,
20 Thos. Hister,
21 Elijah Owen,
22 Wm. Hutchinson,
23 Elisha Coffin,

24 Joshua Hillmon,
25 Daniel Caulk,
26 Aaron Binny,
27 Tilmon Clark,
28 Robert Burney,
29 John Nickolson,
30 Wm. Claton,
31 Lemuel Oaks,
32 James Hutchinson,
33 James Bevill,
34 Taylor Holloway,
35 Moses Elliott,
36 Henry Bevill,
37 James McCuiston,
38 Hartwell Knight,
39 Turner Irby,
40 Jos. Simmons,
41 Alexander Hutchinson,
42 James Loar,
43 Ellis Hoskins,
44 Isaac White,
45 Wm. Wilson,
46 Wm. Dennis,

47 Agbert Landingham,
48 Wm. Knight,
49 Robert Spivert,
50 Mark Caps,
51 Tandy Bell,
52 John Starnt,
53 Benj. Allen,
54 Shadrach Allen,
55 James Brown,
56 Electris Johis,
57 Robert Fleming,
58 John Perdue,
59 Henry Anthony,
60 Nickolas Edward,
61 James Tobin,
62 Marmon Strawn,
63 David Burney,
64 Robert Middleton,
65 Abraham Burt,
66 George Kinnodle,
67 Beniah Fleming,
68 Hugh McCain,
69 Amous Wilson,
70 David Madaris,

71 Thos. Daugherty,
72 James Clark,
73 Harvey King,
74 John Pegram,
75 Henry Wilson,
76 Garrison Justice,
77 Jesse Knott,
78 Hooper Caffer,
79 James Ross,
80 Jasper Gent,
81 William Shelby,
82 Thomas Parker,
83 David Loyd,
84 Adam Boyd,
85 David Edwards,
86 Elias Morgan,
87 Robert Russel,
88 Samuel Barney,
89 George Donner,
90 David Allin,
91 Henry Clark,
92 Wm. York,
93 Harbert Brown,
94 Sutton Taylor.

GUILFORD COUNTY—SECOND REGIMENT.

1 Wm. Clapp, Captain,
2 Henry Humphreys, Lieut.
3 Robert Ervin, Ensign,
4 Aaron Williams,
5 Andrew Garenger,
6 Adam Trollenger,
7 Andrew Gamble,
8 Daniel Gerringer
9 David Edwards,

10 Ephraim Burrow,
11 Enos Frazer,
12 Francis Simpson,
13 George Sullivan,
14 George Stephens,
15 Henry Weatherly,
16 Henry Chaplain,
17 Isaac Wolfingtan,
18 Isaac Lamb,

19 Isaac McDill,
20 Jesse Forbes,
21 Jacob Hager,
22 John Rarden,
23 John Amick,
24 Jos. Shaw,
25 Jacob Coble,
26 Jacob Greason,
27 John Kinman,
28 John Fogleman,
29 James Foster,
30 Zedekiah Smith,
31 Jesse Shaw,
32 James Grissom,
33 John Dickson,
34 Jesse Holton,
35 Joel Lowden,
36 John Boyd,
37 John Tucker,
38 Joseph Quaits,
39 John Ingle,
40 Jonathan Short,
41 John Murphy,
42 James Suduth,
43 John Hemphill,
44 Leonard Philippie,
45 Major Underwood,
46 Martin Fifer,

47 Moses Job,
48 Michael Swain,
49 Moses Gibson,
50 Nemiah Whittington,
51 Obed Gardner,
52 Richard Williams,
53 Robert Morgan,
54 Reuben Dick,
55 Robert Wood,
56 Robert Wilson,
57 Robert Field,
58 Robert Patterson,
59 Solomon Burrow,
60 Samuel Dick,
61 Samuel Irwin,
62 Wm. Thomas,
63 Wm. Fryer,
64 Wm. Simmons,
65 Wm. Swain,
66 Wm. Richardson,
67 Whittenton Sullivan,
68 Wm. Fifer,
69 Winwright Barns,
70 Wm. Humphries,
71 Wm. Watson,
72 Wm. Suits,
73 John Humphreys,

ROCKINGHAM COUNTY.

1 Geo. W. Baker, Captain,
2 Howell Harris, 1st Lieut.
3 David Smith, 2d Lieut.
4 James Fewell, Ensign,
5 Joel Cardwell,

6 John Guy,
7 John Smith,
8 George Jackson,
9 Pleasant Dearing,
10 Pleasant Tod,

11 Reuben Lindsay,
12 Dillard Allen,
13 Josiah Settle,
14 Leonard Carney,
15 Alfred Bethell,
16 Absalom Wall,
17 Philip Gates,
18 Wm. Wall,
19 John Scales,
20 Geo. W. Jennings,
21 Samuel Dalton,
22 Alfred Scales,
23 Green Vernon,
24 Wm. H. Rice,
25 Jos. G. Porter,
26 John J. Wright,
27 Zack Strong,
28 Elisha Hancock,
29 Zack Fewee,
30 Zack Wall,
31 Thomas Smith,
32 James Wall,
33 James Webster,
34 John C. Overton,
35 John Webster,
36 Thos. Barker,
37 John Gilliland,
38 Silas Padge,
39 Joel Fagg,
40 John Barker,
41 Martin Roberts,
42 Robert Hall,
43 James Vaughan,
44 Wm. Whitworth,
45 Jonathan Aldridge,
46 Pleasant Black,

47 Pleasant Webster,
48 Samuel Vernon,
49 Robert Joyce,
50 Philip Ison,
51 Jacob Crawford,
52 Jeremiah Barns,
53 Wm. Reynolds,
54 John D. Vernon,
55 Josiah Vernon,
56 Bartlet Edwards,
57 John Sharp,
58 Willie Dearing,
59 John Parish,
60 Shelton Foster,
61 Thos. Robertson,
62 And Robertson,
63 John Vaughan,
64 Hardiman Strong,
65 Samuel Page,
66 Samuel Moxley,
67 John Cody,
68 James Walker,
69 Milton Grant,
70 Powhattan May,
71 Wm. Duncan,
72 Francis Hains,
73 John Wilson,
74 John Carter,
75 John Geesling,
76 Fountain Purrell,
77 Thos. Carter,
78 James Andrews,
79 Wm. Gedsey,
80 Robert Hudson,
81 Wm. S. Tucker.
82 Freeman Greer,

83 John Tucker,
84 Isaiah Hancock,
85 Alam Boak,
86 Pleasant Gorman,
87 Peter Lyon,
88 Isaac Philipps,
89 David Kellam,
90 Lee Bondusant,
91 Stephen Gibson,
92 Wm. Mangham,
93 Stephen Pratt,
94 Robert Gibson,
95 Robert H. Coats,
96 Anthy N. Millar,
97 Cooper Jordan,
98 Signor Ahorn,
99 George Wright,

100 James Underwood,
101 John Robertson,
102 John Kelly,
103 Benjamin Ladyman,
104 Thos. Underwood,
105 Wm. Small,
106 Edward King,
107 John B. Curry,
108 Noah Cardwell,
109 James Norman,
110 John Smith,
111 John Joyce, jr.,
112 Pleasant Gibson,
113 John Claridge,
114 Eli Hancock,
115 Jos. Bishop,
116 John Dillard.

STOKES COUNTY—FIRST REGIMENT.

1 Sam. Martin, Captain,
2 Thos. Smith, Lieut.
3 Newton Ladd, Ensign,
4 Elijah Nelson,
5 Jacob Nelson,
6 Jeremiah Cloud,
7 James Lawson,
8 Larkin Burge,
9 Joel Ketchum,
10 Edward Yates,
11 Ezekiel Collins,
12 Wm. Blanchet,
13 Benj. Fry,
14 Jas. G. Lyon,
15 Wm. Johnson,
16 Thomas Doss,

17 Bartlet Shipp,
18 Joseph Martin,
19 Wm. Shipp,
20 John Cox,
21 Reuben Tilley,
22 Lambert Dodson,
23 Wm. Stanly,
24 James Hutchens,
25 Benj. Thomas,
26 James Perkins,
27 Matthew Moore,
28 Wm. Young,
29 George Breedlove,
30 Hansford Pollard,
31 John Pollard,
32 Floyd Webb,

33 John Jones,
34 Wm. Camon,
35 Jeremiah Cisk,
36 George Neele,
37 Samuel Angel,
38 Wm. Ladd,
39 James Powers,
40 Benj. D. Angle,
41 Wm. Carr,
42 Wm. Gibson,
43 Robert Neele,
44 David D. Bostick,
45 Thos. Martin,
46 Wm Poindexter,
47 John Tilley,
48 Wm. Slaughter,
49 George Booth,
50 Richard Flynt,
51 James Davis,
52 Wm. Welch,
53 Thomas Evans,
54 John Harvey,
55 John Hoover,
56 Thos. Reddick,
57 Henry Spainhower,
58 James Ridley.

59 Jacob Wolf,
60 Jacob Helsepeck,
61 John Brabin,
62 Jesse Brown,
63 John Edwards,
64 Jacob Fiscus,
65 John Prater,
66 David Spainhower,
67 Frederic Fulk,
68 Wm. Childress,
69 Shedrack Reddick,
70 James Merritt,
71 John Kances,
72 Isaac George,
73 John Hooker,
74 Jacob Denton,
75 James Bowleyjack,
76 Samuel Riggs,
77 Jon Neal,
78 Samuel Neale,
79 Jesse Dunlap,
80 Kelly Shirley,
81 Jesse Banks,
82 John Brown,
83 Arthur Muskram.

STOKES COUNTY—SECOND REGIMENT.

1 John L. Hauser, Captain,
2 Benj. Briggs, Lieut.
3 Solomon Fulps, Ensign,
4 Duncan C. McCocklin,
5 Alex. McKay,
6 Wm. G. Parish,
7 Peter Shammell,

8 David Jean,
9 Jacob Neal,
10 John Myers,
11 Thos. Snow,
12 John Snow,
13 Matthew Marshall,
14 Martin W. Marshall,

15 James Allen,
16 John Boswell,
17 Thos. Marshall,
18 John Bibee,
19 Christian Waggerman,
20 Stephen McFerson,
21 Wm Frazier,
22 Matthias Maston,
23 Thos. Walker,
24 Owen Walker,
25 Israel Robinson,
26 James Lawrey,
27 Elijah Harrell,
28 Fredrick Millar,
29 Fracis Rose,
30 Jacob Huphines,
31 Charles Vest,
32 Wm. Blackburn,
33 Thos. Jinkens,
34 Robert Cornelious,
35 Henry Fidler,
36 John Oens,
37 John Karney,
38 John Strape,
39 John Haning,
40 Jacob Shamel,
41 Daniel Hauser,
42 Abram Lash,
43 Henry Ripple,
44 John Fidler,
45 John Rell,
46 Thos. Rell,
47 Charles Chube,
48 John Todd,
49 Philip Huffman,

50 Abram Johnson,
51 Elisha Johnson,
52 Jonathan Sell,
53 John Styers,
54 John Johnson,
55 Richard Clampit, jr.,
56 Joseph Idol,
57 John Whitehead,
58 Hampton Bynum,
59 Julius Patterson,
60 John Blume,
61 Christian Ebert,
62 David Patterson,
63 John D. Salmons,
64 Wm. Golding,
65 Andrew Bowman,
66 Thos. Westmoreland,
67 Elijah Fowler,
68 Seth Hamm,
69 George Lenville,
70 Moses Lenville,
71 John Forrester,
72 John Campbell,
73 Wm. Branson,
74 Lawrence Angel,
75 John Sprinkle,
76 Wm. Branson,
77 Godfrey Millar,
78 Isaac Church,
79 Robert Hill,
80 John Cornelius,
81 Harman Millar,
82 Mickael Sailer,
83 Henry Doub.

SURRY COUNTY—FIRST REGIMENT.

1 David Freeman,
2 Joseph Bunham,
3 Michael Teag,
4 Enock Stone,
5 Henry Fulks,
6 Joel Bray,
7 Joseph Chandler,
8 Ezekiel Denny,
9 Jesse Lam,
10 Jesse Peal,
11 James Martin,
12 Edmund Fleming,
13 Mordecai Fleming,
14 John M. Fleming,
15 James Bays,
16 Wm. B. McCraw,
17 James Roberts, jr.,
18 Wm. Williams,
19 Coleby Cruid, jr.,
20 Abraham Cruid,
21 Hail Snow,
22 Thos. Snow,
23 Elijah Aubury,
24 Jesse Prichet,
25 Wm. Golden,
26 Matthew Davis,
27 Robert Ship,
28 James Cockram,
29 James Smyth,
30 Charles Tucker,
31 James Smith, jr.,
32 Solomon Centor,
33 Isaac Bartlett,
34 Elijah Thompson,
35 John Thompson,
36 Stephen Potter,
37 Henderson Thompson,
38 Barnard Franklin,
39 Joel Canada,
40 Andrew Willie,
41 Wm. Mash,
42 Thos. Franklin,
43 John Mash,
44 Wm. Paul,
45 Jesse Burch,
46 Lemuel B Jones,
47 John Collins,
48 John Whitlock,
49 Jacob Jones,
50 Aaron Andres,
51 Isaac Wintrey,
52 James Kyle,
53 Jacob Dobbins,
54 Jesse Jones,
55 John Thomason,
56 Wm. Car,
57 Jesse Whitaker,
58 Achilus Key,
59 Littleton Isbell,
60 James Fitzgerald,
61 Lawrence Morris,
62 James Harrison,
63 Asa Earley,
64 John Aulberty,
65 Wm. Whitaker,
66 Isaac Whitaker,
67 Charles Hunn,
68 James McDonald,

69 Richard Studard,
70 Daniel Griffith,
71 Zachariah Clandler,
72 Barajah Reynolds,
73 David Love,
74 James Rorden,
75 Lewis Folkner,

76 Isaac Norman,
77 Eli Tansey,
78 Jeremiah Rorden,
79 Robert Blackville,
80 Wm. Holifyeld.
81
82

SURRY COUNTY—SECOND REGIMENT.

1 Abner Carmichall, Capt.
2 John Welch, Lieut.
3 George Hudspith, Private.
4 Richard Walker,
5 Wm. Petty,
6 George Debode,
7 Willie Harp,
8 Daniel Brandle,
9 Henry Millar,
10 Aaron Nooton,
11 Samuel Speak,
12 John Parks,
13 Benj. Brewer,
14 George Tipps,
15 John Brown, jr.,
16 Wm. Sparks,
17 Joel Sparks,
18 Stephen Denny,
19 Joshua Fenny,
20 Joseph Horton,
21 Nathan Ratcliff,
22 Jonathan Ratcliff,
23 Wm. Hunt,
24 Abraham Swain,
25 Davis Bagley,
26 Hawkins Cook,

27 Nickolas Cook,
28 Hempley Hart,
29 Jesse Collins,
30 John Southan,
31 Levy Johnson,
32 Thomas Hampton,
33 John Castephens,
34 Neal Bohannon,
35 Joshua Carter,
36 Isaac Vestal,
37 Joseph Carter,
38 Berry Paterson,
39 Charles Davis,
40 George Hobson,
41 Jonathan Hinshaw,
42 Lewis Wyles,
43 Henry Hoots,
44 John Frady,
45 Charles Stedman, jr.,
46 Fredric May,
47 John Rutledge,
48 Matthew Johnson,
49 Edmond Lovelepe,
50 Wm. Eaperson,
51 Henry Peace,
52 Benj. Pitell,

53 Wm. Lane,
54 Benj. Glenn,
55 Bennet Philips,
56 Henry Shore,
57 Wm. Robertson,
58 Edmond Philips,
59 Isaac Jarrat,
60 Francis A. Poindexter,
61 James Ball,
62 Benj. Kelly,

63 John Spillman,
64 Henry Skidmore,
65 George Ball,
66 John Pilcher,
67 Francis Moreland,
68 Thos. Thornton,
69 Giles Coe,
70 John McGuire,
71 Peter Vest,
72 Peter Sprinkle.

WILKES COUNTY.

1 Ambrose Carleton, Capt.
2 Andrew Vannoy, 1st Lieut.
3 Saml. Johnston, 2d Lieut.
4 Elijah Coffey, 3d Lieut.
5 Lewis Walters, Ensign,
6 David Allison,
7 Hiram Pipes,
8 Martin Livingston,
9 Moses Stansberry,
10 Samuel Brown,
11 Samuel Neathery,
12 Thos. Barlow,
13 Wm. Hagler,
14 Thomas Steed,
15 Hughs Napper,
16 Thos. Potts,
17 John Allen,
18 John Ferguson,
19 Joel Watters,
20 Edward Watkins,
21 Benj. Foster,
22 Christopher Gullet,
23 Daniel Gullet,

24 Eli Hamby,
25 Jacob Lipps,
26 John Craine,
27 Joel Vannay,
28 Thos. Summers,
29 Wm. Church,
30 James Bradley,
31 Hezekiah Paisley,
32 Cowen Humphry,
33 Isaac Hogler,
34 Joshua Hendrickson,
35 Peter Elerod,
36 John Coffey,
37 Archibald Brown,
38 Wm. Murphy,
39 Joshua Brown,
40 Elijah Barns,
41 Solomon Saunders,
42 John Barns,
43 John Pearson,
44 Larkin Kerly,
45 Samuel Newsom,
46 Simon Shaw,

47 Charles Vickers,
48 George Gilbreath,
49 Helen H. Gilbreath,
50 Frederic Tyser,
51 Javan Ball,
52 Marshall McDaniel,
53 Allen Robinett,
54 Hiram Gilbreath,
55 John Rains,
56 Gideon Gilbreath,
57 Hiram Smoot,
58 Wm. Smith,
59 John Norris,
60 Joel Johnson,
61 Reuben Hamby,
62 James Morgan,
63 Daniel Holderfield,
64 Sylvester Adams,
65 Benj. Treble,
66 George Barns,
67 Wm. Morgan,
68 Larkin Sheppard,
69 Gibson Adams,
70 Whitfield Brown,
71 Eli Brown,
72 Isaac Adam,
73 David Trusty,
74 John Bruce,
75 Daniel Hayes,
76 John Robards,
77 John Brown,
78 Wm. Walsh,
79 Peter Brown,
80 Wm. Amburgy,
81 Malachai Lawrence,
82 John Sparks,

83 George Crouse,
84 John Dunkin,
85 Thos. Rigsby,
86 George Sparks,
87 Jeremiah Caudill,
88 Wm. V. Lyon,
89 John Gilliam,
90 James Tucker,
91 Thos. Wood,
92 John Bensel,
93 Wm. Toliver,
94 Joshua Parks,
95 Elisha Brown,
96 George Sparks,
97 Joseph Gregory,
98 Robert Layle,
99 Wm. Gray,
100 Joseph Brown,
101 Elisha Felts,
102 Robert Perdue,
103 Ramsome Shore,
104 Jonathan Sparks,
105 Daniel McDaniel,
106 Presly Bussill,
107 Daniel Norman,
108 Levi Wilsen,
109 Charles Bewsey,
110 James Lewis,
111 James Morgan,
112 George Norman,
113 Luke Rash,
114 Wm. Combs,
115 Wm. Darnall,
116 Ezekiel Brown,
117 Hezekiah Sebastian,
118 Jonathan Walsh,

119 Jesse Adams,
120 Hopkins Pratt,
121 Edward Turner,

122 Samuel Spier.
123

ASHE COUNTY.

1 Gideon Lewis, Captain.
2 Isaac Weaver, Lieut.
3 Wm. Toliver, Ensign,
4 Henry Graybeal,
5 Eli Ragon,
6 Henry Millar,
7 James Duncan,
8 David Graybeal,
9 David Carpenter,
10 Samuel Griffith,
11 Isaac Taylor,
12 Frederick Staley,
13 Isaac Lewis,
14 Wm. Morefield,
15 Abraham Miller,
16 John Millar,
17 Mark Weaver,
18 Peter Hart,
19 Absalom Bower,
20 John Faw,
21 Jacob Mikel,
22 David Hartzog,
23 Aaron Owens,
24 Peter Feese,
25 Andrew Shearer,
26 Wm. Cox,
27 Isaac Smith,
28 Wm. Mink,
29 Edmond Tilley,

30 Joshua Pennington,
31 David Horton,
32 Phineas Horton,
33 Reuben Hartley,
34 Lewis Fairchilds,
35 Jacob Ingerham,
36 Levi Blackburn,
37 John Shearer,
38 Joel Dugger,
39 David Dugger,
40 Thomas Swift,
41 Henry Hately,
42 John Vanderpool,
43 Wm. Brewer,
44 Jacob Brinegar,
45 John Hoppass,
46 John Brower,
47 Wm. S. Edwards,
48 Young Edwards,
49 Alex. T. Conley,
50 Enock Passmore,
51 Joel Rose,
52 Richard Perry,
53 Wm. Vanover,
54 Joseph Colwell,
55 Enock Baldwin,
56 John Rutherford,
57 John Quinley,
58 John Williams,

59 William Taylor, 61
60 62

RANDOLPH COUNTY—FIRST REGIMENT.

1 Zebidee Rush, Captain,
2 Wm. Welborn, Lieut.
3 —— ——, Ensign.
4 Isaac Elliott,
5 Laza Merril,
6 John McGee,
7 Seth Dickson,
8 Isaac Hannah,
9 Matthew Davis,
10 Mark Stud,
11 Solomon Hannah,
12 Wm. Crawford, jr.,
13 Wm. Morris,
14 John Hannah,
15 Wm. Coggin,
16 Solomon Farmer,
17 Jeremiah Bailey,
18 Benj. Fuller,
19 James Skeen,
20 Stephen Hulgan,
21 John Gibson,
22 Richard Gallimore,
23 Jos. Nicolson,
24 James Harvey.
25 John Mills,
26 Jesse Blair,
27 Robert Gray,
28 Andrew Johnston,
29 Benj. Sanders,
30 Nathan Hoedridge,
31 Lewis Walton,
32 Isaac Coltrane,
33 Thos. White,
34 Reuben Rush, Sergt.
35 Thos. Pearce,
36 Wm. Varner,
37 Benj. Cooper,
38 Andrew Fouts,
39 Whitlock Crage,
40 Jacob Lamn,
41 Reuben Alexander,
42 Benj. Wright,
43 Enock Spinks, Sergt.
44 Branson Lawrann, Sergt.
45 Enock Tucker,
46 Wm. Pearce,
47 Michael Cole,
48 Daniel Cast,
49 John Bowdown,
50 John Haskitt,
51 Wm. Swafford,
52 Joseph Hinson,
53 John Wormington,
54 Micajah Brewer,
55 Jonathan Moffet,
56 Wm. Macon,
57 Doran Yeorgan,
58 Thos. Yeorgan,
59 Thos. Pain,
60 Samuel Milliken,
61 Thos. Clark,
62 Daniel Bobins,

63 John Miller,
64 John Jordan,
65 Nathan Goddin,
66 George Williams,
67 Wm. Presnall,
68 Barnabas Hobbs,
69 Johnson King,
70 Benj. Page,
71 Isham Hancock,
72 Jos. Luther,
73 Wm. Laitham.

RANDOLPH COUNTY—SECOND REGIMENT.

1 John Ramsour, Captain.
2 Minos Ward, Lieut.
3 Richard Richardson, En.
4 Elias Hayes, Sergt.
5 Ivy Richardson, Sergt.
6 Aaron Moffet, Sergt.
7 Nathan Swafford, Fifer.
8 Enock Swafford, Drum.
9 Samuel Aldridge,
10 Christian Brower, jr.,
11 David Ameck,
12 Samuel Royer,
13 Aaron Kivet,
14 Jabaz York,
15 Goshen Gennings,
16 Timothy Onde,
17 Reuben Aldrel,
18 Adam York,
19 Wm. Lochlan,
20 James Lowe,
21 John Wren,
22 Isaac McCollum,
23 David Campbell,
24 Wm. Norman,
25 Samuel Russell,
26 Moses Johnston,
27 Wm. Underwood,
28 Daniel Smith,
29 Charles Jones,
30 Vestal Besson,
31 Thos. Underwood,
32 Ira Richardson,
33 Joseph Lamb,
34 Gabrial Lamb,
35 Michael Swean,
36 John Robbins,
37 Marmaduke Vickery,
38 Wm. Robbins. [of Danl.,]
39 John Ruston,
40 Benjamin Johnston,
41 James Philips,
42 Henry Williams,
43 Richard Caveness,
44 James Warren,
45 Joshua Brown,
46 James Cruthes,
47 Ezekiel Matthews,
48 Henry Moffet,
49 John Cravan,
50 Eli Lambert,
51 John Deaton,
52 Wm. Vestal,
53 Gabriel Lamb

SIXTH REGIMENT.

ROWAN COUNTY—FIRST REG'MENT.

1 Thos. Matthews, Capt.
2 Truth Wood, Lieut.
3 Johnsten Neblock, Lieut.
4 Richman Hughes, Lieut.
5 David Cowan, Ensign.
6 Thos. Allison,
7 Michael Bruner,
8 John Albright,
9 Henry Allemony,
10 Jos. Daniels,
11 Zekial Dekison,
12 Jacob Delow,
13 John Weaver,
14 Jos. Chamblers, sr.,
15 Thos. Reaves,
16 Joseph Agnor,
17 George Dunn,
18 Wm. Gardnor,
19 Samuel Bunch,
20 Littleton Rainey,
21 Philip Rumple,
22 Wm. Rogers,
23 Daniel Murphy,
24 Caleb Curfuse,
25 Christ Blackwelder,
26 Jacob Corisher,
27 Judson Brown,
28 John Minster,
29 Michael Biley,
30 Wm. Williamson,
31 Elijah Marlin,
32 Wm. Thompson,
33 Wm. Rice,
34 Peter Traxler,
35 Levi Mays,
36 Wm. Henlin,
37 Jos. Marlin,
38 James Sammons,
39 John Yost,
40 Adam Eddleman,
41 Andrew Boston,
42 John Shulleberger,
43 Wm. Rose,
44 Abraham Zickler,
45 Henry Arenhart,
46 Henry Snider,
47 Nathan Morgan,
48 Jonathan Miller,
49 John Paim,
50 Noah Parks, jr.,
51 Jacob Shover,
52 Michael Pittman,
53 James Hutson,
54 George Knox,
55 Joseph Clotfelter,
56 John Mills,
57 Samuel Graham,
58 Samuel Reaves,
59 Zekiah Cowan,
60 John Cowan,
61 Reuben Yearborough,
62 Kisman Linn,

63 John H. Brandon,
64 Henry Hill, jr.,
65 Wm. Anderson,
66 Henry Stillar,
67 Enock Philips,
68 Fred Menos,
69 Wm. Barber,
70 Jos. Cowan,
71 Walter Rigdon,
72 Burrage Davenport,
73 John McConnihery,
74 John Craig,
75 Thomas Willis,
76 Jacob Weant,
77 Jacob Cross,
78 Thomas Craig,
79 William Long,
80 Samuel Anderson,
81 Solomon Hall,
82 William Anderson,
83 William Price,
84 Matthias Phifer,
85 John Weab,
86 Thomas Renshaw,
87 Wilson Niblock,
88 Daniel Bogar,
89 Martin Clutz,
90 Anthony Pealor,
91 Peter Cruse,
92 John Lippert,
93 John Wasnor,

94 Jacob Poole,
95 John Thomas,
96 Valentine Rimer,
97 George Waller,
98 Thomas Cunningham,
99 Hermon Walton,
100 Peter Brown,
101 Jerry Arey,
102 George Smithall,
103 John Crotzer,
104 John Hartman,
105 George Eller,
106 Peter Agnor,
107 John Gardener,
108 Daniel Swink,
109 Jacob Thomas,
110 Henry Castor,
111 Philip Edlinian,
112 George Agle,
113 Christian Rinehart,
114 Fred Holshausen,
115 Jacob Fulwider,
116 Joseph Cowan, sr.,
117 Joseph Cowan, jr.,
118 Timothy McNealey,
119 David Cooper, B. S.,
120 Samuel McLaughlin,
121 James Short,
122 James McLaughlin, sr.,
123 James Brigs,
124 James Locke.

ROWAN COUNTY—SECOND REGIMENT

1 George Smith, Captain.
2 George Miller, 1st Lieut.
3 John Wilson, Ensign.
4 David Billiny,

5 Samuel Spafford,
6 Elisha Word,
7 Peter Frank,
8 Henry Workman,
9 Isaac Kinney,
10 George Gregson,
11 Peter Whitaker,
12 John Gregor,
13 William McCarn,
14 William Jarrat,
15 John Garvay,
16 Lennard Smith,
17 William Peacock,
18 James Jackson,
19 Jesse Pealer,
20 John Houser,
21 Walter Northern,
22 Mashack Green,
23 John Goss,
24 John Briggs,
25 Jonathan Barclay,
26 Joseph Goss, jr.,
27 Isaac Cobble,
28 Isaac Margan,
29 Alex. Yarborough,
30 Joseph Clark,
31 William Stout,
32 Jesse Harris, jr.,
33 Edward Davis,
34 Peter Riley,
35 William Hughs,
36 Joseph Shoulse,
37 David Garner,
38 James Hughes,
39 Jonathan Coggins,
40 Isaick Russell,

41 Cornelius Loftin, jr.,
42 Edmond Smith,
43 Henry Shemeel,
44 Isaac Thompson,
45 James Johnston,
46 John Shipton,
47 John Davis, jr.,
48 Robert Lacey,
49 James Morgan,
50 William Sorrat, jr.,
51 James Davis,
52 Abraham Owen,
53 James Wiseman,
54 David Smith,
55 James Elliot,
56 Ebenezer Moore,
57 Noah Hunt,
58 Ezekiah Owen,
59 David Grub,
60 John Shoaf,
61 Martin Owen,
62 James Womack,
63 Warren Roberts,
64 Hugh Cunningham,
65 George Grub,
66 Michael Sink,
67 Thismothy Wiseman,
68 John Macray,
69 Thomas Sullivan,
70 Joseph Black,
71 David Bower,
72 Adam Black,
73 Ruedolph Yonce,
74 John Wortman,
75 Philip Myre,
76 William Goodman,

77 John Moss,
78 Daniel Myre,
79 Michael Myre,
80 Matthew Byrns,
81 Christopher Hepler,
82 Nathan Lambeth,
83 Philip Hapler,
84 John Beck,
85 Jacob Hasby,

86 Thomas Owen,
87 Lewis Robling,
88 Peter Winklar,
89 William Ball,
90 John Hill,
91 James Pickler,
92 James Dedman,
93 James Coaths.

ROWAN COUNTY—THIRD REGIMENT.

1
2
3
4 Thomas Mumford,
5 Ishmael Cordle,
6 Jacob Lain,
7 Daniel Click,
8 William Call,
9 James O'Neal,
10 Jesse Hendricks,
11 Drury Jones,
12 Abraham Allen,
13 Enoch Ellis,
14 John Peck,
15 David Harris,
16 William Guy,
17 Thomas Skinner,
18 William Dulin,
19 Stephen Williams,
20 William Edwards,
21 Samuel Poyner,
22 Joshua Hindrix,
23 Isaac Twoney,
24 Jesse Swan,

25 John Hare,
26 William Madden,
27 Samuel Gray,
28 Joseph Forcum,
29 John Taylor,
30 John Brandon,
31 Joseph Beal,
32 William Dockins,
33 Saul Price,
34 Thomas Smoot,
35 Laurence Hudson,
36 John Gabard,
37 Alfred McCullock,
38 George Wilson,
39 Charles Detheridge,
40 John Smart,
41 Thomas Hendrix,
42 Christoper Killer,
43 Frost Nelson,
44 John Ijams,
45 Daniel Earnest,
46 Johnsey Gaither,
47 Daniel Helter,
48 William Nelson,

49 Jacob March,
50 Wilson Austin,
51 John Bryan,
52 John Douge,
53 Peter Mock,
54 John Etchison, jr.,
55 Henry Brickhouse,
56 Jesse Bowden,
57 William Chapman,
58 Elijah Adams,
59 John West,
60 Isaac Creef,
61 Samuel Ward,
62 Smith Cox,
63 Thomas Chaffin,
64 John Renair,
65 Hamilton Gatten,
66 William Foster,
67 Thomas Foster,
68 Thomas Foster,
69 Ignatius McDonnell,
70 John Phillips,
71 William Hainline,

72 Abraham March,
73 Thomas Owens,
74 William Batey,
75 Elisha Leach,
76 Henry Hendrix,
77 Jonathan Cronfell,
78 Jonathan Jones,
79 John Pierce,
80 John Johnson,
81 William Humphries,
82 William Holomon,
83 Abijah Irwin,
84 Conrad Mires,
85 George Gullet,
86 Anthony Silvey,
87 John Sparks,
88 David Sleets,
89 John Thornton,
90 George Howard,
91 Samuel Brannock,
92 Henry Call,
93 William Johnson,
94 John D. Ballard.

ROWAN COUNTY—FOURTH REGIMENT.

1 Moses Welborn, Captain.
2 Moses Welborn, jr., Lieut.
3 Adam Huffman,
4 Christian Zimmerson,
5 Cage Ferril,
6 David Bodenhamer,
7 David Clinard,
8 Daniel Motsingen,
9 David Weer,
10 David Michael,

11 Emsley Burton,
12 George Zink,
13 George Grimes,
14 George Jush,
15 Henry Little,
16 Henry Sawers,
17 Henry Wood,
18 Henry Mires,
19 Hugh Robertson,
20 Henry Barrier,

87 Lovin Bennet,
88 David Sedberry,
89 Jacob Luken,
90 John Mills,

91 Jesse Haygood,
92 Kenneth McClenon,
93 Thomas Williams,
94 Moses Batton.

MONTGOMERY COUNTY—SECOND REGIMENT.

1 David Green, 1st Lieut.
2 Chas. Culpepper, 2d Lieut.
3 George Little, Ensign.
4 Burwell Braswell,
5 William Buress,
6 Andrew Bird,
7 Stephen Crump,
8 Abraham Cooper,
9 Washington Coaley,
10 Leonard Cagle,
11 Thomas Cox,
12 George W. Davidson,
13 James Floyd,
14 Daniel Ford,
15 Richard Greene,
16 Isham Honeycut,
17 Samuel Honeycut,
18 George Hearn,
19 Philip Hegler,
20 Reuben Honeycut,
21 Jacob Hartsell,
22 Leonard Hartsell,
23 Willie Harris,
24 John S. Kindall,
25 Henry Kimry,
26 Henry Kipley,
27 Stephen Kirk,

28 William Lyerly,
29 Joseph Milton,
30 Frederick Mossman,
31 William Moss,
32 Jonathan McDonald,
33 Matthew Parham,
34 George Poplin,
35 Jarrot Pritchard,
36 Jesse Poplin,
37 Michael Ritchie,
38 George Read,
39 Joel Rowland,
40 Jordan Russel,
41 George D. Smith,
42 John Smith,
43 Richard Stoker,
44 George Sydes,
45 James Townsell,
46 William Tomlinson,
47 Jonathan Wilkerson,
48 Hewet Weaks,
49 John Walker,
50 George Whitley,
51 George Palmer,
52 Farley Hopkins,
53 Bennet Solomon,

MECKLENBURG COUNTY—FIRST REGIMENT.

1 James Wilson, Captain.
2 Thos. Boyd, Esq., 1st Lieut.
3 Jos. Blackwood, 2d Lieut.
4 Isaac Price, 3d Lieut.
5 Chas. Hutchinson, Ensign.
6 William Carson,
7 John Wynens,
8 Barzilla Garner,
9 James McCombs,
10 John Barnett,
11 William McKelvia,
12 John Hawkins,
13 Amos Barnett,
14 Ezekiel Alexander,
15 William Shelvey,
16 John C. Garrison,
17 James Means,
18 Thomas Hope,
19 Robert Coldwell,
20 John Price,
21 John Parkes, sr.,
22 Samuel Johnston, jr.,
23 William Wolles, jr.,
24 Mathew Wallis, jr.,
25 Samuel Parks,
26 Robert Coldwell, jr.,
27 Ann Wynns,
28 John Sadler,
29 John Barnhill,
30 Jacob Julin,
31 James Henderson,
32 Elisha McCracken,
33 Christopher Jove,
34 Robert Dunn, jr.,
35 Andrew M. Parish,
36 William Dunn,
37 Andrew Lewing, jr.,
38 Francis Perry,
39 John Farra,
40 John Lewing,
41 James Carothers,
42 James Dinkins,
43 Robert Bigham, jr.,
44 John Johnston,
45 William Johnston,
46 Samuel Neeley,
47 David Reed,
48 Joseph Whiteside,
49 Augustus Miles,
50 Mathew West,
51 Thomas Connel,
52 William Benhill,
53 Robert McKnight,
54 Michael Baker,
55 Abel Baker,
56 Hugh McDowell,
57 William Kerr,
58 John Hawkins,
59 Aaron Baker,
60 Andrew Walker,
61 James Porter,
62 John Beaty,
63 Samuel Bigham,
64 Simon V. Pelt,
65 John Beaty,
66 Peavon Jackson,
67 John Blackburn,
68 John Wilson, jr.,

69 John Brown,
70 William S. Norman,
71 Daniel Baxter,
72 Benjamin Wilson,
73 Thomas Elliott,
74 James Conner,
75 Daniel Davis,
76 William Elliott,
77 Richard Hartley,
78 George Duckworth,
79 James Meek,
80 James Alexander,
81 Joel Jones,
82 James Sloan,
83 Isaac Morrison, jr.,
84 John Parker,
85 James Mentith,
86 Joseph Williams,
87 Andrew Prim,

88 Robert A. Orsburn,
89 John White,
90 Michael Channels,
91 Gabriel Ferrel,
92 Giles Irwin,
93 John Ferrel,
94 Joseph Wallis,
95 Henry Hunter, jr.,
96 William Ferrel,
97 James Steele,
98 Nelson Gray,
99 John Steele,
100 Robert Montgomery,
101 Richard Peoples,
102 James A. Braddy,
103 Joseph McKellerand,
104 George Goforth,
105 John D. Alexander.

MECKLENBURG COUNTY—SECOND REGIMENT.

1 David Moore, Captain.
2 John Wilson, 1st Lieut.
3 Solomon Reed, 2d Lieut.
4 William John, 3d Lieut.
5 Albertes Alexander, En.
6 Richard Barflet,
7 Matthew McCall,
8 James McCall,
9 Henry Thompson,
10 Alexander Stewart,
11 William Cheery,
12 James Robertson,
13 Samuel Yandles,
14 James Harbeson,

15 William Shelby,
16 Gideon Freeman,
17 John Morrison,
18 John Allen,
19 John Forsythe,
20 Games Barnes,
21 Moses Purser,
22 Micajah Barns,
23 Osburn Wilkinson,
24 Robert Allen,
25 Groves Vinson,
26 William Helmes,
27 Charles Helmes,
28 Fredric Starns,

29 Nathaniel Starns,
30 Morris Shehorn,
31 William Yerby.
32 James Rone,
33 John Belk,
34 Dan'l. Rich,
35 John Junderbusk,
36 Henry Flowers,
37 David B. Yaudles,
38 Salamachus Alexander,
39 Abdon Alexander,
40 Osburn Smart,
41 Elisha Smart,
42 John McCullock,
43 Robert Cook,
44 Stephen Hanson,
45 Moses Craig,
46 Wm. McCoy,
47 Robert Howood,
48 William Woodall,
49 Jacob Gray,
50 Aaron Howie,
51 Andrew King,
52 Joshua Finsher,
53 Samuel Rape,
54 Samuel Rener,
55 James Hambleton,
56 Moses Vick,
57 John Phillips,
58 James Train,
59 George Berns,
60 William Fisher,
61 Daniel Button,
62 Hugh McAlroy,
63 Jess Ivey,
64 John Hauley,

65 Benjamin Spravey,
66 Joseph Reed,
67 Adam Karr,
68 John Matthews,
69 George Parke,
70 William Reed,
71 Wm. Downs,
72 Wilson Taylor,
73 John Maglauchlin,
74 Joseph Hall,
75 William Maygechee,
76 Henry Hargett,
77 William Hargett,
78 Joel Helmer,
79 John Crowel,
80 Peter Chainey,
81 David Harkey,
82 George Tuter,
83 Elias Stilwell,
84 James Morrison,
85 Moses Tomberlin,
86 Edward Reak,
87 Neel Morrison,
88 James Costley,
89 Thomas S. Cochran,
90 Wm. Housten, jr.,
91 Robert Cochran,
92 Hugh Wilson,
93 Reuben Hood,
94 Charles Dennis,
95 Samuel Neele,
96 John Harkey,
97 James Rogers,
98 Robt. Harrison,
99 John Hodge,
100 Richard Lambert,

101 David W. Story,
102 John Fuller,
103 James Shaw,

104 Lewis Webb,
105 James Story, sr.

CABARRUS COUNTY.

1 Even S. Willey, Captain.
2 George Fogleman, Lieut.
3 Christopher Milken, En.
4 Alex. W. Harris, 1st Sergt.
5 Ozni Rogers, 2d Sergt.
6 John Long, 3d Sergt.
7 A. Kemmons, 4th Sergt.
8 Peter Alles, 1st Cor'l.
9 John Drye, 2d Cor'l.
10 Daniel Drye, 3d Cor'l.
11 Andrew Trulman, 4th do.
12 Daniel Mooss,
13 Daniel Ritengous,
14 Henry Hover,
15 Andrew Blackwater,
16 John Nusman,
17 John Goger,
18 Jacob Overcast,
19 Jonathan Stanford,
20 Alexander Bain,
21 Methias Passenger,
22 Jacob Stirwatt,
23 William Bell,
24 John Hall,
25 William Pelt,
26 Samuel Neel,
27 James Ross,
28 George Long,
29 James Gray,
30 George Kegle,

31 David White,
32 John Mathews,
33 James Love,
34 James McMahew,
35 John Haskey,
36 Adam Ritchey,
37 George Trutman,
38 James Buchanon,
39 John Snider,
40 George Miller,
41 Moses Conel,
42 Andrew Yaw,
43 Jacob Bager,
44 John Bager,
45 David Nisler,
46 William Scott,
47 Jacob Croner,
48 Christopher Hattaman,
49 John Mitchell,
50 Peter Walter,
51 Paul Walter,
52 Charles Hartman,
53 George Letort,
54 Jacob File,
55 Cirus Alexander,
56 Silas McCinlay,
57 Richard D. Plunkett,
58 James Welch,
59 John Eliot,
60 Andrew Wolker,

61 John Clay,
62 John Davis,
63 John Morris,
64 Robert Dixon,
65 Isaac McClerland,
66 Hugh Dixon,
67 Hezekiah Davis,
68 Jacob Goodman,
69 John McCinley,
70 John Bradshaw,
71 Isaac Howell,
72 John Johnston,
73 William Houston,
74 John Mullen,
75 John Green,
76 William Simons,
77 John McLain,
78 Joel S. Houston,
79 Henry Petery,
80 Jacob Cline,
81 Tobias Mesthinghams,
82 James Hadley,
83 James Nicholson,
84 John Davis,
85 William G. Harris,
86 David Winecof,
87 Samuel Holebrooks,

88 Cirus Wedenton,
89 George Goodnight,
90 David McRee,
91 William Houston,
92 Tobias Goodman,
93 Joseph G. Spires,
94 John Garman,
95 Beverly Gray,
96 John Sossiman,
97 Christopher Osburn,
98 Durum Cuzine,
99 Caleb Blackwater,
100 Moses Archabb,
101 Samuel H. Cochran,
102 John Cuzine,
103 David Linker,
104 Adam Cariker,
105 David Miskingham,
106 Jacob Tucker,
107 Jacob Hegles,
108 Jacob Funn,
109 Daniel Funn,
110 David Fink,
111 Matthias Miskingham,
112 Henry Himpman,
113 George Barnhart.

IREDELL COUNTY.

1 John McKee, Captain.
2 William Kerr, Lieutenant.
3 Thomas Forterner, Ensign.
4 Andrew McKenzie, -
5 William Hicks,
6 Charles Summers,

7 Alexis Alexander,
8 James Crawford,
9 William Jacobs,
10 John Bone,
11 Alexander Watts,
12 John Freeland,

13 Alexander Hall,
14 Andrew W. Davidson,
15 John Woodard,
16 Daniel Brawley,
17 Aaron Downs,
18 James McKnight,
19 John Sloan,
20 John Huggins,
21 John Atwell,
22 James Maulholland,
23 Robert Brawley,
24 Ruel Walles,
25 Hiram Lawson,
26 James McRee,
27 John McDate,
28 Robert Elliott,
29 David McRee,
30 Jeremiah Whiley,
31 James B. Thomas,
32 Angus McRoy,
33 Robert McFarland,
34 Samuel McFarland,
35 Ralph Stewart,
36 Henry Morrison,
37 James Alexander,
38 Jacob Bostion,
39 John Carter,
40 John Wilkinson,
41 Tobias Miller,
42 Martin Cryder,
43 Thomas Elliott,
44 Hamelton McClatchy,
45 Abner Feamster,
46 George Irwin,
47 James Gilley,
48 William Morrison,
49 Jaran Fortune,
50 Joseph Wright,
51 Andrew Davis,
52 Rhoda Westmoreland,
53 Abner York,
54 Samuel Honeycutt,
55 Alfred Kerr,
56 Robert Timpleton,
57 Richard F. Houston,
58 James Alley,
59 Peterson Westmoreland,
60 William Mayhew,
61 Joseph Rogers, jun.,
62 James Randels,
63 John Lippard,
64 Joseph Parks,
65 Matthew Calaher,
66 Windle Holshouser,
67 Abraham Ritchey,
68 David Clodfelter,
69 Neal McKay, jun.,
70 John Wilson,
71 Neal McKay, sen.,
72 Andrew Neil,
73 John Fleming,
74 James Morten,
75 John Erwin, sen.,
76 John Steel,
77 William Lipperd,
78 William King,
79 John Harchie,
80 William Allison,
81 William Gay,
82 Samuel Archibald,
83 Ninia Steel,
84 Robert McGuire,

85 Thomas Allison,
86 Maxwell Chambers,
87 George Mair,
88 Samuel Timpleton,
89 Daniel Lewis,
90 Kinchen Walls,
91 Robert Lazenby,
92 Lebishes Gaither,
93 Greenberry H. Johnston,
94 John Fitzgerril,
95 David Holleman,
96 Leonard Wishon,
97 William Mason,
98 Solomon Summers,
99 John McLelland,
100 John Claggett,
101 William Summers,
102 Humphrey Tomlinson,
103 Thomas Kerney,
104 James Thompson, Captain.
105 Isaac Smith, Lieutenant.
106 Perry Tomlinson, Ensign.
107 Ezekiel Morgan,
108 Jacob Privit,
109 William Mitchell,
110 James Williams,
111 John Mears,
112 Robert Coleman,
113 Mark Marlow,
114 Gideon Deboard,
115 Anderson Johnson,
116 Ezekiel Mires,
117 William Bogle, -
118 Charles Hatten, jun.,
119 Elisha Farmer,
120 Isaac Kena,

121 James Bogle,
122 James Reynold,
123 James King,
124 James Haroin,
125 Lemuel Beckham,
126 Samuel Meadows,
127 William Jolley,
128 David Roberts,
129 James Barnard,
130 Henry E. Williams,
131 Enock Gaither,
132 John Dillard,
133 Adam Campbell,
134 William Marlow,
135 Archibald Cast,
136 Plesabo Hueston,
137 Isaac Wailes,
138 David Marmon,
139 Thomas Marmon,
140 John Maiden,
141 Joseph Milsaps,
142 Alexander Lackey,
143 Dearling Allen,
144 Elihugh King,
145 John Guider,
146 Nathan Guiltney,
147 William Guiltney,
148 Robert Guiltney,
149 Wallis Privit,
150 John S. Patterson,
151 John Griffith,
152 Ruton Jordan,
153 Ezekiel Edis,
154 George Flowers,
155 James Dishman,
156 Richard Cook,

157 James Bentley,
158 John Arrington,
159 Alexander McHague,
160 Arnold Holland,
161 John Maxwell,

162 Joseph Shelby,
163 Alexander Long,
164 James King,
165 James Gregory,
166 John King.

LINCOLN COUNTY.—FIRST REGIMENT.

1 James Finley, Captain.
2 Wm. J. Wilson, 1st Lieut.
3 Richard Cowan, 2d Lieut.
4 Andrew Barry, 3d Lieut.
5 John Beard, Ensign.
6 Ambrose Gaultney,
7 Andrew Slinkard,
8 John Hogan,
9 Henry Sadler,
10 George Berry,
11 Jacob Troutman,
12 William Short,
13 James Graham,
14 Isaac Murrell,
15 John Hunt,
16 Benedict Jetton,
17 Benjamin Proctor,
18 John Litz,
19 William Little,
20 Richard Proctor,
21 William Nance, jun.,
22 James White,
23 William Nance,
24 William Tucker,
25 Ambrose Cobb,
26 Jacob Cloninger,
27 Samuel Pew,
28 Thomas Sadler,

29 Needam Wingate,
30 David Smith, jun.,
31 Robinson Moore,
32 William Meginess,
33 John Rhodes,
34 John Meginess,
35 William Sutton,
36 John Mahew,
37 Bedford Childers,
38 Thomas Tucker,
39 Samuel Abernathy,
40 Red Errowood,
41 Robert Lucky,
42 Charles Edwards,
43 Anthony Long,
44 Freeman Shelton,
45 Reuben Grice,
46 John Bynum,
47 William Hill,
48 Willis Ballard,
49 William Killian,
50 Robinson Harris,
51 Anthony Hinkle,
52 Ashman Gwin,
53 James Hicks,
54 Daniel Killian,
55 Frederic Killian,
56 Edward Carroll,

57 John Jinkens,
58 Thomas Dickson,
59 John Venable,
60 Austin Ford,
61 Peter Titman,
62 James McCarver,
63 William Rockford,
64 Robert Alexander,
65 William McCarver,
66 Wiertt Jenkins,
67 Reuben Jenkins,
68 Jacob Rhine,
69 Adam Rhine,
70 Solomon Rhine,
71 John Rhodes,
72 John Bynum,
73 David Costner,
74 Jacob Smith,
75 George House,
76 Amos Robeson,
77 Alexander McCullock,
78 Keece Price,
79 Moses Grissom,
80 Thomas Groves,
81 Hiram Harris,

82 James Shannon,
83 Jacob Fite,
84 Ezekiel McClure,
85 John Merner,
86 Samuel Williams,
87 James McClure,
88 William Lettimore,
89 John Damon,
90 Anderson Wells,
91 William Hamilton,
92 John Leeper,
93 John Glover,
94 Alexander Rankin,
95 William Reed,
96 Steward Jinkens,
97 William Bluford,
98 John Hanks,
99 Ebner Rumfelt,
100 John Carthy,
101 Jacob Kenedy,
102 John Oats,
103 John Parmer,
104 William Adams,
105 John Blackwood.

LINCOLN COUNTY—SECOND REGIMENT.

1 Daniel Hoke, Captain.
2 John B. Harris, 1st Lieut.
3 Gilbert Milliken, 2d Lieut.
4 Isaac Mauney, 3d Lieut.
5 Peter Hoke, Ensign.
6 John Carpenter,
7 Henry Huffsteddler,
8 Moses Barr,
9 Jacob Plunk,
10 William Carpenter,
11 Joseph Black,
12 William Ferguson,
13 Cudias Smith,
14 Jonas Rudisil,
15 Peter Mauney,
16 David Kezer,

17 Peter Eaker,
18 George Seller,
19 Peter Costner,
20 John Huffsteddler,
21 William Guntlessey,
22 Daniel Glotfelder,
23 Elias Glotfelder,
24 John Teague,
25 George Glotfelder,
26 Rudolph Glotfelder,
27 Lewis Huet,
28 Philip Skerd,
29 Thomas Smith,
30 John Bumgarner,
31 Willie Hops,
32 Archibald Cobb,
33 Elisha Saunders,
34 Joshua Hunter,
35 Conrade Heldebrand,
36 Peter Reymer,
37 Bostian Best,
38 John Housar,
39 Solomon Shoup,
40 Samuel Bigham,
41 William Willis,
42 Charles Williams,
43 James Chapman,
44 Nathaniel Pew,
45 Jacob Houser,
46 John Watterson,
47 Joseph Wear,
48 James Patterson,
49 Preston Goforth,
50 Hugh Spurlin,
51 Isaac Mullinax,
52 James Elliott,

53 Thomas Earswood,
54 George Goforth,
55 Jacob Harman,
56 Robert Barber,
57 Young Marden,
58 Thomas Black,
59 David Dickson,
60 Hardy Long,
61 Solomon Childers,
62 Christopher Carpenter,
63 James Endsley,
64 Anthony Clerk,
65 David Bookout,
66 Archibald Endsley,
67 John Wright,
68 Thomas Crags,
69 Philip Haynes,
70 John Whitworth,
71 Joshua Howell,
72 Samuel Collins,
73 John Monser,
74 Casper Bolick,
75 George Bowman,
76 Henry Lickman,
77 Matthew Boovey,
78 Charles Ward,
79 William Harman,
80 David Huntley,
81 Martin Lickman,
82 George Turner,
83 Abraham Tray,
84 Henry Lickman, jun.,
85 Samuel Sullivan,
86 Christian Bollinger,
87 Christopher Hope,
88 Michael Ingle,

89 William Cline,
90 John Shafer,
91 Henry Houser,
92 Ransom Husky,
93 Matthias Barringer,
94 Michael Dillinger,
95 Daniel Blackburn,
96 Jacob Harner,
97 Aaron Moore,
98 David Dick,
99 Joseph Heldebrand,
100 Joseph Lenhart,
101 James Lemons,
102 Daniel Fullbright,
103 Francis Summitt,
104 Daniel Summitt,
105 Nicholas Carpenter,
106 Peter Lorance,
107 Joseph Ashe,
108 John Earney,
109 Alfred Sherril,
110 Elias Shine,
111 Conrade Ward,
112 Avery Guant,
113 Andrew Yant,
114 Phillips Hedrick,
115 Benedict Levant,
116 John Cowan,
117 George Shook,
118 Jacob Fullbright,
119 Leonard Kagle,
120 Ephraim Christoph,
121 William Echard,
122 John Hadrick,

123 Aaron Downson,
124 Peter Kellar,
125 Gabriel Isaac,
126 Samuel Peterson,
127 Frederic Knup,
128 Francis King,
129 Peter Raby,
130 Michael Sattonfield,
131 Jonathan Robinson,
132 Miles Abernathy,
133 David Hawn,
134 Valentine Taylor,
135 John Stamy,
136 Peter Frey,
137 James Gilleband,
138 John Snyder,
139 James Bridges,
140 James Jones,
141 Benjamin Newman,
142 Sterling Singleton,
143 John Ward,
144 John Gottelder,
145 James Fisher,
146 Samuel Selton,
147 William Black,
148 David Warlic,
149 Elisha Winson,
150 Nimrod Winson,
151 Henry Killian,
152 Solomon Killian,
153 Daniel Coulter,
154 Henry Coulter,
155 John Shufford,

RUTHERFORD COUNTY—FIRST REGIMENT.

1 John Oliver, Captain.
2 John Moore, 1st Lieut.
3 Joseph Taylor, 3d Lieut.
4 Lindsey Fortune, Ensign.
5 Adam Hampton,
6 Vincent Wood,
7 John McHan,
8 James Hill,
9 Jonathan Mullens,
10 William Hicks,
11 Jonathan Hampton,
12 Harbert Horton,
13 Ransom Edgarton,
14 David Womack,
15 Hamilton Freeman,
16 Carter Johnson,
17 Reuben Melton,
18 Robert Webb,
19 Leonard Deck,
20 John Melton,
21 Richard E. Allen,
22 Thomas Wamock,
23 Jeremiah Webb,
24 Asaph Hill,
25 Moses White,
26 Samuel Bickerstaff,
27 Robert Johnston,
28 John Crow,
29 Thomas Stockton,
30 John Bradey,
31 Josiah Jones,
32 Isaac Rhom,
33 Benjamin Grayson,
34 William Grayson,
35 William Melton,
36 Elijah Pool,
37 William Hunt,
38 Elijah Sparks,
39 Thomas Brackett,
40 Simon Steet,
41 William Hutchins,
42 William Steet,
43 James Taylor,
44 Hugh Watson,
45 Daniel Watson,
46 William Reed,
47 John Guffy,
48 Archy Reed Guffey,
49 James S. Guffey,
50 Jesse W. Grove,
51 Benjamin Andrews,
52 James Thompson,
53 James Moore,
54 George Ross,
55 James Irvine,
56 William Sprat,
57 Richard Newcam,
58 David Hodge,
59 Rial Hill,
60 Henry Camp,
61 Noah Sergant,
62 Benjamin Ketor,
63 Wade Bates,
64 Eli Hanes,
65 James Ketor,
66 William Marshall,
67 Micajah Bankenship,
68 James Nancy,

69 Ephraim Cook,
70 William Wallace,
71 Jacob Venzant,
72 John Cook,
73 Howard Williams,
74 Henry Morris,
75 Zedekiah Harris,
76 William Whiteside,
77 Sterling Lewin,
78 John Hunter,
79 Mark Moore,
80 William Harris,
81 Andrew H. Elliott,
82 James Ward,
83 Miner Winn,
84 Jesse Morgan.

RUTHERFORD COUNTY—SECOND REGIMENT

1 Abraham Irvine, Captain.
2 John Fonetren, Lieut.
3 Joseph Willis, Ensign.
4 Micah Davis,
5 John Blonton,
6 Bayard McCraw,
7 James Wilkins,
8 Jesse Blanton,
9 John Rippy,
10 Elijah Hamrick,
11 Richard Bridges,
12 Samuel Fonetren,
13 Absalom Ellis,
14 Nehemiah Padgett,
15 Benjamin Burns,
16 Valentine Martin,
17 Richard Lea,
18 George Bridges,
19 Jesse Rippy,
20 Samuel McIntire,
21 Robert Smith,
22 Joseph Laguire,
23 Henry Ledbetaer,
24 Daniel King,
25 James McIntire,
26 Henry Weston,
27 Thomas Downey,
28 James Wilson,
29 Alfred Moore,
30 James Crane,
31 Samuel Wilson,
32 Jesse Braddy,
33 Solomon Harrelson,
34 David Lissum,
35 John Bailey,
36 Henry White,
37 Alfred Moore,
38 Constant Brooks,
39 James Wilson,
40 James Dickus,
41 Jenky Jenkins,
42 Lewis Johnson,
43 Elisha Stacy,
44 William Holland,
45 Zekariah McDaniel,
46 John Green,
47 Darlin Webb,
48 Gilbert Harrel,
49 Richard Bostick,
50 Henry Grigs,

51 Jacob Willis,
52 Jacob McKinney,
53 John White,
54 Henry Workman,
55 William Newton,
56 John Rooker,
57 Hugh McRannolds,
58 William York,
59 Blueford Randal,
60 James Arrowood,
61 Jesse Grigg,
62 Bannester Grigg,
63 Richard Gibbs,
64 William Wilkey,
65 Mosse Black,
66 Samuel Julin,
67 Jabez Murry,
68 John Smith,
69 John Barker,
70 James Chitwood,
71 Jesse Ledford,
72 Thomas Hill,
73 Abel Beaty,
74 William Dedman,
75 Allen Mathis,
76 John Handcastle,
77 Martin Beam,
78 Samuel Mode,
79 Thomas Garner,
80 William McEntire,
81 Isham Julin,
82 John Alexander,
83 Elijah Holifield,
84 Robert Scruggs,
85 Joel Williams,
86 Abraham Pagett,
87 William Lea,
88 Elias Scruggs,
89 John Robeson,
90 David Beheler,
91 John Amos,
92 David Pope,
93 Arther Clarke.

RUTHERFORD COUNTY—THIRD REGIMENT.

1 Ephraim Carruth,
2 James Braden,
3 William Newman,
4 Andrew Thompson,
5 Leander P. Carruth,
6 James Ruth,
7 Joseph Wood,
8 Robert Baicly,
9 William Colier,
10 James Crawford,
11 Noah Hampton,
12 Austen Musuck,
13 Thomas Prator,
14 Gabriel Wilmath,
15 John Ownsby,
16 Sims Ownsby,
17 John Lowther,
18 Isaac Goforth,
19 Cornelius Clemmons,
20 Greenbury Griffen,
21 John Dolton,
22 David Turlly,

23 John Going,
24 William Wootan,
25 Charles Edwards,
26 Pleasant Whirly,
27 Elijah Dolten,
28 Thornton Randal,
29 Dennis Duff,
30 Edward McGuin,
31 Ephraim Jackson,
32 Luke Woldson,
33 John Hiflin,
34 Samuel Thompson,
35 John Skipper,
36 Burges Smith,
37 Jonathan Ellison,
38 George McKinney,
39 Jeremiah Smith,
40 William Thompson,
41 Robert Cockrum,
42 Joseph Studman,
43 James Menice,
44 John Sutton, jun.,
45 Thomas Dills, sen.,
46 James Henderson,
47 William Giles,
48 William Sutton, jun.,
49 John Logan,
50 James Miller Erwin,
51 William Wilson,
52 William Clinton,
53 Edley Hambleton,
54 George Musick,
55 Archibald Sohlar,
56 An'd Young,
57 Claton Brown,
58 William Ownby,
59 John Dillbark, jun.,
60 Burrel Utly,
61 Thomas Blackurl,
62 George Fry,
63 Caleb Williams,
64 Joshua Wells,
65 Thomas Steedman,
66 Solomon Blackurl,
67 Richard Sisemore,
68 Joseph Wilson,
69 John Smith.

BURKE COUNTY—FIRST REGIMENT.

1 Frederick Sluillei, Captain.
2 Elrod Pobete, 1st Lieut.
3 John F. O'Neil, 2d Lieut.
4 John Riel, Ensign.
5 William Brittain, 1st Serg't
6 Jacob Keller, 2d Sergeant.
7 John Walker, 3d Sergeant.
8 Henry M. Oneal, 4th Serg't
9 Swipton Lowdon, Drum.
10 Stephen Ballow, Fifer;
11 Ezekal England,
12 Peter Wisenghunt,
13 John Williams,
14 Peter Mull,
15 Frederick Bottles,
16 Garrat Garratson,
17 James Largant,
18 Thomas Moody,

19 Philip Pitts,
20 William Sorrals,
21 Joseph Thompson,
22 James McFalls,
23 Reuben Walker,
24 Samuel Lockrage,
25 William Oglesby,
26 Archibald Oglesby,
27 Thomas Michaels,
28 Robert Good,
29 William Reed,
30 Andrew England,
31 Joseph Baker,
32 John Bottles,
33 Elijah Walker,
34 John Good,
35 William Hartley,
36 Joseph Murphy,
37 John H. Singling,
38 Philip Shufler,
39 Joseph England. M.
40 William England, jun.,
41 Solomon Good, jun.,
42 John Powell,
43 Michael Wisinghunt,
44 Demmon Dossey, jun.,
45 John Derryburry,
46 Alexander Deal,
47 Henry Deal,
48 John Jones,
49 John Poteete,
50 Peter A. Bry,
51 Michael Wehunt,
52 John Martin,
53 William Deal,
54 John Black,
55 John Kennedy,
56 John Hartley,
57 Abraham Deal,
58 William Brackett,
59 John Airwood,
60 George Reider,
61 William Wenters,
62 John Eavins,
63 Elijah Powell,
64 Lewis Powell,
65 Henry Wilds,
66 John Bial,
67 Jacob A. Bey,
68 Andrew Kincaid,
69 James McDowell,
70 John Hayse,
71 Elijah Hayse,
72 Isaac Tunmire,
73 Henry Winker,
74 John Killian,
75 John Purson,
76 Thomas Bryant,
77 Perian Daniel,
78 Jesse Smith,
79 John Smalley,
80 Henry Kyles,
81 William Pyott,
82 Archibald Gibbs,
83 James Hill,
84 Micajah Lisk.
85
86
87
88

BURKE COUNTY—SECOND REGIMENT.

1
2
3
4 Larkin Kerby,
5 Andrew Reid,
6 Joel Williams,
7 William Turner,
8 William Roberts,
9 James Collins,
10 John Fincannon,
11 Thomas Bean,
12 Jesse Berry,
13 Abraham Melone,
14 Samuel Smith,
15 John Bovey, jun.,
16 John King,
17 Leps Helton,
18 Joshua Harshaw,
19 Henry Cook,
20 Alexander Campbell,
21 John Ernest,
22 Solomon Crisp,
23 James Fletcher,
24 William Coffey,
25 Colbert Hays,
26 John Harriss,
27 Reuben Coffey,

28 James Gilbert,
29 John Sumpter,
30 Joseph Owens,
31 John Prock,
32 Alexander West,
33 Samuel Howell,
34 Thomas Blair,
35 Justice Beech,
36 Frederick Tucker,
37 John Brown,
38 Christian Haas,
39 John Litten, (in dispute)
40 Robert Riner,
41 Philip Rough,
42 Joseph Kerby,
43 Jonathan Penly,
44 Lemuel Holt,
45 John Fritt,
46 William Reed,
47 Matthew Winkler,
48 Daniel Whittenburg,
49 Thomas King,
50 Enock Pressnill,
51 Thomas Dorsett,
52 Eli Justice,
53 Thomas Forrester.

BURKE COUNTY—THIRD REGIMENT.

1 Jason Carson, Captain.
2 James Burgen, Lieutenant.
3 Pleasant Cashin,
4 Burret R'ckets,

5 James Smith,
6 Jonathan Allison,
7 John Ross,
8 Dennis Ross

9 Ben. Curtis,
10 Lavender Fortune,
11 George Darmald,
12 Alexander Portet,
13 George Edmison,
14 Johnson Allison,
15 Samuel Cockhorn,
16 William Barley,
17 Swinefield Heil,
18 Henry Crown,
19 William Guy,
20 Jesse Henil,
21 William Hughs,
22 Andrew McKinly,
23 Abner Devenporte,
24 William Waldriss,
25 Elis Waldriss,
26 Thomas Devenporte,
27 Manual Lamb,
28 William Dickson,
29 William Voun,
30 Austin Pack,
31 William Bright,
32 Joab Goodbread,
33 Joseph Lanner,
34 Thomas James,
35 Thomas Gribble,
36 Mitchel Parham,
37 William Henderson,
38 Joseph Civins,
39 John Queen,
40 John Morris,
41 William Duncan,
42 John W. Carson,
43 Stogdol Wilson,
44 David Curtis,
45 Man Shots,
46 Thomas Hancy,
47 Daniel Morrow,
48 John Biddicks,
49 James Reves,
50 Jacob Martin,
51 William Jones,
52 William Lackey.

BUNCOMBE COUNTY—FIRST REGIMENT.

1 Clayton Neel, Captain.
2 Andrew Wilson, Lieut.
3 John Sutton, Private.
4 Samuel McCarson,
5 Charles McLain,
6 Lewis Herrin,
7 William Wilson,
8 James Brevard,
9 Robert Wilson,
10 Thomas Jones,
11 Charles Adams,
12 James Erwin,
13 Cajer Smith,
14 Abraham McGuffee,
15 George Justin,
16 James Jones,
17 Nathan Fletcher,
18 John Justice,
19 Jesse Casse,
20 Andrew Lockhart,
21 James Maxwell,
22 William Justice,

23 William Case,
24 Andrew Lockhart,
25 James Maxwell,
26 Archibald Edmiston,
27 James S. Smith,
28 Jesse Causby,
29 William Carn,
30 Davis Rhodes, .
31 Ninnion Edmeston,
32 William Cincard,
33 Ezekiel Sandelin,
34 John Osborn,
35 Jeremiah Osborn,
36 Daniel Allen,
37 Henry Studer,
38 Matthias Little,
39 Samuel Corn,
40 James Tweed,
41 Hugh Johnston,
42 David Evins,
43 Enock Williams,
44 Robert Orr,
45 James Nickolson,

46 Peter Sheperd,
47 William W. Lain,
48 Richard Sceutill,
49 Daniel Hefner,
50 Eli Mearill,
51 Ballard Lake,
52 John Clayton,
53 George D. Davis,
54 David Fains,
55 Burges Lake,
56 George Erwin,
57 Samuel King,
58 Walter Burwell,
59 James Clark,
60 Matthew Wilson,
61 James Kitchins,
62 David Johnson,
63 Alexander Jordan,
64 Jonathan Lincard,
65 Grady Johnson,
66 Solomon Farker,
67 John Galloway,
68 Lewis Ransom.

BUNCOMBE COUNTY—SECOND REGIMENT.

1
2
3 John Smith,
4 John Hawkins,
5 Aaron Javette,
6 Elsy Rundles,
7 Joseph Gudger,
8 John Gooch,
9 Joseph Wright,
10 Nimrod Merril,

11 Amos Lanning,
12 Eli Rimon,
13 Aaron Banks,
14 Andrew Rorran,
15 Thomas Snelson,
16 Thomas Rogers,
17 George Lindsey,
18 John Frisby,
19 William Spivey,
20 David Rogers,

21 David Vance,
22 James Wever,
23 William Button,
24 David K. Baty,
25 George Corn,
26 Richard Daff,
27 James Dillard,
28 Robert Britton,
29 James Rogers,
30 Jacob Carber,
31 Joseph Carver,
32 Joseph Millsaps,
33 William Mason,
34 David Millar,
35 Malley Reeves,
36 Thomas Jones,
37 Irea Javiette,
38 Joseph Hays,
39 George Brock,
40 Elisha Spivey,
41 Jacob Fortunberry,
42 Abraham Penland,
43 Aswell Phillips,

44 James Rice,
45 William Crage,
46 Samuel Mafee,
47 William Murray,
48 John M. Patton
49 William Wafer,
50 John Henry,
51 John Palmer,
52 Andrew Garron,
53 John Gearron,
54 William H. Murrey,
55 M. Haustin Patton,
56 Jacob Jaron,
57 William Gudger,
58 Thomas Murry,
59 Thomas Taylor,
60 Samuel Jinkins,
61 Adam Garron,
62 John Patton,
63 Cilas Rhea,
43 Azra Jinkins,
65 Samuel J. Mavey.

BUNCOMBE COUNTY—THIRD REGIMENT.

1 Levi Bailey, Captain.
2 Joseph Shepard, 1st Lieut.
3 David Hughey, Ensign.
4 William Keith,
5 Henry Keith,
6 James Wood,
7 Mark Roberts,
8 Thomas Roberts,
9 Edward Robertson,
10 Reuben Keith,

11 John Cody,
12 Tavner Moore,
13 Joseph Ponder,
14 Thomas Gaines Roberts,
15 Nimrod Buckner,
16 Robert Roberts,
17 Jesse Giles,
18 John Green,
19 William Carson,
20 John Greenwood,

21 James Hurstle,
22 Samuel Hughey,
23 Shadrack Guthry,
24 Garrat Dewesee,
25 William Williams,
26 Augustine Prestwood,
27 John Lams,
28 James Lams,
29 Britain Williams,
30 John Arrewood,
31 Benjamin Webb,
32 Richard Holland,
33 Joseph Callihorn,
34 Absalom Medcalf,
35 Sperlin Bowman,
36 John Cornwell,
37 John Garrett,
38 John Stanton,
39 John Slanlon,
40 George Stanton,
41 John Randolph,
42 George Robertson,
43 William Byrd,

44 John Edwards,
45 Samuel Byrd,
46 William Dayton,
47 James Edwards,
48 William Taylor,
49 Jacob Silver,
50 James Angel,
51 James Killian,
52 James McMahan,
53 Maxamilian Harriss,
54 Uriah Honeycutt,
55 Angel Cook,
56 John Anglin,
57 John Poteet,
58 James Poteet,
59 William Calliway,
60 Abner State,
61 Jesse Radford,
62 Edmond Edwards,
63 Thomas Wilson,
64 Thomas Lawson,
65 Joseph Ray.

HAYWOOD COUNTY.

1 John McClure, Captain.
2 Elijah Dever, Lieut.
3 John Dever, Ensign.
4 John Welsh,
5 Joseph Cathey,
6 Jethro Cathey,
7 Christian Howel,
8 Benjamin Hatfield,
9 Jonathan Hains,
10 James Campble,

11 Andrew McClor,
12 William McClure,
13 Benjamin McMullen,
14 Charles Evenes,
15 Richard Clark,
16 Abraham Eaton,
17 William Goodwin,
18 Lazarus Eaton,
19 James Chambers,
20 William Chambers,

21 James McFarland,
22 Bailey Fleming,
23 Champ Langsford,
24 David Elder,
25 John Dillord,
26 John Oliver,
27 Benjamin Enlos,
28 Edward Coiter,
29 Jesse Enloe,
30 James A. Ellis,
31 George Penland,
32 William Rogers,
31 James Williams,
34 John Telley,
35 Robert Penland,
36 Hirom Gray,
37 William Murray,
38 William Crawford,
39 Josiah Crawford,
40 Joseph Chambers,
41 John Lord,
42 Andrew McLeon,
43 Joseph Dunn,
44 John Bell,
45 Andrew Bryson,
46 John Middleton,
47 Jonas Denton,
48 Andrew Hopper,
49 Jonathan Denton,
50 James Peterson,
51 Malachai Boland,
52 John Middleton,
53 William Watson,
54 John Nelson,
55 Henry Anderson,
56 Martin Hefley,
57 Nicholas Massey,
58 William Montgory,
59 George Hiffley,
60 John Anderson,
61 Isom Gurly,
62 James Welsh,
63 Hugh Donalson,
64 Mark Colmer,
65 Elisha Foller,
66 John Mann,
67 John Tollor,
68 Samuel Corter,
69 Samuel Robeson,
70 Thomas Watson,
71 John Watson,
72 James Love,
73 Loyd Heyson.

The following Counties of the Detached Militia of 1814, were called into service at Norfolk, in Virginia, by orders issued in September, A. D., 1814, to-wit: Granville, Wake, Johuson, Franklin, Warren, Halifax, Southampton, Nash, Edgecombe, Martin, Bertie, Hertford, Gates, Chatham, Orange, Person.

N. B. The Detached Militia from the Counties of Chatham, Orange and Person were ordered to return to their respective homes before they arrived at Gates Court House, the place of rendezvous.

The Detached Militia from the following Counties were called into service at Wilmington, North Carolina, by orders issued September 29th, A. D., 1814, to-wit: New Hanover, Brunswick, Bladen, Columbus, Robeson, Cumberland, Duplin, Sampson.

The following Counties of the Detached Militia were called into service at Newbern, North Carolina, by orders issued September 17th, A. D., 1814, to-wit: Pitt, Wayne, Green, Jones, Lenoir, Craven, Beaufort.

The Detached Militia from the following Counties were called to Hillsborough, the place of rendezveus, on the 28th of November, A. D., 1814, where they were organized, and from thence marched to Norfolk, in the service of the United States, agreeable to a requisition made by the President to the Governor of this State: The Counties to-wit: Orange, Chat-

ham, Person, Caswell, Ro\
Stokes, Surry, Wilkes.

The officers of this regiment w
RICHARD ATKERSON, of Person,
SAMUEL HUNTER, of Guilford, as
JAMES CAMPBELL, of Rockingham,
JOSEPH WINSTON, jun., of Stokes, ι

A requisition was made by Major General Thomas Pickney, for one regiment to march to the defence of the southern frontier of the Sixth Military District of the United States. In consequence of which, orders were issued from this office, calling forth the De'ached Militia from the following counties, to-wit: Anson, Richmond, Moore, Cabarrus, to rendezvous at Wadesborough, Anson county, on the 24th of February, 1815. Also, to Ashe, Wilkes, Burke, Rutherford, Buncombe, Haywood, to rendezvous at Wadesborough, in Anson county, on Wednesday, the 1st day of March, A. D. 1815.

Of this regiment the following officers were designated to the command, to-wit:

ANDREW IRWIN, as Lieutenant Colonel Commandant.
JOHN McGIMPSEY, of Burke, as Lieutenant Colonel.
JESSE ALLEN, of Wilkes, 1st ⎱ Majors.
THOMAS LENOIR, of Haywood, 2d ⎰

N. B. The orders from this office were dated on January 25th, A. D. 1815.

I do hereby cert:
that the foregoing ... true c...
and Soldiers of the Detached Mili...
pursuance of a requisition of the Pres.
States, in virtue of an act of Congress, passed 1c

     ROBERT W. HAYWOOD,
      Adjutant General, of the
       Militia of N. Carolina.

     ADJUTANT GENERAL'S OFFICE,
      Raleigh, March 6th, 1873.

I certify that the foregoing list of Officers and Soldiers of the war of 1812, in the Detached Militia of North Carolina, is a true copy of the records of this office.

     JOHN C. GORMAN,
      Adj. General of North Carolina.

www.ingramcontent.com/pod-product-compliance
Lightning Source LLC
Chambersburg PA
CBHW021835230426
43669CB00008B/976